THE FIVE AND TEN MEN

TEN MEN WHO REDEFINED DISTANCE RUNNING

RICHARD AMERY

2019

Front cover: **Vladimir Kuts celebrating one of his two Olympic victories. Melbourne 1956**

The Five and Ten Men
© Richard Amery 2019

Title: The Five and Ten Men: Ten Men Who
Redefined Distance Running
Author: Richard Amery

Subjects
Sport and Recreation: History
Sport and Recreation: Running and Jogging
Sports and Recreation: Reference

ISBN: 978-0-6485614-0-8

Cover design by Nicola Day

Interior design by Green Hill Publishing

WHY THIS BOOK?

I HAVE ALWAYS BEEN interested in distance running. Not quite sure why. It is certainly not because of any great ability on my part. On the distance running continuum I would place myself as average – not completely hopeless, but a long, long way from world class. My only ever decent run was somewhat tainted – being disqualified (later re-instated) after winning the state marathon title many years ago. The crime? Wearing the wrong coloured shorts. Let's just say that my interest and enthusiasm for the sport far outweighed my ability.

It is this interest, and the wish to impart something of the history of the sport that brought me to the point of writing this book. The subjects chose themselves. Of the many record holders over the classic distances of five and ten thousand metres, there have only ever been ten who have held both records. Were it to be a book on the ten greatest distance runners the list would probably not be much different. Each in their own way played a significant part in showing just what was possible, and in so doing raised the bar for those to follow.

I often say that the hardest world record to break or gold medal to win is the 100metres, simply because probably just about everybody at some stage runs a 100m race. If you have some ability it is going to become apparent pretty early. Training will build upon whatever natural ability is present. The distance events are probably not far behind. Requiring little in the way of equipment or facilities, just about anybody can find out fairly easily if they have an aptitude for the sport. That of course is the easy part. The hard part is maximizing what ability they might have.

RICHARD AMERY
ADELAIDE, SOUTH AUSTRALIA
OCTOBER 2019

CONTENTS

INTRODUCTION: STANDING ON THE SHOULDERS OF OTHERS

COMPARING THE SPORTING PERFORMANCES of different eras is not easy. In both "qualitative" and "non qualitative" sports, to say that a performer from one era is superior to that of another is difficult. Was Muhammad Ali a better boxer than Joe Louis, or Roger Federer a better tennis player than Rod Laver? One can look at their records – who they beat, what tournaments they won, their sporting longevity, etc., but in the end any decision is to a great degree subjective.

Times change, and change brings with it different training techniques, different equipment, and differences in the frequency and standard of competition. Thus while in modern tennis, for example, it is relatively easy to say at any given time who is the best player, it is quite another to say that the best player today would be better than the best player of thirty or forty years ago.

There is little doubt that the top players of today hit the ball much harder than their forbears, but much of that is almost certainly due to the revolution in tennis racket construction over the last few years. Put an old wooden frame racket in the hands of today's stars, and the playing field becomes much more even for the stars of old. Also, the increased frequency of competition where top players regularly play each other for big prize money must also serve to raise standards.

One might think that in sports where performance is directly measurable, such comparisons would be far more easily made. In swimming for example, the top female performances of today leave the men of only a few years ago far behind. On times, the great Dawn Fraser would not have a hope of making the Australian national team, let alone winning the one hundred-metre freestyle at three successive Olympics. And yet, does anyone really believe that if a young Dawn were competing today she would be so convincingly thrashed by the present generation?

And so to the sport of distance running. On times, the best women of today would leave the likes of Paavo Nurmi in the five and ten thousand metres well behind. In the marathon, Paula Radcliffe (the present world record holder) would finish some eight minutes ahead of the great Zatopek.

It was not until 1939 that the thirty minute mark was beaten for ten kilometres. Seventy years on, the new target is twenty-six minutes! At his best, Nurmi would be almost lapped twice in a five thousand metre race against the record holder of today. Yet once again, the question begs to be answered. Would that really happen? The answer is – probably not.

If a young Nurmi could be dramatically transported to the twenty first century, and given the benefits of synthetic tracks, pace makers, year round training, altitude training, along with the best sports medicine advice available, what times might he run? Of course it is all conjecture, but surely no one would deny that it would be much faster than his records of the nineteen twenties.

To look at it another way. Were a Haile Gebrselassie or Kenenisa Bekele transported back eighty years and trained for only part of the year (at sea level), raced on frequently sub-standard tracks, and knowing that the world mark for five thousand metres was in the fourteen thirties instead of the twelve thirties, what times might they run?

Distance running, in line with most other sports, has undergone great changes over the last eighty years or so in the period during which the individuals covered in this book competed.

Let us consider for a moment some of these changes. Until the sixties, tracks were made of cinders. Some were better than others, but the one thing they all had in common was their susceptibility to weather conditions. Rain could turn an otherwise good track into something more akin to a cross-country course than the modern synthetic track of today.

In top competition today, one no longer sees athletes covered in mud at the end of a race – no matter how much rain might fall. The other factor to consider with the tracks of old was the way in which frequent use could soften the inside lanes, making the going much harder for the runners. It was no coincidence that distance races were often run more in the second lane than the inside one, simply because of the firmer footing.

Two of the last three Olympics to be run before the introduction of synthetic tracks had distance events that were on either a soft track (Melbourne), or a very wet track (Tokyo). Besides the "weather proofing" that the modern artificial surface affords, the generally firmer and consistent footing has affected times.

Opinions vary as to how much, and it probably varies somewhat from runner to runner. General consensus seems to put the difference at about a second a lap in the distance events. This alone puts those record holders up to and including Ron Clarke perhaps between twelve seconds or so better off over 5,000 metres and twenty five seconds over the longer distance vis a vis those who came after them.

Few modern records in the distance events have been set without pace makers. Probably the most famous example was Roger Bannister's carefully orchestrated attempt on the four minute mile. He showed what was possible with cooperative colleagues. Almost certainly, given a similar situation, athletes such as Hagg of Sweden or Landy of Australia would have been capable of achieving the same feat that he did.

Following Bannister's example, the Hungarians (running the year after the Englishman's breakthrough) showed what could be done with planning. In their case this was possible because under the guidance of Igloi, there was a trio (Tábori, Rózsavölgyi, and Iharos) who were both capable and happy to help each other. It would not really be until some years later and the advent of financially lucrative incentives that pace makers became pretty much the norm in most non-championship races of note. Given such conditions, it is interesting to contemplate what times athletes such as Ron Clarke or Kipchoge Keino may have run at their best.

Without doubt, one of the biggest changes in distance running over the years is the country of origin of the various record holders whose stories make up this book. Until the Second World War, only Finland provided entries on the list. After the war, the countries changed, but still remained firmly within Europe. While athletes from Czechoslovakia, Hungary and Russia replaced Finns, there was little in evidence that the situation would change too dramatically in the foreseeable future.

However, with the wisdom of hindsight, there were signs. The marathon wins by Abebe Bikila in both the Rome and Tokyo Olympics gave an indication of what the future might hold. The floodgates opened for the Africans (especially the Kenyans and Ethiopians) at Mexico City in 1968. African runners placed second in the 800 metres, first in the 1,500, first, second and third in both the 5,000 and 10,000, first and second in the steeplechase, and first in the marathon. No doubt the results were skewed because of the altitude factor, but the writing was well and truly on the wall.

While six of the first seven dual record holders were from Europe (with Ron Clarke being the sole exception), the last three were all out of Africa. Not only that, the annual world leading times became increasingly dominated by African runners. In most present day world-class distance events, a fair skinned runner near the front is a cause of some note. For many outside of Africa, athletes are often competing not with an expectation of winning, but rather to be the first "non African" across the line.

The causes of this dramatic change have been the subject of considerable debate and conjecture. The true reason is almost certainly a combination of factors.

One of the more obvious ones was the scarcity of opportunity for African runners prior to the nineteen sixties. While a sporting framework was well developed in European countries and most English speaking nations, the same could not be said of most African nations. Had there been such a framework, the African domination may well have occurred much earlier.

As mentioned above, the marathon win in Rome by Bikila showed that Africans could indeed run. The win itself was almost an accident, as he very nearly did not make the Ethiopian team. The next Olympics in Tokyo showed that while Bikila was the undoubted star of Africa, he was not the only runner of note from the continent. In the form of Kipchoge Keino and others, it was also apparent that Ethiopia was not the only African country capable of producing world-class runners.

The results from Mexico City in 1968 proved two things. The first was that there were many Africans who could run, the second was that living and training at high altitude was a definite advantage. With those two revelations, the world of distance running would never be the same again.

Modern distance running at the top level today has become almost an African championship; such is the degree to which that continent dominates those events. The men have done so for some time; the women took a little longer, but are now just as dominant as their male counterparts. At the same time, while standards are rising in Africa, in much of the world they are falling. Once again, the reasons for this are probably manifold.

The "glamour sports" for many in the traditionally strong sporting regions of Europe, North America and Oceania, is not athletics, but the various football codes (especially soccer), tennis, golf, and basketball. It is sports such as these that attract the crowds, the television coverage, and of course the money. In this time of full professionalism, the most handsomely rewarded distance runner would be considered a pauper in comparison to the best golfers, tennis players, or soccer players. However, in most African nations, the availability of golf courses and tennis courts is somewhat limited, not to mention the cost of equipment for such sports. Running and soccer have no such requirements and so it is not surprising that the African countries have found success in both pursuits.

Both require minimal equipment and little in the way of facilities. Both also provide a means of breaking free from the extreme poverty found in many of the African nations. Signing a professional soccer contract or winning a big city marathon can mean earning more money virtually overnight than would otherwise be possible over a lifetime.

At a time when the standards of distance running are continuing to rise, it is obvious that such a rise is far from uniform. Almost all the raising of standards has been African based. Europe – for long the nursery of all distance record breakers – is virtually nowhere to be seen. The rise in African standards has been balanced by a steady decline in standards in most – if not all – of Europe, and indeed much of the rest of the world.

The causes of this decline are no doubt due to a number of factors, but the growing popularity of other sports and the increasingly sedentary western lifestyle would have to rank highly in any list. Studies of East African athletes have shown that many (but not all) walked or ran quite long distances to school each day. Thus by the time they had completed schooling, they had undertaken many thousands of kilometres of "training" before embarking on a proper distance running programme. As the twig is bent, so it shall grow.

Not to be ignored is the psychological aspect of so many Africans running so well. A defeatist attitude among many non-Africans may well be a contributing factor leading to their declining standards. If a task is deemed impossible, why attempt it?

Of course training has always played a part in record breaking. Hard and consistent training is nothing new. Well over a century ago professional endurance runners were training hard – often for several hours a day, covering distances that are rarely approached today.

As training knowledge has increased and become more widely disseminated, probably the biggest change has been the number of talented athletes training with both high volume and intensity. Natural ability – no matter how great – is by itself not enough to compete in distance running at the highest level. It is easy to look at the top Africans and put their success down to natural talent, but this overlooks the simple fact that they train extremely hard.

The training sessions undertaken by some of the top runners are little short of amazing. The former steeple-chase and 5,000 metre record holder Moses Kiptanui could complete 6x1,500 metres in 3:47-3:49, with a 4-5 minute recovery between. Hicham El Guerrouj, the 1,500 metre and mile record holder could complete sessions of 10x400 metres in 53-4 seconds with only 30 second recoveries, while his predecessor as the dual record holder, Noureddine Morceli, could reportedly complete 15x400 metres in 54-5 seconds with a 90 second recovery. At various parts in this book, other examples of such training are given. Clearly, talent allied with such training gives rise to great results.

The monetary rewards available to the modern athlete make the "under the table" payments of earlier years seem laughable. There is, however, both an upside and a downside to such payments. Over the last few years there has been a trend for many of the most talented young runners to virtually begin their careers as marathon runners. The conventional wisdom for a long time was that only after a career of track racing should one move to the roads. No longer. Increasingly, lucrative big city marathons and championships are won by runners barely out of their teens.

The reason for this is fairly obvious. The winning of one major marathon may bring a greater financial return than perhaps two or three seasons of high quality five and ten thousand metre running. It is no coincidence that the standard of marathon running has exploded over the last few years. Runners, who would previously have opted for the track, instead begin training specifically for the marathon at an early age – probably to the detriment of their shorter distance performances.

There are two principal factors that determine the level of performance that an individual might attain. They are training, and the genes one is born with. There is no escaping the fact that to be a top-level performer in endurance events, one has to choose one's parents very carefully!

For a number of factors that limit performance, there is a genetically determined upper limit. For example, an individual's maximal oxygen uptake (the maximal amount of oxygen an individual can take in and utilise) is determined by a combination of training, lifestyle, and genetics. All the training in the world seems to increase it by a maximum of about 30%. Thus, if one is born with a VO2 max. of 40-50 mls/kg/min (as it is normally expressed), an increase of 30% will still be well short of the 70-85 levels recorded by world-class performers.

A similar story applies with other factors that affect performance. For example, running economy (essentially the ability to run efficiently) is a combination of both heredity and training. The simple fact is that some people are innately more efficient at running – despite it being a fairly basic skill – than others.

Gene profiling is unearthing an increasing number of genes that can influence distance-running ability. With an increase in the numbers of competitors, the likelihood of individuals appearing with a more favourable set of genes also increases. The top runners of today race at speeds that are beyond the realm of all but a tiny percentage of the population as a whole.

From a purely statistical viewpoint, it is hard not to believe that in certain regions of Africa – notably parts of Kenya and Ethiopia – there is a strong genetic component in their success. It is also worth noting the influence of extended family relationships (not confined to Africans!) on distance running success. Training alone would not seem an adequate explanation.

Environment of course plays a crucial role in almost any sporting success. Access to facilities, supportive parents, the esteem in which top sportsmen and women are held, along with financial rewards are all factors leading to success. For many, sport is a way of escaping from poverty. It is probably this latter reason as much as any, that has been responsible for the rise of the Africans in distance running.

The big money available for top athletes has coincided with the increasingly sedentary lifestyle of western nations. Little wonder that the centre of distance running has moved from Europe (predominantly) to Africa. With the vastly differing lifestyles, it is hard to see any immediate reversal of the situation. This is not to say that non-Africans can never again be world-beaters at the longer distances, just that the chances are not great. Put simply, the pool of talent appears that much greater in some of the African nations, and the motivation to work hard is that much higher.

As an example, in one month alone in 2009, no fewer than 24 Kenyans ran faster than 2:09 for the marathon, with another 16 running between 2:09 and 2:10 for the distance. Impressive as those figures are, there were some notable absentees who were preparing for major races later in the year. Many countries with a tradition of athletics would be happy to have a single runner in that category. Ten years later the situation has only become more pronounced, with the fastest twenty-four marathon runners of all time being from either Kenya or Ethiopia, and the time required to make the list being 2:04.27. Of the twenty-four, a number have run under that time on multiple occasions.

So what does the future hold? In a way, one could argue that the superiority of the East Africans has been bad for the sport of distance running. Such is their present degree of dominance that world championships and Olympic Games – along with the lucrative big city marathons – have become something akin to de facto African championships.

At the time of writing, it is hard to see the situation changing dramatically in the immediate future. Almost certainly there will be some great non-African talent that will come to the fore. Logic would seem to dictate that there will be individuals born with a favourable set of genes and the desire and enthusiasm to make the most of their natural talent. Such individuals need not necessarily be African. Probably the main factors counting against such an individual reaching the very highest standard are the lack of similar numbers in non-African countries, and in most cases the all too comfortable upbringing that most western youth have.

The prevalence of television, computer games, cars and fast food is hardly the ideal environment from which world-class distance runners might emerge. Probably these latter factors, as much as any, have been responsible for changing the face of world distance running.

Future record holders, if the current situation continues, will most likely – but not necessarily - be out of Africa. With annual rankings dominated by that continent's runners in all the distance events, it would be a brave man to bet against Africans claiming future records. However, the fact that athletes from Germany, Australia, and the US have run below thirteen minutes for five kilometres shows that it is possible for non-Africans to perform at the very highest level. Sooner or later, one may well come along with the physical qualities, the mental strength, and the right training to push the boundaries of endurance even further than has so far happened.

PAAVO NURMI

"All that I am is because of my mind."

Every picture tells a story. Nurmi in
typical stance. Aloof, alone, unsmiling
after victory in the 10,000m at the
1920 Antwerp Olympics.

It would be hard to imagine, taking into account both geographical and political factors, a country less likely to dominate the world of distance running than Finland. Situated in the far northern latitudes, the small population experiences severe winters where even the southern most parts of the country regularly have weeks on end with temperatures well below zero. Low temperatures, heavy snowfalls, and long periods of little or no daylight during the long winters would hardly seem the ideal climate for the development of distance runners. Consider also that Finland was long seen as the poor relation among the Scandinavian countries (certainly no longer the case due to the emergence of companies such as communications giant Nokia on the world stage). As if that would not be enough, the twentieth century history of the country would seem to put paid to almost any athletic aspirations the country might have had, encompassing as it did both a bloody civil war and an invasion by their Russian neighbours.

So much for theory. History shows that no country has ever dominated distance running the way Finland did prior to the Second World War. A few facts and figures should suffice as examples of the Finnish dominance. In the five kilometre event, the world record was broken five times between 1912 and 1939. On every occasion the runner was Finnish. In the ten kilometre event, Finnish runners held the world record continuously between June 22, 1921, and June 11, 1949; just on twenty eight years before another country could lay claim to it. During this period the record was broken eight times. Of the world leading times for the year, between 1921 and 1939 (nineteen years), on only three occasions did the leader in each of the distances not have the word Finland follow their name. There were six Olympic festivals held between 1912 and 1936. Of the twelve gold medals on offer for the longest track races, only twice was the winner not from the land of the midnight sun. Of the total of thirty-six Olympic medals on offer for these events, the score was Finland 22, the rest of the world 14. In each of these games, Finland finished second only to the United States in the total athletics medal tally. But for the advent of war in 1939, the

Finnish Olympic record would almost certainly have been even more noteworthy.

The above are only the highlights; they do not include the large number of Finns who dominated the yearly ranking lists during the interwar years. One would have to look very hard indeed to find a sport so dominated over such a long period, and this from a country that even today boasts such a small population. With this in mind, one could perhaps be forgiven for wondering not why such a country has more entries in the "five and ten" record holder list than any other, but perhaps why they do not have more, such was their degree of dominance.

What brought about such dominance? Despite the harsh winters, summer in Finland can be often ideal for physical pursuits. The country itself is characterized by thousands of lakes and seemingly endless forests. While the winter days are short (or non-existent), the days in summer are long, with even the southern areas experiencing no true darkness for weeks on end during the summer months. The country has long had a tradition of physical activity, especially in the endurance fields of cross-country skiing and running. Go to any small country town, and there will almost certainly be an athletics track to be found, along with markers in place to signify ski tracks for the winter months. The place of physical education in the school curriculum was accepted in Finland long before most countries thought it might be of some value. Another fact that perhaps says something about Finnish culture and the attitude toward sport is the statistic that there is approximately one sauna for every two people living in the country.

Another factor often put forward to try and explain the Finnish success is the concept of "sisu" – probably most simply explained as a combination of perseverance, pride, and just being stubborn – perhaps in part a response to the climate, and perhaps in part a response to the history of the country. That history has been most heavily influenced by having a large and powerful (and not always benign) neighbour sharing a common border. Russia had occupied Finland three times – in 1721, 1743, and 1809. Unlike the first two occasions, after 1809 they did not withdraw. Thus it was, that in the pre World War One era, Finland competed in the Olympics, not as an independent country, but as an adjunct of Russia. Although competing in prior Olympic festivals, it was the 1912 version in Stockholm that really set Finland on the path it was to follow so successfully until 1940. The responsibility for this direction could fairly be laid at the feet of two men. The first was Hannes Kolehmainen. The second was the boy who was inspired by his Olympic deeds – Paavo Nurmi.

It would be no exaggeration to say that Kolehmainen's feats in Stockholm inspired a generation of Finnish runners. For the first time, both the five and ten kilometre events were held at the Olympics, and he won both. The most memorable race was undoubtedly the shorter of the two events. Prior to this no one had been inside fifteen minutes for the distance. In the final, the two standout performers were the Finn and the French athlete, Jean Bouin. From the outset, it was clearly a two-man race. As was often the norm for the times, the pace was anything but steady; rather, the early pace was at a level that clearly could not be maintained. Kolehmainen led early, but the Frenchman took over and led for the majority of the race. Only in the last few strides did the Finn edge past to record the narrowest of victories – 14:36.6 to 14:36.7. The world record (now officially recognized by the newly constituted International Amateur Athletic Federation) had set a standard that would have been unthinkable to most prior to the race. Completing a demanding programme, the undoubted hero of the Games also won the ten kilometre event (in which heats were also conducted), the cross country (then an Olympic event over 8 kilometres), and also set a world 3 kilometre record as part of the teams event (despite Finland failing to make the final).

Following his Stockholm exploits, Kohlemainen went to live in New York, working as a stonemason and further enhancing his reputation as the premier runner of his era. Returning to Olympic action after a war induced eight-year hiatus, he added to his reputation with a marathon victory in Antwerp. Sadly, his great rival from the Stockholm games was not a competitor. Bouin had been struck down and killed early in the Great War, a victim of so-called "friendly fire." Kohlemainen finally returned to his homeland in 1921, and although still competing, his best days were behind him. His last notable exploit was to light the Olympic flame at the 1952 Helsinki Olympics, at age 62. He received the torch from the boy he had helped inspire all those years ago – Paavo Nurmi.

Between the 1912 and 1920 Olympics, Europe had spent much of the time in military and political upheaval. Finland, until its final break from Russia, had been a partly autonomous state within the Russian empire. However, during the late nineteenth and early twentieth century, attempts to "Russify" the Finnish state served, if anything, to have the opposite effect of that intended. Russian defeat at the hands of the Japanese in 1905 showed the Finns that their rulers were not invincible, and exploits such as those of Kohlemainen served to further the awakening of Finnish nationalism. The final straw came with the Russian revolution in October 1917, and the overthrow of the old Tsarist regime. With it came a breakdown of Finnish society. The Finnish Senate declared its independence on December 6, and this was recognized by the new Soviet state on January 4, 1918. For Finland, the solution of one problem brought with it the creation of another.

Just as Russia fought a bitter civil war after the overthrow of the old regime, so Finland slid into armed civil conflict just at it rid itself of its old master. Similar to the Russian experience, the country divided into Red and White armies each comprising some 80-90,000 Finns. Although each of the armies was overwhelmingly Finnish, the Whites received assistance (primarily from Germany in the form of some 13,000 troops), while the Reds had the assistance of a lesser number (less than 10,000) of Russians. Although the war lasted less than four months, some 37,000 died, due to a combination of combat deaths, executions, and prison camp fatalities. The great majority of deaths were inflicted on the Reds. Following the cessation of hostilities, many prison camp inmates still succumbed to the effects of both malnutrition and the influenza epidemic that swept the world in 1918.

The social effects, not surprisingly, impacted on Finnish society long after the war finished. By the end of 1918, the great majority of Red prisoners had been pardoned and released, but the very last few prison camp inmates were not repatriated until 1927. The final ghost of the Civil War was not laid to rest until 1973, when the Finnish government paid compensation to over 11,000 citizens who had been imprisoned following the Civil War.

If ever a country needed a unifying force and something to instill pride in their new-found independence it was post war Finland. Living as we do in an age where the term "celebrity" has been so greatly devalued, it is hard to envisage the impact that a figure such as Paavo Nurmi had. Slightly built at 1.74m and 65 kilograms, he was not a likely candidate for the status of national hero. However, like very few other celebrities (in any field) he was truly larger than life. His demeanor, characterized as it was by an apparent aloofness, served only to add to an aura that was based on being so superior to nearly all his contempories.

His reign as probably the best-known sportsman in the world lasted for over ten years, and his eventual disbarment from Olympic competition, if anything, served only to add to the mystique that surrounded his superlative career. His fame spread well beyond national boundaries and sport, and the bare statistics of his career- encompassing as it did some twelve Olympic medals and twenty two world records - do not by themselves explain the esteem in which he was held. Over sixty years after his last Olympic triumph, the IAAF voted Nurmi the greatest 5,000 metre and second greatest 10,000 metre runner of all time.

This greatest of all Finnish athletes was born on June 13, 1897, in the southern city of Turku. From his earliest days, life was not easy, and his upbringing in a poor but religious family colored both his approach to running and to life in general. He said in later life that on Sundays while other children his age could play, he was expected to walk to church with his father. The eldest of five children, Nurmi was only twelve when his father (a carpenter) died, leaving him to help make a living for the family. His first job was as an errand boy for a local company, and he later credited the effort involved in pushing often heavily laden carts up and down the streets of Turku with laying the foundations for his future running success.

Early in life Nurmi decided that running was for him. No doubt the often solitary aspects of the sport appealed to his personality, and once he had made the decision, it only seemed to reinforce that aspect of his nature. As an eleven year old, his talent for running was noticed by Fabian Liesinen, then one of the better Finnish runners. Asked by Nurmi to time him over 1500 metres, he was impressed by his time of 5:02 – a fine effort for one so young.

Although knowing where his sporting future lay, he did not compete in proper competitions until 1914, and even then decided to concentrate more on training than actually competing. He had joined the club Turun Urheiluliitto as a fifteen year old, and would continue to represent it for the rest of his career. In 1914, he won the junior national 3,000 metre title, but the following year his 1500 metre best was a very ordinary 4:37.8. Reflecting his preference for the longer distances, probably along with his lack of speed training, his 1500m best was still only 4:29 at age twenty one. His approach from his earliest years was as if he was looking to the future, not just the satisfaction of short-term success.

In the modern world of instant communication and the "knowledge society", it is worth contemplating the vastly different place the world was in the early twentieth century. Coaching and sporting knowledge (i.e. how to train) was almost non-existent. As a result, the young Nurmi had to derive a system of training largely by himself. This he began in earnest when he was fifteen but as was the norm, did not involve training during winter. Also, the various types of training that are now taken for granted did not appear on the athletic scene until much later. Thus, his early training largely comprised little other than steady runs in the forests and roads around Turku. This, he would later say, delayed his development as he almost completely neglected to incorporate any sprints or faster running into his training regime.

Despite his club membership, he rarely trained with others, and where this did happen, it was usually only in the form of indoor gym work during the winter months. At the age of 21 he was called up for military service. This event had a dual benefit for the young Nurmi. Firstly, it gave him more time to train, and secondly, it exposed him to different types of training; most notably incorporating various types of faster running into his daily regime. Despite these benefits, he later reflected that his training was really not sufficient for what he wanted to achieve, beginning as it did only on the first of April each year.

As a recruit, Nurmi first came to the attention of his superiors when he was required, along with other recruits, to undertake a twenty kilometre route march in full uniform in addition to carrying a rifle, ammunition, and a weighted pack. Running was permitted, and he completed the course so far ahead of the others, there were initial suggestions that he must have taken a shortcut.

Until 1924, daily training consisted mainly of a morning walk, followed by an afternoon running session that might include a series of short sprints. In the spring of 1924, Nurmi increased both the volume and intensity of his training, bringing with it his best results. Certainly, the type of training he was undertaking was quite severe for the times. A typical training day would involve a morning walk of 10-12 kilometres (with a few short sprints included), followed by some gym work. After an hour or so of rest, the second session of the day would be quite intense, involving a series of short sprints, a timed run over 400-1000 metres, and finish with a 3-4 kilometre steady run (accelerating over the last lap). The evening session would comprise a cross country run of perhaps five to seven kilometres, aiming to raise the pace over the last kilometre or so. This would be then followed by a series of short sprints. As can be seen from these examples, Nurmi's great achievements were not based purely on natural physical talent. Rather, he trained in a regular, systematic fashion that was quite advanced for its time. During his career, he remained a believer in the benefits that regular walking (incorporating some sprints en route), could bring to a training programme. However, reflecting on his training in later years, he was of a view that walking was of little value, and that the main thing he lacked in his training was more speed work.

Such regular training and competition brought more success, and by 1920, Nurmi had set his first national record. The race was over 3,000 metres at Turku, on May 28. The time was 8:36.2, a far more noteworthy performance than his 1500 best that had improved to a still relatively mediocre 4:05.5. However, at this stage he was certainly not considered to be a likely winner at the forthcoming Antwerp Olympics. As it turned out, he was selected to run in both the five and ten kilometre events, as well as the cross-country (then an Olympic event).

His first event was the shorter of the two track races. Held at 3:15 p.m. on Tuesday, August 17 (an extremely hot day), Nurmi assumed the lead after three laps and attempted to run away from his pursuers with a first half in 7:12. With one exception the plan succeeded, but he was out sprinted in the closing stages by the diminutive twenty year old, chain smoking Frenchman, Joseph Guillemot (14:55.6 to 15:00). This would prove to be the only time that Nurmi would lose an Olympic final to a foreign runner.

The two met again at the longer distance on Friday, August 19, the day following the heats. The time of the final was put forward two hours to accommodate the wishes of the Belgian king. Biding his time, Nurmi did not look a genuine threat until the last kilometre. With a lap to go, only the Finn and the five kilometre winner were left at the front. Nurmi slowed with some three hundred metres left, allowing Guillemot to take the lead, before coming from behind in the final straight to win (31:45.8 to 31:47.2). The Frenchman, having indigestion problems caused by the change in schedule, vomited on Nurmi's shoes after the race. In the cross-country event, Nurmi was again successful, winning from the Swede Erik Backman (27:15 to 27:18), as well as leading Finland to the team gold medal. Nurmi had left Finland as a little known competitor; he returned a national hero.

Following the Antwerp Games, Nurmi set about cementing his position as the outstanding runner of his era. Between 1921 and 1923 he competed throughout Europe setting numerous official and unofficial world records. His first world mark came over 10,000 metres at Stockholm on June 22, 1921. The time was 30:40.2, eclipsing the record of 30:58.8 established by Jean Bouin some ten years earlier. 1921 also saw Nurmi show a hitherto unseen turn of speed at shorter distances. With no specific training for the event, he was second in the national 800 metre title, and then startled most observers with the third fastest mile on record – a 4:13.9 in Stockholm on July 10. This run missed the European record set only eight days earlier by the narrowest of margins – 0.1 second.

In addition to his world marks, there were numerous instances where intermediate times en route to longer distances were also under existing records, but not officially accepted. Thus, for example, in his first ten kilometre record, his six mile time of 29:41.2 did not achieve ratification. Despite his new-found ability at the shorter distances, Nurmi obviously found the longer distances more to his liking. The 1922 track season was highlighted by him breaking world records at 3,000, 2,000 and 5,000 metres on successive weekends. However, while Nurmi was busy rewriting the record books, the rest of the world was not standing idly by.

Sweden had a Finnish born schoolteacher in the form of Edvin Wide who they believed could challenge the dominant Finn for running supremacy. A late developer, Wide's 1,500 best was only 4:04.4 in 1921, but by 1923 he had run a number of times well inside four minutes. A challenge was put to Nurmi who surprisingly elected to race Wide at his best distance (the mile), rather than go for a longer distance where victory would be almost guaranteed. His decision to opt for the shorter distance was no doubt made easier by a race earlier in the month when he ran 3:55.6, less than a second from the world 1500 mark.

On August 23 in Stockholm, a crowd of some eighteen thousand turned out to see the match race take place on a 385 metre track. After the first 440 yards, with Wide leading in 60.1, Nurmi took over the lead and gradually pulled away, his lead at the end being some fifteen metres. His winning time of 4:10.4 was a new world mark, while Wide finished in a very creditable 4:13.1. Intermediate times at 1500 metres were 3:53.0 and 3:54.2; both well under the existing record. Remarkably, running on the same track the next day, Nurmi again beat Wide and broke a world record, this time over three miles (en route to a 5,000 metre victory). To complete his remarkable season, on September 10, he broke his own 3,000 metre record, running 8:27.8 in Copenhagen.

By the end of the 1923 season Nurmi held the global marks for the mile, 2,000 metres, 3,000 metres, 5,000 metres, and 10,000 metres, as well as unofficial marks for 1,500 metres, three miles and six miles. He remains the only athlete to simultaneously hold the mile, 5,000 and 10,000 records. During the Finnish summer, he stepped down even further in distance, winning his national title over 800 metres in a time (1:56.3) good enough to rank twentieth in the world for the year.

While Nurmi espoused the view that even paced running would bring records and victories, in reality his races did not always follow this script accurately. He was able to adapt to situations as they arose, and proved more than capable of either leading all the way, or coming from behind in the closing stages with a sprint finish. After his experiences at the 1920 Olympics he often trained and ran with a stopwatch, and before races would nominate a winning time; asserting that if the opposition ran a faster time, they would win. This, of course, rarely happened.

While the years 1921-1923 made him the pre-eminent runner of his time, it was his 1924 season that raised his reputation to that of mythology. That same year also saw the emergence of another athlete who could most closely be called a genuine rival rather than merely a contemporary. That athlete was Ville Ritola, the fourteenth of twenty children, with but two years of formal education, who had emigrated to the US from Finland as a seventeen year old in search of a better life. But for the presence of his more famous countryman, Ritola would almost certainly hold a more revered position in the annals of distance running. Living as they did on different continents, clashes between the two occurred usually only during the Olympics and events immediately preceding or following such festivals. By all accounts, the two were not the best of friends during this period.

Ritola did not have the systematic approach to training that Nurmi did, but did come into contact with, and received advice from Hannes Kohlemainen while the two were living in New York. Not able to return for the 1920 Olympics due to work and marriage commitments, he nevertheless forged a noteworthy running career in his adopted country, setting a number of national indoor records, as well as a second place in the 1922 Boston Marathon. He returned to the land of his birth in 1971, by which time Nurmi's attitude had changed markedly; organizing an apartment for Ritola and his wife in a building he owned. He also became a regular visitor to his old rival.

Returning home shortly before the 1924 Olympics, (his trip paid for by the Finnish authorities), Ritola immediately showed his ability with a new 10,000 metre world mark (30:35.4) on May 25 in Helsinki. Finishing well over a minute ahead of the second place getter, and with the final kilometre being the fastest, it looked as if at last Nurmi may have had a genuine rival. However, Nurmi was not to be outdone. Wishing to capitalize on his new-found speed, Nurmi had decided to enter both the 1500 and 5,000 metre events at the forthcoming Paris Olympics. There was a problem however – and a seemingly insurmount-able one. The finals of the two events were scheduled only thirty minutes apart. After lobbying by Finnish officials, the gap between the finals was lengthened by some twenty-five minutes, surely little more than a token gesture. To make matters worse, while training on icy roads over Easter, Nurmi slipped, injuring his knee in the process. Unable to walk for two weeks, he missed valuable training at such a crucial time, and when he did return his progress was initially disappointing.

Despite this setback, he decided to push ahead with his plan to run the double, and planned for a dress rehearsal on June 19 at Helsinki, some three weeks prior to the events in Paris. Both events were virtual time-trials, such was his margin of victory. Despite this, the evening would be remembered as one of the great moments in athletic history.

Conditions were pleasantly cool, certainly better than they would be in three weeks time. The 1500 started at 7:05 p.m. Leading from the start, Nurmi went through the first lap in 57.3 (much faster than the 61 he had planned) with the 800 being timed at 2:01. The third lap took a more reasonable 65 seconds, with the finish line being crossed in 3:52.6, a new world record. With barely an hour to "recover", Nurmi toed the line for the start of the 5,000 metres at 8:10 p.m. Starting with an opening kilometre in 2:48.6 (14:03 pace), he then settled into a more even pace, but still had enough in reserve for a final lap in 64 seconds.

The 1924 Olympic 5000m. Ritola
leads from Nurmi and Wide.

The result was another world record of 14:28.2. Convinced of his condition, he was determined to see his plan through to its fulfillment.

The Paris Olympics were very much a showcase for Finnish distance running. With the whole running programme squeezed into just eight days, there was minimal recovery time for many of the competitors. The first race, on July 6, was the 10,000 metres. Nurmi was not an entry. The reason for his absence was apparently made by team officials, ostensibly to save their star performer for the rest of his arduous programme. From a team perspective it certainly had some logic to it, seeing as they had the newly crowned record holder as their main entry, and conditions were much warmer than they had come from in Finland. The result was an overwhelming victory to Ritola in yet another world record – his second in barely six weeks. Second place went to Edvin Wide, with the Finns Berg and Sipila rounding out the first four positions. The following day (July 7) Ritola won his steeplechase heat in 9:59. The next day, both Nurmi and Ritola qualified for the 5,000 metre final comfortably, Nurmi winning his heat, Ritola finishing third in his. July 9 saw them both in action again, Nurmi winning his 1500 heat in 4:07.6, while Ritola took the steeplechase final in 9:33.6.

July 10 saw Nurmi's day of days. At 7:05 p.m. he took his place at the start of the 1500. The track was a 500 metre oval, and it was his aim to complete each of the first two laps in 75 seconds. As per his dress rehearsal in Helsinki earlier, his first lap was faster than planned. He went through the first 400 in 58, the first lap in 73.2, and 800 metres in 1:58.5. By this stage the only real competition was from the third rated American Ray Watson, the rest of the field being at least twenty metres behind. Watson was unable to maintain the pace, despite it having slowed (the 1000 metre mark being passed in 2:32), and slipped out of contention. Entering the final lap with a forty metre lead, Nurmi tossed the stopwatch he had been carrying to the infield, and ran steadily to the finish. While the battle for the minor placings raged furiously behind him, he did just enough to win comfortably. His final time (3:53.6) was just a second from his world record, with Scharer of Switzerland second in 3:55. As evidence of the struggle behind the winner, the third place-getter, Stallard of Great Britain, did not regain consciousness until thirty minutes after he crossed the line. While most of the other finishers stood or lay in various states of distress, Nurmi merely picked up his warm-up clothes, and jogged to the change rooms to rest before his next event. He did not have long.

At 8:00 p.m. he was at the start for his second event of the evening. His two main rivals, Ritola and Wide, assumed that their best chance for success lay in capitalizing on the obvious fatigue of the 1500 winner. With this in mind they set off at a furious pace, the first kilometre taking only 2:46.4 – 13:52 pace, when the world mark was over thirty seconds slower. At times Nurmi was up to forty metres behind, but he knew what he was doing. Referring to his watch for guidance, he took the lead about halfway through the race, and narrowly held off Ritola for the win (14:31.2 to 14:31.4). The time was second only to his world record on the all time list. Wide finished over thirty seconds behind in third place.

Despite the efforts of that day, the very next saw both Finns in action again, this time in heats of the 3,000 metre team race. Finland qualified for the final, with Nurmi recording the fastest time (8:47.8). The following day was the cross country, held in appalling conditions with temperatures around 36^0. If ever an event was to showcase Nurmi's superiority over his fellow runners, this was it. Despite facing the ten kilometre winner, he simply ran away from his pursuers as if it were a cool day. Of the thirty-eight starters over the 10,650 metre event, twenty three failed to finish, while many of those who did, completed the race at little more than a jog. Nurmi left Ritola some eighty five seconds in arrears for second place, with third over another minute further back. Several were hospitalized after their exertions; Nurmi merely prepared for the next day's competition.

The last day of competition saw the running of the 3,000 metre team race. With Finland fielding both Nurmi and Ritola, the event was probably considered a foregone conclusion to most, and thus it turned out to be. Finland won comfortably from Great Britain, with Nurmi well ahead of Ritola – 8:32.0 to 8:40.6. The third Finn across the line was Elias Katz in fifth place. To say that Finland dominated the distance events at the Paris Olympics would be something of an understatement. Their athletes won the 1500; finished first, second, and fifth in the 5000 (not counting Wide who finished third); finished first, third and fourth in the 10,000 (again not counting Wide who was second); finished first, second and fifth in the steeplechase; finished first and second in the cross country; won the 3000 metre team race; and for good measure another Finn, Albin Stenroos won the marathon. Including his team medals, Nurmi finished with five golds, Ritola with four gold and two silver. However, there was little doubt as to who was the overwhelming star of the games. One rumor that Nurmi himself would neither confirm nor deny regarded his non-participation in the ten kilometre event. The story was that while that race was being run, he ran a solo time trial, easily breaking the world record in the process. Certainly, after what he had accomplished over the nine days in Paris, few would have doubted his ability to do just that.

The return of the ship to Helsinki carrying the Olympic team drew a crowd of thousands to welcome home the new national heroes. Nurmi himself was touchingly handed a bunch of roses by his landlady as he descended the gangplank. There followed a reception later at a Helsinki sports field, where the Olympic victors were presented with a garland of flowers by the daughter of the Finnish president. All then completed a lap of honor. The shy Nurmi was certainly not at ease in such situations.

Following his Olympic heroics, the Finnish government commissioned a life size statue by the well-known sculptor, Waino Aaltonen. Although Nurmi did model for the monument, it was decided to be a depiction of Finnish runners in general, rather than purely a likeness of Nurmi. The end result was cast in bronze in 1925, and five replicas made. Besides the best known one outside the Helsinki Olympic stadium, there are others at the Helsinki Art Museum, the University of Jyvaskyla, and the city of Turku. The fifth one is located at the IOC headquarters in Lausanne, Switzerland.

Returning to competition, Nurmi completed his season in a manner that dispelled any doubt as to who was truly the best Finn, and hence the world's best. Running a virtual time trial in Kuopio on August 31 (he won by three and a half minutes), Nurmi took the ten kilometre record down to 30:06.2 (rounded up to the nearest fifth of a second). The first half took 14:52.5, the second 15:13.6. Six miles was passed in 29:07.1. There seems little doubt that a sub thirty minute time was within his capabilities. In two further races he was matched against Ritola, and on both occasions he won convincingly. The first time was over 5000 metres at Turku, on September 14. He won by twenty seconds in 14:43.8. The second time was over 10,000 metres at Tampere, on September 15. Nurmi ran 30:20.9, to easily account for Ritola who finished in 30:44.5.

Having taken all before him in Europe, American officials and promoters were anxious to get the all conquering running legend to take part in meetings on their side of the Atlantic. They had initially approached him in 1922, but had been put off firstly by studies he was undertaking, and then by his preparation for the Olympics. Following his Paris exploits, there was even greater enthusiasm for him to make the crossing. This he finally did in November 1924 aboard the steamship Celtic. Nurmi was accompanied by his masseur, Eino Hakoniemi, and upon arriving in America, Hugo Qvist, chairman of the New York Finnish American Athletic Club became his advisor and interpreter. Training on board ship during his trip over was not easy, in part due to Nurmi's reluctance to train in front of other passengers during the day. Upon his arrival on December 10, he received an enthusiastic welcome by several hundred Finnish-Americans. At an official welcoming ceremony at City Hall, he was given the keys to the city by the mayor.

Between the time of his arrival and his first race, Nurmi trained hard in preparation for what would prove to be an exhausting campaign. His first race was in Madison Square Garden on January 6. Setting the scene for what was to follow, the promoters had organized a repeat of his Paris 1500 – 5000 metre double within the hour, the only difference being that the shorter race was replaced by the mile. In this, the two top Americans, Joie Ray and Lloyd Hahn looked likely winners, but were caught at the end by Nurmi in a new indoor world mark of 4:13.5. The longer race pitted him against his Paris rival, Ritola. There was little separating the two until just over a lap to go of the 160 yard track, whereupon Nurmi pulled away convincingly to win in 14:44.6 - his second world mark of the evening.

After that opening night, his programme was enlarged as promoters clamored for his services. In the modern age of jet travel and luxury hotels, it is worth looking back at his schedule. All told, over a four and a half month period (his last race was on May 26), he covered over 50,000 kilometres, ran fifty five races, set twelve indoor world records, gave numerous running exhibitions, and took part in a variety of PR commitments. He failed to win only twice – once when forced to withdraw due to a stomach complaint, the other in his last race of the tour over 800 metres. There were two other occasions when he failed to be the first to finish, but these were handicap events. During the time of the "roaring twenties" in America it seems incongruous, to say the least, that the shy, introverted runner who did not give a single interview or seem to court publicity should be such a huge draw card. President Coolidge made sure that he met him, and the New York Times ran over seventy feature articles covering his tour.

As a portent of what was to happen later in his career, Nurmi, Quist, and Ritola were investigated on charges of demanding excessive expenses in violation of their amateur standing. No doubt, due to some creative accounting procedures, the charges were dismissed. While his American sojourn was an undoubted triumph, Nurmi was never again quite the runner he had been after such a mentally and physically draining tour. He would repeat a similar tour again in 1929, but in a shortened and much less demanding format.

The following year was highlighted by Nurmi twice setting new records over 3000 metres – at Berlin on May 24 (in 8:25.4), and Stockholm on July 13 (in 8:20.8). The latter race was against his great Swedish rival Edvin Wide, who managed to gain some sort of revenge later in the season. In a Berlin meet held on September 11-12, the almost unthinkable happened when Nurmi lost two world records in as many days – and he was running in both races. In the first, the German Otto Peltzer won the 1500 metres in 3:51.0, Wide second in 3:51.8, with Nurmi third in 3:52.8. The following day, Wide again finished ahead of Nurmi, this time over two miles in 9:01.4 to 9:05.0. Also, during the season, Nurmi had time to turn out for his club, as they twice broke the world mark for the 4 x 1500 relay.

1927 was an ordinary year by Nurmi's standards – just the one world record; this time over 2,000 metres in Kuopio on June 18, in 5:24.6. It appeared as if both his enthusiasm for the endless grind of training and competition, along with his physical powers were on the wane. He was by no means a definite starter in the Olympics to be held the following year. Eventually he changed his mind, however; partly due to the recognition of what more Olympic glory might do for his asking price in America.

The Amsterdam Olympics of 1928 were held in a stadium designed to hold 40,000 spectators, and built specifically for the Games. They were notable for being the first Olympics to admit female competitors (despite objections from such notables as Baron de Coubertin and Pope Pius XI). Amsterdam also saw the introduction of the Olympic flame that remained alight for the duration of the Games.

The first of Nurmi's events was the 10,000m, held on Sunday, July 29, the first day of athletic competition. Unlike his previous Olympic effort over the distance in 1920, this time there were no heats, just the final. By the half way mark the race had developed into a three-way tussle between Nurmi, Ritola, and Wide. The rest of the field was a good hundred metres in arrears. Another four laps and it became a race in two as Wide was forced to concede. Ritola stayed ahead, but was out sprinted by Nurmi at the end in a time only twelve seconds outside his own world mark (30:18.8 to 30:19.4). Wide finished well back in third (31:00.8). The second race in Nurmi's Olympic programme was the 5,000 metre qualifying heat two days later (Tuesday, July 31). With the four fastest qualifying, he was happy to get through in the easiest manner possible, finishing in fourth place after a hotly contested final sprint.

The next day saw him running the qualifying heat for the 3,000 metre steeplechase, an event he had only run twice before. His decision to enter this event was largely made on the basis that he had not qualified for the Finnish team in the 1500, and the cross-country was no longer an Olympic event. The very first water jump proved a disaster, as his spikes dug into the top of the barrier, sending him spinning into the water. Despite eventually winning the heat, the fall resulted in injury to his hip and foot.

The 5,000 metre final two days later (Friday, August 3), saw both Nurmi and Ritola carrying injuries – Nurmi with his hip sore from the steeple chase fall, Ritola with a sprained ankle. After two laps Nurmi went to the front, but the pace was not fast enough to worry the rest of the field unduly. As a result, Ritola took the lead at the half way mark, despite visibly favouring his ankle. With a kilometre left, the race was between the two Finns, Wide, and Lermond of the US. Ritola started his final run for home with six hundred metres to go. Only Nurmi was able to respond, and it looked like he would again out sprint his rival. Things did not go to plan, however. Just as Nurmi launched his final attack, Ritola summoned a final sprint of his own, and pulled away to victory. At the end Nurmi had his hands full warding off the fast finishing Wide. The final times were Ritola --14:38.0, Nurmi - 14:40.0, Wide - 14:41.2.

His final event, the steeplechase, followed the next day. Still feeling the effects of his injury and the 5,000 metre final, the race was an ordeal for Nurmi. Not a great hurdler at the best of times, his painful hip only served to highlight this shortcoming. As part of a planned strategy, the best of the Finish steeple chasers (Toivo Loukola) went to the lead after two kilometres and established a thirty metre lead on the rest of the field being led by Nurmi. Making no attempt to catch his team mate, Nurmi ran steadily, allowing Loukola to build up a winning lead. Only in the last lap did Nurmi leave the rest of the field behind to finish with the silver medal. The third Finn, Ove Andersen completed a clean sweep of the medals for Finland, with both Loukola and Nurmi under the old world mark.

Following the Olympics, three more world records fell to Nurmi. At Berlin on October 7, he ran ten miles in 50:15, and then continued on to claim the one-hour mark (19,210 metres), and the 20,000 metres in 1:04:38.4. Shortly afterwards, in December, he left for his second North American tour. His racing proper did not start until January the following year, and his itinerary was much reduced compared to his previous trip.

The years leading up to the 1932 Olympics were to show that despite his age and constant racing, he was still the one to beat. In 1930 he broke the world six mile record at Stamford Bridge in London (albeit in a time markedly inferior to his ten kilometre best), in 29:36.4. The following year his best performance was an attack on the world two mile record, resulting in him becoming the first man under nine minutes at Helsinki on July 27 (time – 8:59.6).

With the Los Angeles Games approaching, Nurmi appeared to gain renewed motivation, and probably trained harder than at any time in his career. On a personal level, 1932 was also a landmark year, bringing as it did marriage to local beauty Sylvi Laaksonen early in the year. In December of the same year, his only son, Matti, was born.

Deciding to finish his Olympic career in dramatic fashion, Nurmi entered the Finnish Olympic marathon trial, held at Vilpuri, on June 26. Bearing in mind the Olympic race was scheduled for August 7, recovery time between the two events would be considered inadequate by today's standards. No doubt in part due to the fact that the first and last ten kilometres was run on a track, a huge crowd was in attendance to see the race. In an unusual twist, Nurmi decided to wear spikes, despite over half the race being on road. His reasoning was that spikes (albeit shorter than usual) would give him greater traction, especially for the track sections of the race. By twenty-five kilometres (reached in a fast 1 hour, 27:43), it was Nurmi and Armas Toivonen side by side, accompanied by a large group of cyclists. At this stage, after a brief conversation, Nurmi increased his pace and one kilometre later had a lead of 150 metres. For the remainder of the race his lead increased, until it reached just on two kilometres. Despite the race being scheduled for the full marathon distance, Nurmi announced to officials that he would be stopping some two kilometres short at the traditional Scandinavian distance of 40.2 kilometres. His time of 2:22:03.8 equated to about 2:29:00 for the full distance, well under world record pace. Toivonen, who completed the full distance in 2:35:00, went on to finish third in the Olympic event (only 36 seconds behind the rapidly fading gold medalist, Zabala of Argentina). As it was, his selection trial marathon had brought on an injury to his achilles tendon that persisted during his time in America. That, however, was only the start of his problems.

The disqualification of Nurmi from the 1932 Los Angeles Olympics deprived him of the chance to emulate the feat of his boyhood inspiration, Hannes Kohlemainen, twelve years before. His disqualification (on the grounds of having accepted excessive allowance money for a series of races in Germany the year before) was an event waiting to happen. The fact that Nurmi had long profited financially from his athletic prowess (despite it never being formally proven) was never really in doubt. Certainly, he was not the only one to have done so. His problem was that during his era there was a growing idealism within both the International Amateur Athletic Federation and the International Olympic Committee toward a strict interpretation of the amateur ideal. Sport, it was argued, should be above the world of politics and commercialism.

The chief proponents of this view were the Swede, Sigfrid Edstrom, president of the IAAF, and his deputy, the American Avery Brundage – both wealthy businessmen. The former had been the inaugural president of the governing body of world athletics, (a position he would hold until 1946) while the latter would go on to rule the Olympic movement for two decades (1952-1972) as if it were his personal fiefdom. Both approached the upholding of the amateur ideal with religious like zealotry. This approach persisted at the highest level until the 1970s, the final break coming with the election of Samaranch as IOC president in

Alone and in front.
Nurmi leads the Finnish
marathon trial for the
1932 Olympics.

1980. Nurmi had traveled to America with the Finnish team, and his official exclusion from the Games was not announced until July 28, 1932 – only three days before the official opening of the Games. The international career of the greatest of runners was over.

While his international career was finished, Nurmi was still able to compete domestically as a "national amateur". Bearing in mind the quality of Finnish distance running vis a vis the rest of the world, his banning probably made little difference to the quality of opponent he met. He was still good enough to win his national 1500 metre title in 1933. His final competition was over 10,000 metres at Viipuri, on August 16, 1934. He won. He was thirty-seven years old.

With the conclusion of his running career, Nurmi set about preparing for the rest of his life. Running had brought him both public esteem and considerable financial reward. He had invested his earnings astutely in the stock market, and this gave him the capital to begin his first business venture after retirement – opening a clothing store. Shortly after, he moved on to other ventures, notably in construction and real estate, where he proved to be a very successful businessman. Proving as resolute and determined at business as he was at running, Nurmi adopted a "hands on" approach to his ventures, constantly visiting construction sites and dealing personally with those doing work for him. During the post war construction boom, he did very well.

While he had retired from running, Nurmi had certainly not retired as a public figure. He was without doubt the best known ambassador the country had. In 1940, he toured America again, not as a runner, but as a manager / publicist with Taisto Mäki (the new 5 and 10 kilometre record holder), to raise funds for the Finnish defense against the invasion by the Soviet Union in the Winter War of that year. During the visits to Finland by various dignitaries he was often one of the invited guests. Among his interests were classical music and art.

Without doubt the most famous public performance by Nurmi following his retirement was his appearance at the 1952 Helsinki Olympics. Held in the stadium originally designed for the 1940 Olympics, as was customary, the final bearer of the Olympic torch remained a closely guarded secret. When the final runner of the torch relay proved to be Nurmi, virtually every athlete broke ranks to get the best possible view of the legendary runner. After completing his leg of the relay, he handed the torch over to his boyhood idol, and later friend, Hannes Kohlemainen.

Throughout his life, Nurmi had shown little or no interest in his celebrity status, and with retirement this did not change. In a rare exception to this rule, he reluctantly agreed to a radio interview on the occasion of his seventieth birthday. The key point in agreeing to the interview was that the main interviewer was a former national high jump champion, who had fought hard on Nurmi's behalf to have his disqualification from amateur ranks overturned. That high jumper had since gone on to become one of Finland's most revered presidents, Urho Kekkonen.

Nurmi had always taken care of his physical well being both during and after his running career. It thus came as a shock that at the age of sixty he suffered a heart attack, despite having none of the known risk factors. Both his blood pressure and cholesterol levels were considered normal, and he had remained active following his retirement from competition. No doubt as a consequence of his own affliction, in 1968 the Paavo Nurmi Foundation was established. The aim of the foundation was to fund research involving cardiovascular disease. The funds were to be drawn against earnings from investments and properties donated by Nurmi to the foundation.

Ten years after his initial heart attack, Nurmi suffered a stroke, and finally succumbed to complications from atherosclerosis on October 2, 1973. He had lived just long enough to see Finnish distance running glory revived in the form of Lasse Viren. He was seventy-six. As a contrast, he was outlived by his two main rivals. Ritola was eighty six when he died in 1982, while Wide lived to be one hundred and was still often seen jogging in his nineties. Just as Nurmi had been a pall-bearer, along with other Finnish greats, at the funeral of his friend and inspiration Hannes Kohlemainen, so a later generation did the same for him. Eight days after his death, he was given a state funeral in the magnificent Old Church in Helsinki, before being laid to rest in his hometown of Turku. In his typical methodical manner, he had brought a gravestone back from the US in the 1920's to serve as a memorial for the family.

The latter years of Nurmi's life had not been kind to him. While retaining his keen mind and mental faculties to the end, the one thing that was so important to him – his physical well being – proved elusive. In the end it left him somewhat embittered. Increasingly he questioned the value of his own contribution and that of sport in general, to society. This opinion, mentioned in one of his increasingly common moments of melancholy, downplayed the important part he had played in helping foster national pride and identity for the newly independent Finland.

As measures of the esteem in which he was held both during and after his athletic career, were the instances in which his memory was preserved. Besides the previously mentioned statues, there were postage stamps in his honour, a ten mark note issued by the Bank of Finland in 1987 carried his picture, the national airline (Finnair) named an aircraft after him, and even a minor planet was named in his honor.

Perhaps the best summary of Nurmi's running career and life in general, is given by his former team mate, and later President of Finland, Urho Kekkonen. Speaking of the reasons for his success he said: "In my opinion character was the most important. He was resolute to the point of stubbornness, and unyielding – a mercilessly tough man. He had the intelligence to plan his training programme, the courage to set his goal high and the will-power in training and competition to achieve the goal he had set".

TAISTO MÄKI

The Rekola Herd Boy

Mäki finishing his record
breaking 5000m in
Helsinki in14:08.8.

FOLLOWING PAAVO NURMI'S ENFORCED retirement from international competition in 1932 (due to professionalism), the pre-eminent position of Finland in world distance running seemed a little shaky. While Finns remained the main contributors to the annual list of top performances, there were some signs that perhaps they would not continue to have things all their own way.

The first real sign occurred in the lead up to the 1932 Los Angeles Olympics. On June 19 of that year, two of Nurmi's venerable records were broken, and only one of the two was claimed by a Finn. In Helsinki, Lauri Lehtinen took a huge chunk off Nurmi's 5,000 metre record. Running what was then an unusual negative split (i.e. the second half of the race being faster than the first), he reduced the record by over eleven seconds as he came home in 14:16.9. Another Finn, Volmari Iso-Hollo was also well under the old time in second place (14:18.3). Meanwhile, in Antwerp, the Pole Janusz Kusocinski reduced Nurmi's 3,000 metre record to 8:18.8. Unlike Lehtinen's effort, his second half was considerably slower than the first.

The Olympics themselves put the Finns well and truly to the test. The 10,000 metres was run on July 31, and Kusocinski made his intentions clear from very early in the race. Taking the lead almost from the start, he set a pace that was well below that required to break Nurmi's record time for the distance. Passing 5,000 metres in 14:56.6, he was shadowed by two Finns and John Savidan of New Zealand. The Finns were the second and third place getters from Lehtinen's 5,000 metre record race – namely Volmari Iso-Hollo and Lauri Virtanen.

Despite slowing somewhat over the second half, the Pole's relentless pace dropped all of his pursuers except for Iso-Hollo, but a final lap of sixty two seconds proved too much for the Finn as Kusocinski proved victorious by 1.2 seconds. His time of 30:11.4 was second only to Nurmi's world mark.

Five days later was the 5,000 metre final. With Kusocinski not running, and the newly crowned record holder Lehtinen well ahead of the rest of the field on times, a Finnish victory seemed assured. However, a hot day and a determined home town rival almost proved their undoing. The two Finns, Virtanen and Lehtinen went into the lead early and pushed the pace. However, after a fast 2:46 first kilometre, they were forced to slow considerably. Going into the last kilometre, Virtanen was still with his countryman, but so was the local hope, American Ralph Hill. Primarily a miler, he stayed with Lehtinen as Virtanen began to fade. The final straight saw one of the tightest finishes of any Olympic distance race. With both men on the verge of exhaustion, Hill tried to get by twice, but on both occasions was thwarted by the Finn veering into his lane.

Lehtinen finally prevailed, with both being given the same time (14:30.0). Virtanen took the minor medal fourteen seconds later as the large partisan crowd loudly voiced their displeasure at the result. A final lap of barely under seventy seconds was some indication of the fatigue of the competitors. Despite some encouragement, Hill refused to lodge a protest, and Lehtinen's victory stood.

Following Lehtinen's 5,000 metre record in 1932, times for both the five and ten kilometre distances stagnated somewhat for the next four years. After his great 14:16.9 in the Olympic year, the best he could do in 1933 was only 14:41.4. Despite the time being so far outside his best, it was still good enough to lead the world rankings. For the next two years no one got below 14:35, while in the same period, Nurmi's 10,000 metre record easily withstood all challengers.

As is often the case, an Olympic year brings forth new talent, as well as serving as an added incentive for veterans to push themselves to new heights. Berlin in 1936 was such a case. By the end of 1935, Finland had resumed their seemingly rightful place at the top of the distance pyramid. Over 5,000 metres Finns had recorded the seven fastest times for the year (albeit with the fastest being almost twenty seconds outside the record for the distance), while over the longer distance they had the two fastest, and four of the top ten.

The Berlin Olympics proved to be another showcase for Finnish distance running. First up was the 10,000 metres. The Finnish trio of

Salminen, Askola and Iso-Hollo controlled most of the race, the only true interloper being Kohei Murakoso of Japan. Murakoso had come into the games with the fastest time of the year (30:41.6), but at the business end of the race had to concede to all three Finns.

For Salminen, it was a fitting victory for the veteran. Having missed both previous Olympics, his major win prior to Berlin was the initial version of the European championships in 1934 where he won the 10,000 metres. Two years later (at age thirty three) he eventually showed his true ability. He picked the perfect time to improve his personal best (to 30:15.4), and his best was needed as he held off Arvo Askola by only 0.2 second.

Five days later, on August 7, the Finns again demonstrated their superiority. Gunnar Hockert, considered by many of his countrymen as the greatest talent of them all, won the 5,000 metres in a sprint finish from Lehtinen in 14:22.2. Sadly for Salminen, he fell with two laps remaining and had to be content with sixth. Hockert would go on to set new world marks for both three thousand metres and two miles after the Games, while Salminen would finally break Nurmi's long standing 10,000 metre mark the following year at age thirty four.

With such talent around, the thought that a runner who took until age twenty two to break sixteen minutes for 5,000 metres (and then by the barest of margins – 0.1 second) would end up being the fastest Finn of them all looked unlikely to say the least. Despite the apparent lack of early promise, this runner – Taisto Mäki - would eventually rise to be not just the best in Finland, but in the world.

Of all the dual five and ten thousand metre record holders, Mäki is almost certainly the least recognised, at least outside his homeland. The reason for this lack of recognition is fairly simple. His greatest races took place in the weeks immediately preceding the outbreak of the Second World War in late 1939. As a result, he never had the chance to demonstrate his prowess on an Olympic stage, and his best results were quickly overtaken by world events that relegated even the greatest sporting results to only minor importance.

Taisto Armas Mäki was born in the Finnish capital of Helsinki on December 2, 1910. The youngest of three boys, his early life was not easy. His mother (Sylvi) died from the effects of diphtheria when he was just five, and four years later his father (Antti, a self employed carpenter) died after contracting pneumonia. Shortly before his death, the family had moved from Helsinki to what was then a small town on the outskirts of the city – Rekola.

After losing both parents, Taisto and his two older brothers (Voitto and Lennart) were taken in by their grandmother, continuing to live in the cottage their father had provided. The village of Rekola has long been swallowed up by the expansion of Helsinki, and is now located in the municipality of Vantaa. Mäki would live in Rekola for the rest of his life, and because of his early farm work would earn the nickname "Rekola herd boy". As an indication of the tough economic times, Mäki only completed six years of formal education – two in Helsinki, and a further four in Rekola. It was then that he had to leave school and begin farm work. For the young Taisto, these were not easy times, highlighted as they were by frequently long days and hard physical labour. The farm work lasted for three years.

When seventeen (in 1927), he joined the local sporting club (Rekolan Urheilijat), and two years later, in November 1929, enlisted with others of his age for a years compulsory military service – a requirement still in force in modern Finland. Following his military service, Mäki went to live with an uncle in Viitasaari in central Finland for six months, working in the forestry industry. He returned to Rekola in the spring of 1931.

Like many young men of his age, Mäki had tried his hand at a number of sports – notably skiing, soccer, and baseball, along with some athletics. However, it was not until his return from central Finland that he had his first proper running competition. The forestry work had been hard, and left no time for training, so his first races back in Rekola (organised by his local club) relied almost solely on natural talent. His first two races were over 1500 metres, and while showing some promise, they were not enough to persuade him to give the sport his full attention. The following year (1932) he took part in a 3,000 metre event for novices in Helsinki. This was really his first formal competition. He won. Later that same year he ran 5,000 metres in 15:59.9. Following those efforts, he began to train regularly.

Despite his increasingly serious approach to training for running, he still decided to try his hand at soccer the following year. However, he soon realised that his true talent lay elsewhere. Certainly, it was recognized by his club president, Viljo Partio, who suggested that he put all his energies into running. As an example of good sporting advice, it would be hard to beat.

That year (1933) his best 5,000 metre time improved – but only to 15:48.0. It was certainly no indication of what was to occur the following year. That same year he decided to try his hand at a new type of job. After a six month training course, he embarked on a new career in the police force. This proved to be very much a short-term venture, and after only two months Mäki decided that the life of a police officer was not for him.

The following year (1934), he got a job that would be his employment for the rest of his working life, until 1972. The company he worked for was appropriately called Alko – the state owned company that produced and sold alcohol. For the first four years, he was employed in the warehouse, and after 1938 was a salesman for the government product to shops in the region. It was not unusual for promising sportsmen of the time to be given "special consideration" for such jobs. Between 1945 and 1950 he was selling the company's product in Kerava (a small town some thirty kilometres outside Helsinki), and between 1950 and 1971 did the same job at a variety of shops in Helsinki.

His new job was in fact organised by his new club, Helsingin Kisa-Veikot (HKV), which he joined in 1934. Obviously deciding to give distance running his full attention (no doubt influenced by fellow sport loving employees), he began training very hard. He frequently rose at 4:30 a.m. and covered some 10-15 kilometres in training before catching the 6:15 train from Rekola to work. After a full days work, a second session would involve running up to 23 kilometres home in the evening. The evening session often involved varied pace running. It was not unusual for him to cover some 200 kilometres in a week. Running had become a serious undertaking, and it would not be long before the results of such training would be evident.

1934 was also the year in which Mäki was married (to Gerda). They already had a daughter (Maire, born in 1930), and would later have a son (Aarre, born in 1942). Three years later they moved to another house in Rekola, which would remain the family home for the rest of their days.

The new job, the more settled family life, not to mention the far more serious training quickly brought results. After a 5,000 metre best of 15:48 0 in 1933, his result at the national championships in Tampere the following year was a shock to say the least. Despite the presence of two Olympic champions (one from 1932, the other yet to be crowned in 1936), Mäki ran away with the 5,000 metre title in 14:49.2. Lauri Lehtinen (the 1932 Olympic champion over the distance), and Gunnar Hockert (later to become the 1936 gold medallist) were left in his wake. Despite his new-found status as national champion, his winning time (which remained his best for the year) was only sufficient to rank him as the thirteenth fastest of the year on the world list.

Selection for the inaugural European Championships in Turin would have been a formality for the newly crowned national champion, but such was not to be. The week after his breakthrough win he was injured while taking part in a triple jump competition in Rekola. Not able to run due to the injury was a heavy price to pay for what had been little more than some light relief from the more serious aspects of training.

As it turned out, in the championship 5,000 metre event, the Frenchman, Roger Rochard improved his personal best by almost ten seconds, to comfortably win from the 1932 Olympic gold medallist over 10,000 metres, Janusz Kusocinski, in 14:36.8, whilst third place was taken by the late blooming Ilmari Salminen. The latter would also narrowly take honours in the longer track event, after a close tussle with his fellow Finn Arvo Askola. The fact that Rochard's winning time was some thirteen seconds better than Mäki's best for the year is an indication that even his best may not have been good enough to prevent the French victory.

It is interesting to note that these first continental championships took only three days to complete, and they were a male only affair. Women did not join the competition until 1946.

After his sudden breakthrough in 1934, any assumption that Mäki's career would be plain sailing from that point was rather quickly proved wrong. This was Finland in the nineteen thirties, and top distance runners seemed to be everywhere.

Despite improving his 5,000 metre best to 14:40.4 in 1935 (winning from Salminen, Lehtinen, and Virtanen), competition for places in the team for the Berlin Olympics the following year would obviously be tough. Beside his 5,000 metre improvement, other notable bests for that year included 2,000 metres in 5:24.6, 3,000 metres in 8:36.5, and in an early portent of what would later follow, 10,000 metres in 31:40 (his first attempt at the distance).

After his 1934 national championship win, and his continued improvement the following year, Mäki's hopes for the Olympic year of 1936 would no doubt have been high. However, in an Olympic year, things do not always go as expected.

In the Olympic trials (held in Helsinki on July 12), Mäki could only finish third (14:41.6) behind Hockert and Salminen (with defending Olympic champion Lehtinen dropping out). Four days later, in Kouvola, Mäki would again be beaten, this time by Lehtinen, in 14:43.0. The result of this race determined the third Finnish entrant for Berlin, meaning that Mäki would not be on the team. Perhaps significantly, his two best times for the year over the five kilometre distance, were both in races where others finished ahead of him. His best 5,000 metre time for the year (his 14:41.6) was good enough to rank twelfth internationally, but there were still six of his countrymen faster over the distance.

As mentioned earlier, the Berlin Olympics were again a showpiece for Finnish distance running. After their relative disappointment at the

Los Angeles Olympiad four years earlier, it was as if the natural order had been restored.

If 1936 had been something of a disappointment as a result of missing the Berlin Olympics, the following year showed that it was only a temporary setback. Mäki began his competitive year by winning the national cross country, and during the course of the Finnish summer proceeded to improve his 1500 metre best (from 3:57.1 to 3:55.2), and his 5,000 metre best (down to 14:28.8). All told, he had four times over the latter distance superior to his best of the previous year.

In a season of over thirty races, Mäki lost only five times, and significantly won both the national title and the prestigious Finland – Sweden dual meet over 5,000 metres. Despite his fine series of victories, one of his best performances came in a losing effort. On August 26 at the Elaintarha track in Helsinki (home of Mäki's HKV club) the American Archie San Romani claimed the 2,000 metre world mark, winning in 5:16.7. Mäki was also under the old mark (by 0.2 second), as he finished second in 5:18.2. This would be the last world record set at the old track, as its future use would be as a warm up venue for the Olympic stadium that would be officially commissioned on June 12 the following year.

1938 began as per the previous year with a win in the national cross country, followed by a series of victories over distances between 1500 and 5,000 metres. However, he did experience defeats over his favourite distance; firstly, at the hands of the Swede, Henry Jonsson, in Helsinki on June 21, then at the hands of fellow Finn, Kauko Pekuri in the Finland – Hungary meet on July 10 (again in Helsinki), and again in the national championships where he could only manage fourth (Helsinki, August 7). Four days later, he again lost, this time to Salminen.

Despite these losses, Mäki still managed to gain selection for the forthcoming European Championships, to be held in Colombes, near Paris. In line with the recent standardization of tracks, the upgraded stadium circuit was now at the newly adopted 400 metres, down from the previous stadium distance of 500 metres.

In the championship event over 5,000 metres, Mäki, and the fellow countryman who would feature in so many of his races – Kauko Pekuri – alternated the pace at the front. The one runner who refused to concede was the Swede Jonsson, who had beaten Mäki earlier in the year. Mäki finally prevailed, but only by 0.6 second, while Pekuri finished 1.8 seconds behind the Swede. The winning time was 14:26.8.

The next day, the longer track event was won by Salminen, who managed to hold off the Italian Giuseppe Beviacqua by just 0.8 second, winning in 30:52.4. The remarkable Finn proved to be one of the truly great 10,000 metre runners. Not only was he a double European champion over the distance, he was also Olympic champion, and had displaced the venerable Nurmi as world record holder over the distance. That event took place in Kouvola, on July 18, 1937. Despite beating the previous time by only 0.6 second, the fact that the last two kilometres were the fastest of the race was perhaps an indication that he was capable of better than his final time of 30:05.5 indicated. That however, was to remain his personal best for the distance.

After his championship triumph, Mäki would compete five more times before calling an end to his season. Perhaps surprisingly, he lost more than he won, but one race would more than make up for the losses.

His first race (and loss) came five days after his win at Colombes. Over 3,000 metres in Stockholm, the first three placegetters from that race again filled the top three places here. The only difference was that Jonsson replaced Mäki in the top spot, with Pekuri again finishing third. Eight days later in Helsinki, the European champion over 5,000 metres faced up against the 10,000 metres champion, over the longer distance. Despite losing to his senior countryman, Mäki dramatically revised his best time over the distance, as both were given the same time of 30:13.4, with Mäki's regular adversary Pekuri finishing a close third in 30:14.0. Despite that gruelling effort, the very next day Mäki was in the central Finnish town of Lahti to run over 5,000 metres. Perhaps unsurprisingly, his winning time was a somewhat pedestrian 15:13.1.

After his 10,000 metre effort against Salminen earlier in the month, Mäki realised that he was capable of better. He had the chance to show just how much better on September 29 at Tampere. Despite coming after the European titles, the event served as the national championship race. The track at Tampere had not yet been changed to the standard 400 metres, and was set at 3331/3 metres.

Being the national championship race, just about all the best Finns were present, including Salminen, Lehtinen, Heino, and Pekuri. In Salminen and Heino there were the present and future record holders over the distance. But this day was not to be theirs. Mäki was in great form, and after a first half in 14:59, covered the second half only slightly slower to come home in 30:02.0 to shave three and a half seconds from Salminen's world record. Salminen had a day to forget as he was lapped by the new record holder, finishing fifth in 31:04.6, the minor placings being taken by Pekuri (30:18.2) and Arvo Askola (30:48.8).

Finishing the year as the European champion over 5,000 metres, and the new world record holder over 10,000m, Mäki could rightly claim the mantle as the worlds best distance runner, his final race of the year (a slow 5,000 metre defeat) notwithstanding. Perhaps fittingly, the winner in that race was Pekuri.

If 1938 had been a good year for the newly crowned record holder, it was only a prelude for what was to occur the following year. In a succession of races over distances between 1500 and 5,000 metres (including a cross country event over 4.5km), Mäki was undefeated as he lined up for an international 5,000 race on June 16.

The race was held in the new stadium that was to become the venue for the 1952 Olympics. It was originally intended as the venue for the 1940 Games, after Tokyo had been stripped of their right to hold them that year as a result of that country's increasing military aggression. Because of the World War between 1939 and 1945, Finland would wait a further twelve years to host the greatest sporting event of them all, while Japan would have to wait double that time.

That however, was all in the future as Mäki, along with the best of his countrymen faced the starter. As was often the case, Pekuri was not afraid to take his share of front running duties. After a fast opening kilometre (2:46), chances of a new record may have slipped away as the next three kilometres passed in the 2:52 – 2:53.5 range. However, over the last kilo, Mäki changed gear and finished the final thousand metres in 2:44.3, to be rewarded with a time of 14:08.8, taking 8.1 seconds from Lehtinen's world mark. For his efforts, Pekuri also finished under the old world mark in 14:16.2, while Salminen, getting better with age, finished third in a personal best 14:22.0 at age 37. Mäki's three mile time en route of 13:42.4 was also a new world mark.

After another series of races between 800 and 5,000 metres (including two relays for his club), his next truly great effort was on July 7 in Helsinki over two miles. Despite being the obvious favourite after his earlier record breaking effort, Mäki had to work hard for his win. In the end he won by a scant 0.3 second from Veikko Tuominen – 8:53.2 to 8:53.5 – with Pekuri third in 8:54.8, as all three broke the previous world mark of 8:56.0 held by the Hungarian Miklos Szabo.

His next three races included a personal best over 1500 metres in Tampere (winning in 3:53.5), another 1500m in Stockholm (losing to the Swede Jansson in 3:54.0), and even a 400 metre race (finishing fifth). Then followed the annual Sweden versus Finland dual meet. For many years this had been one of the true sporting highlights for both countries. Despite the two longest track events being held on consecutive days, Mäki's form was such that he was selected for both. He did not let the selectors down.

First up was the 5,000 metres, with the world record holder winning by a second from the Swede Jonsson in a good 14:17.8, with Pekuri filling third spot. The next day (July 28) resulted in maximum points for the Finns as the world record holder beat the Olympic champion – Mäki 30:35.4, Salminen 30:35.6.

The national championships in Helsinki were a month later, but Mäki was not taking it easy. Among his races leading up to the nationals were races in Great Britain and Sweden, but probably his best effort was over a mile in Helsinki nine days before the national titles. Despite his 4:12.0 being a losing effort, it was still good enough to rank ninth in the world for 1939, as the winner's (Joseph Mostert of Belgium) time (4:10.4) was the second fastest for the year.

The national championships began for Mäki on August 27 with a heat win over 1500 metres, however he decided against running the final the next day. Instead he concentrated on the longest of his two trademark events. Finishing well clear of the rest of the field, he ran a fine 30:09.4 to finish over half a lap ahead of Salminen, with Iso-Hollo and Heino filling the third and fourth positions.

Allowing himself a three day break after his championship win, Mäki then had three races in as many days, over 3,000, 1500, and 5,000 metres, all in mediocre times, and losing the 1500 metre race. He then had another week without racing, before a relatively slow 5,000m (beating Salminen in 14:54.8), and then five days later a much faster effort, winning from Jonsson in Stockholm in 14:19.8. Two days later he was ready to add another chapter to distance running history.

September 17 dawned as a pleasant clear day. In the morning, Mäki ran (and won) an easy club race over 1500 metres at a suburban track. The slow time of 4:23.0 was no indication of what was to follow later in the day. In the afternoon, on the bigger stage of the new Helsinki stadium, he set out with the aim of becoming the first to finish the ten kilometre distance in less than thirty minutes.

A first kilometre in 2:55.5 made his intentions clear, and despite slowing somewhat, reached the halfway mark in 14:58.2. After a too slow seventh kilometre in 3:04, Mäki picked up the pace and ran the last three kilometre segments in 2:54.0, 3:00.4, and 2:54.2, to finish full of running in 29:52.6. He had taken just on ten seconds from his own record, broken the six mile record on the way (28:55.6), but most importantly become the first sub thirty minute runner over the distance. Behind Mäki, fellow Finns Tauno Kurki (30:16.0) and the evergreen Salminen (30:26.2) filled the minor placings.

Mäki's last race for the season was over 5,000 metres ten days later, where he failed to finish. At the end of the 1939 season, Finns had four of the top five over 5,000 metres, and all top five over 10,000 metres. Of course, they also had the reigning European and Olympic champions over both distances, along with the world record holder for both. With a hometown Olympics the following year, to say the future looked bright would be an understatement of epic proportions.

While many in Finland had been preoccupied with the feats of their athletes, those involved in international relations had other more serious concerns. The storm clouds of war had been gathering for some time, and for the Finns, the signing of the so-called non-aggression pact between Nazi Germany and Soviet Russia had the potential to be a death sentence for the country. Mäki's final race for 1939 was on September 27. By November 30, Finland was at war

The Winter War that lasted from November 30, 1939 until March 13, 1940 was the first of Josef Stalin's two great blunders of the Second World War. The second would be his failure to adequately prepare for Hitler's invasion of his country (despite numerous very specific warnings) in 1941.

The outbreak of the Second World War was brought about by the German invasion of Poland. As part of the Soviet – German treaty (the so-called Molotov-Ribbentrop pact), signed shortly before the invasion, Stalin got to control a large section of eastern Poland. Along with the division of Poland, there was also German agreement that they would not intervene in a subsequent Russian annexation of the Baltic States and Finland (a section of the secret protocols enacted as part of the treaty). The Baltic States realised they had little alternative, but Finland was a different matter. They decided to make a stand.

No doubt emboldened by the ease with which Poland was over-run, along with the subsequent subjugation of the Baltic States, it was assumed by Stalin that Finland would fall just as easily. With the overwhelming numerical advantage of the Soviets in both man- power and equipment, they thought (along with the rest of the world), that any war would be a short-term affair. Certainly, Stalin expected to have the entire country under his control shortly after any invasion. The reality was somewhat different.

The invasion of Finland was treated with near universal disdain by the world community. The Russians were expelled from the League of Nations and a number of overseas Finns returned home to fight, along with other nationals. Despite general admiration for Finland from the international community, little of such admiration translated into what was needed – military aid.

Despite their huge advantage in troop numbers and equipment, the invasion was a disaster for the Soviets. The failure was due to a combination of factors, but a great deal of the blame can be sheeted home directly to Stalin and the Communist regime.

The purges of the late thirties had left the armed forces bereft of many of their most experienced and capable leaders – liquidated or exiled by a paranoid leader who saw almost all his countrymen as potential threats to his power. Coupled to this lack of leadership was the command structure. The professional soldiers had to defer to the political commissars attached to all units before a military decision could be made. This hardly made for an efficient fighting force.

Despite being greatly outnumbered, the Finns were far more at home in the conditions. A bitterly cold winter (with temperatures dropping to below – 40 degrees), allied with the ability of most of the locals being able to ski and use guerrilla type tactics, saw enormous losses imposed on the invading forces. In some cases, the Russians lost 10% of their forces due to frost-bite before the fighting even began.

Despite huge Russian losses, the result of the war was somewhat inevitable. The death toll and suffering of the men under his control meant little to Stalin. Sheer weight of numbers meant that the longer the war dragged on, the less would be the chance of Finland (with a total population of less than four million) being able to withstand the onslaught.

Mäki winning over three miles in New Orleans as part of the Finnish relief fund tour in 1940.

A peace treaty was finally signed on March 12, 1940 – but not before an estimated 125,000 Russians were killed, with an additional 260,000 wounded. Finnish losses were about one fifth of the Russian figures (still a large number for such a small country).

While Finland retained its sovereignty, it was forced to concede some 10% of its land (largely in the eastern Karelian region that abutted the then Soviet Union), and 12% of the population was forced to re-locate.

Distance running, along with every other aspect of Finnish life, was in turmoil during the days of the Russian invasion. For example, Hockert, the Olympic champion from Berlin was killed on the Karelian front, while Viljo Heino (later to break the 10,000-metre world mark) was wounded. Heino continued to train, but often undertook such training with a pistol tucked in his shorts.

Mäki himself (now also in the army) was initially sent to the Karelian front, however he was recalled after a short time with a view to undertaking a goodwill / fundraising trip to America. After spending some time training in both Helsinki and Hameenlinna (about 100 kilometres north of the capital), he left Helsinki by ship on January 16 (accompanied by compatriot Paavo Nurmi), arriving there via Norway on February 3, 1940. There was a notable Finnish presence in the US, with such expats as Ville Ritola and Hannes Kohlemainen having made the country their home many years before.

There was considerable support for the Finnish war effort against the naked aggression of their much larger neighbour, with the conflict viewed very much as a David versus Goliath affair. Mäki and Nurmi got considerable publicity and sympathy, along with some money for their country's plight.

By the time of his trip, Mäki was the world record holder in the two miles, three miles, five thousand metres, six miles, and ten thousand metres. He was without doubt the finest distance runner of his time, and the latest example of the "Flying Finns."

Running in America brought mixed results, but most times were well outside his best. This was hardly surprising considering the turmoil in his homeland, and the fact that the trip was primarily to garner support for the war effort at home rather than any promotion of Mäki's running career.

Another factor that contributed to Mäki's less than imposing results in America was the influence of Paavo Nurmi. For Nurmi, there was one of doing things – his way! To suggest there might be an alternative way of training would be seen as little short of heresy in Finland, and arguing with such an iconic figure almost unthinkable.

Nurmi devised a training plan for Mäki for their American tour. Once in New York, training consisted basically of three sessions a day, each of about an hour's duration or longer. The morning run was in Central Park, while the daytime and evening sessions were both indoors on a wooden surface. The bulk of training was steady running, which because of both the volume and the surfaces on which it was run, left Mäki almost constantly tired. As if that were not enough, Nurmi decreed that in buildings, at all times the stairs would be used rather than the lift. At times after training, it was all Mäki could do to make it to their eighth floor apartment. Nurmi returned home in March, while Mäki stayed on in America, not returning to Finland until July 3. While both were in America, a peace treaty was negotiated with the Soviets.

The war years took a terrible toll on the Finnish nation. Beside the Winter War, Finland also fought the so-called Continuation War later during the Second World War. The aim of this conflict was to try and regain the territory lost in their earlier war against Soviet Russia. Unfortunately, that meant siding with Nazi Germany. As with the first conflict, Mäki took part and was on the front until the conclusion of hostilities in 1944.

With the end of fighting, the Paris Peace Treaties of 1947 required the Finnish nation to pay reparations equivalent to three hundred million US dollars to the Soviet Union (at 1938 values). Of all countries, Finland was the only one to fully repay the assigned amount – a huge sum for such a small population.

The war essentially put paid to Mäki's athletic career. True, in 1940 he did win his national title again over 10,000 metres (30:39.4), and his 5,000 metre best of 14:32.0 was good enough to rank sixth on the world list, but over both distances there were other Finns faster – one over the longer distance, and three over the shorter.

Between 1940 and 1945, Finnish dominance of the annual best distance running performances ceased, with the lists being dominated by athletes from either the Axis powers or from neutral countries (notably Sweden). Where the Finns had the top five (and six of the top

Mäki in training for his American tour. New York, 1940.

ten) over 10,000 metres in 1939, by the end of 1941 they had none in a top ten made up of four Swedes, three Hungarians, and one each from Italy, Germany, and Argentina. With the exception of Heino, the world list for the 5,000 metres was very similar.

The following year marked an even more pronounced shift, with the five kilometre event dominated by Sweden. Not only did runners from that country make up eight of the top ten for the year, in Gunder Hagg they had unearthed a rare talent. While his battles with compatriot Arne Anderson over the mile and 1500 metres captivated the sporting world (and almost certainly would have led to one or both of them breaking the four minute barrier for the mile had they not been disqualified for professionalism), it was over 5,000 metres that Hagg made just as big an impact.

During his 1942 season - the start of his record-breaking career - he made one of his infrequent forays into the longer distances, and on September 20 at Goteborg comprehensively demolished Mäki's best over 5,000 metres. Starting with an opening kilometre of 2:40.0 (13:20 pace!), he won by almost three quarters of a lap to become the first under fourteen minutes for the distance, finishing in 13:58.2. His three mile time of 13:32.4 was also well under the old mark. A new era had arrived.

Over the longer distance, Mäki's time would survive another two years. Perhaps fittingly, the record would go to another Finn – Viljo Heino, who completed the twenty five lap journey in Helsinki on August 25 in 29:35.4.

And what of Mäki during this period? As a consequence of his war service, he competed little. He ran in the national championships over 10,000 metres in 1942, but as an indication of his lack of form, his third place finish in a race won by Salminen was almost two minutes outside his best.

After the conclusion of the world conflict in 1945, he did show glimpses of his former self, but it was now six years since his glory days. In 1945 he did enough to rank fourth fastest in the world over 5,000m (a losing effort in 14:27.0), and third fastest over 10,000 metres (winning against Denmark in 30:12.6). The following year, his best of 14:33.8 (finishing second to fellow Finn Sarkama) would rank him thirteenth fastest for the year, while his only start over 10,000 metres for the year (in the Finland – Sweden dual meet) would result in him dropping out.

By 1947, the best he could manage over 5,000 metres was 14:50.8, sufficient to rank just inside the top forty for the year, while his two journeys over the longer distance brought almost identical times – 30:34.0 in the national championships, and 30:34.2 in the dual meet against Sweden. Both times were good enough for only third place, but did place him eighth fastest for the year.

1948 was an Olympic year, and also Mäki's last real year of competition. His bests of 14:39.4 and 31:35.8 were good enough to rank twenty-fourth and forty-sixth respectively, but he was never a realistic chance for Olympic selection. Although he did run in 1949, his 5,000 metre best of 15:30.0 indicated that his running had become more of a recreation than a serious vocation. Another two years later (1951) he lined up for the national cross-country title in Lappeenranta. In what was to be his last real race he finished thirteenth.

Mäki continued to live in Helsinki and remained in his job with the state alcohol company until his retirement. His death on May 1, 1979, at age 68, was a shock to all who knew him. He appeared in robust good health, but died suddenly of coronary thrombosis. At the time, this was not uncommon in Finland, due in no small part to the Finnish diet which comprised large amounts of saturated fats. In later years, due to medical prompting, this aspect of the local diet has improved somewhat.

On one level, Mäki's career as an athlete was an unlucky one, belying the personality of the individual. His misfortune was being at his best at an inopportune time. Had the Olympics been held as scheduled in 1940, he would have undoubtedly been favourite for both of the longer track events. Hagg of Sweden had not yet come on the world scene to be a threat over 5,000 metres, and Heino would not make his mark at the longer distance for another three years. By 1948, however, his window of opportunity had well and truly closed.

An assessment of Mäki's career perhaps suffers due to people putting undue emphasis on Olympic results as the measure of a competitor. Like other such performers – for example in later years Henry Rono, Sándor

Mäki & Nurmi during their U.S.A.
Goodwill tour March 1940.

Iharos and Ron Clarke – politics in various forms conspired to prevent them from showing their best on the Olympic stage.

While on this level, Mäki can be viewed as something of a sad figure, in person he was, if anything, the opposite. From early in his career the opinion had been expressed that he was too outgoing and not serious enough to make it at the highest level. Certainly the 1936 gold medallist Salminen had expressed this opinion to him early in his career. This view was no doubt coloured somewhat by the example set by the introverted, taciturn Nurmi. Photos of Nurmi show him rarely smiling, unlike most photos of Mäki. In the conservative society of pre war Finland, Mäki was something of a bohemian. Once, when asked to explain a disappointing result in an important race, he jokingly referred to the fact that he had drunk too much coffee beforehand.

Mäki's outgoing personality and the fun-loving exterior he presented obviously masked a sometimes more serious side. Clearly, anyone who could train with the determination that he exhibited was not completely carefree. Early on, he had said that he believed in the "miracle of exercise", and was a great believer that if one was enthusiastic, it was possible to both train hard and put in a full days work. He was living proof that such an attitude could pay dividends. Perhaps in these days of the full time professional athlete, many could do worse than reconsider his approach.

Unfortunately, when considering the past greats of distance running, if there is one name omitted, more often than not it is that of Mäki. Yet he really deserves to be ranked as highly as many of his better-known countrymen. He was a European champion, a multiple world record holder, and but for the vagaries of international politics, may well have been a double Olympic champion.

EMIL ZATOPEK

The Human Locomotive

Zatopek training in Helsinki
before his historic Olympic triple
victory. The only runner to have
won the 5000m, 10,000m and
marathon at a single Olympics.

IN SPORT OVER THE years there have been individuals who, for a variety of reasons, have transcended the feats that made them legends in their particular sport. For example, sportsmen such as Paavo Nurmi in running, Babe Ruth in baseball, or Muhammad Ali in boxing, conjure up images of larger than life figures whose influence was far greater than merely being pre-eminent in their particular sporting field. They became world figures, feted equally by national leaders and the ordinary man in the street.

Emil Zatopek almost certainly fits into the above category. There are probably a number of reasons why such individuals assume legendary status, but two predominant ones would have to be their performances, and the other would be their personality.

In each case, they were clearly the best in the world at what they did, but more than that, was the way they did it. Whether it was the introverted, unsmiling Nurmi, the happy go lucky Ruth, or the brash extroversion of Ali, they were all figures that were noticed for more than just their physical ability. They were also all children of their era, whether it was the grim economic times of the twenties and thirties in the case of Nurmi and Ruth, the tumultuous sixties in the case of Ali, or the post war years of Zatopek.

In the case of Zatopek, his influence far exceeded just his own sport. Single handedly he demonstrated just how much training the human body could endure, and as a consequence, just how much it could improve. These principles were recognized first by the athletic frater-nity, probably next by swimming, with other endurance sports following. This is not to say that before Zatopek top athletes did not train hard – in many cases they did; but it was he more than anyone who showed just how hard, and for how long. Also, the fact that he was more than happy to share his ideas on training was in sharp contrast to others who were often secretive when it came to the reasons for their success.

There is an old Chinese adage: "May you live in interesting times." Whether or not Zatopek was familiar with the saying, his life epitomized its spirit. Born on September 19, 1922, in the town of Koprivnice, the country that was to become so dear to him was itself only four years old at the time. In the aftermath of the First World War, Czechoslovakia was created as part of the break up of the old Austro-Hungarian Empire. The predominant ethnic groups of the new country were some seven million Czechs, two million Slovaks, and three and a half million German speaking members (largely concentrated in the region referred to as the Sudetenland).

The youngest of six children, at the age of sixteen Zatopek began working as an apprentice in the Bata shoe factory in Zlin, some ninety kilometres from his hometown. The following year (1938) the German army moved into the Sudetenland, using the desire of the large German speaking group to become part of the greater German Reich as justification. By March the following year, the rest of the country was under German control, including the Bata shoe factory.

As part of a promotion for the company, there was an expectation that employees would participate in a race through the town streets. Thus it was that a reluctant Zatopek faced the start of his first race as an eighteen year old in 1941. He had shown no real desire or apparent aptitude for sport until this time. Despite his initial reluctance, he finished second in the race, and as a result was chosen to represent the company in a 1500 metre track race later in the year. Another second place seemed to awaken a desire to improve, along with a realization that perhaps he had some ability in this new found activity.

The German occupiers were apparently content to allow sporting activities continue largely as normal. Following his 1500 metre effort, Emil began training with some friends, but once the pleasant weather of summer came to an end, it was he alone training after work. The following year he began to win some races, and was noticed for the first time, but only within his own country. This was not really saying a lot, as Czechoslovakia was certainly no Finland or Sweden when it came to distance running. The best of the Czech distance runners could barely break 15:30 for 5000 metres, at a time when the world mark had been lowered to below fourteen minutes.

The first track race for Zatopek beyond 1500 metres was over three kilometres in 1942. Despite a somewhat promising 9:12.2 for the distance, that race along with a fifth place in the national 1500 metre championship in a mediocre 4:13.9, gave little indication of the career that was to eventuate. Training at this stage involved little more than steady running, usually about eight kilometres a day. Even so, it was regular, at a time when year round training was more the exception than the rule.

The following year (1943) was really the turning point for Zatopek, as it was during this period that he decided to change his approach to training. As a result the athletic world, indeed much of the entire sporting world, would never be the same again.

The new type of training in this case, was interval training. The concept of such training was not new; it had been used in some form many years before, notably by the Finns, by Kusocinski of Poland (the 1932 Olympic ten thousand metre champion), and by Dr. Waldemar Gerschler while coaching in Germany in the thirties. However, without a doubt it was Zatopek who popularized it, along with the concept that gradual progression enabled ever increasing workloads to be undertaken.

While such training may have been undertaken before Zatopek, it would be a mistake to assume that knowledge about it was readily available. The ready dissemination of information that we take for granted today, is a far cry from the time when Zatopek was beginning his athletic career. Initially, such methods were decried as foolhardy by many who knew what he was doing. It was only after he began achieving his exceptional results that he changed from a fool to a genius.

The concept of interval training involves periods of work separated by periods of recovery. In Zatopek's case, he initially began running one hundred, two hundred, three hundred and four hundred metre distances followed by recovery jogs of a similar length. At the start of his career, when he was concentrating on the 1500 metres, the total volume of fast running for each workout was between 1500 and 4000 metres. As his career progressed and he came to specialize at the longer distances, so his training changed. The greatest change was in the sheer volume of work undertaken. After a few years of training he ran intervals almost exclusively over two hundred and four hundred metres, with jog recoveries of two hundred metres or less. At times he was running up to one hundred such four hundred metre stretches (spread over two sessions) daily. He came to believe that improvement resulted primarily from an increase in the total training volume.

Although much of his training was done on tracks, a great deal was also done in the forests where he lived. Often such non track training was done in boots, not so much for added resistance, but rather to avoid ankle injuries on the uneven surfaces. One constant was the regularity of the training. Weather was never an excuse to miss running. From extreme heat to snow, training went on. The other key factor was the regular and gradual increase in training intensity and volume. Although a stopwatch was never used, the aim was to make training so hard that races would seem easy by comparison.

The new type of training seemed to be working. In 1943, he lowered his 800 metre time to 1:59.0, and his 1500 metre time of 4:01.0 was the best of the year by a Czech runner. His time of 15:26.6 for 5000 metres was also within striking distance of the national record that had stood for nine years. He also improved one position over his 1942 finish to take fourth in the national 1500 metre title.

The following year saw his training really begin to bear fruit. He finished second in the national 1500 metre title, broke four minutes for the first time over the distance (3:59.5), and then set new national records over both 3000 metres (8:34.8), and 5000 metres (14:54.9). However, although these were noteworthy performances at home, on a world scene dominated by Finland and Sweden during the war years, they were nothing to get too excited about.

By the end of 1943, the tide of war had changed, and over the later part of 1944 and the early part of 1945 the occupiers of Czechoslovakia had changed from German to Russian. Like many his age, Zatopek had been conscripted for military service, but as fighting left his country he was able to put more of his energy into training. His second national record at 3000 metres (in 8:33.4) was among his first races after the German army was driven out, while his first 5000 metre race of the season was a national championship win in a record 14:50.8.

Finding that army life agreed with him, Emil applied, and was accepted for the officer training course. It came as a pleasant surprise for him to find that the officer training school had excellent facilities for training, and also that he was able to find the time to put them to good use – invariably in the evening after completing his military duties.

It is probably no coincidence that all three members of the exclusive "five and ten" club who set their records in the aftermath of the Second World War, namely Zatopek, Iharos and Kuts were all "Eastern Bloc" members of the armed forces. At a time when there were still shortages of basic items, and life was harsh for many, membership of the forces guaranteed regular meals, time to train, and time off for competitions.

Early in the 1946 season Emil lowered his national 5000 metre record to a far more respectable 14:36.6, in addition to bringing his 3000 metre best down three times, culminating in a best of 8:21.0. Because of his excellent early season form he was selected for the first of the post war European Championships. These were held in Oslo, in August. After the cessation of hostilities, there was little reason to believe that the Finnish dominance of distance running so evident up to 1939 would not continue after the war. The new 10,000 metre record holder was yet another Finn (Viljo Heino), while the 5000 metre record holder (the Swede Gunder Hagg) had been disqualified, as per Nurmi, for accepting undue payments.

The championships in Oslo served both as an indication of what the future might hold, as well as a reminder of lost opportunity. Clearly for some, the war had deprived them of their best chance for Olympic glory. In the 10,000 metres, the Finnish world record holder Viljo Heino was the comfortable winner. Had Olympic competition taken place in 1944, he would have been an overwhelming favourite for the event.

Emil entered the 5000 metres, and a clear winner here was more difficult to predict. In the end the victor was perhaps the most unlikely looking champion ever to lace up spikes. Sydney Wooderson was a slightly built, bespectacled solicitor whose physique betrayed a talent for running seen in few. Breaking world records for both the half mile and mile, he was also good enough to win his national cross country title over nine miles. He would have been a definite threat at either the 1940 or 1944 Olympics. A world record holder for the mile at twenty three, and the European 1500 metre champion in 1938, he was now thirty one, and again had the chance to show what he was capable of – and what might have been. Taking the lead in the last two hundred metres, he sprinted away to win in the second fastest time ever recorded (14:08.6).

Heino, the 10,000 metre winner from the previous day finished fourth, while Zatopek finished fifth in a new personal best of 14:25.8. The contrast in styles between the Finn and the Czech could not have been greater. While Heino was renowned as one of the most stylish runners ever to grace a track, Emil could most charitably be described as the exact opposite. His uninhibited style gave the impression that each stride could well be his last. With head bobbing, arms flailing, and mouth wide open, he gave the impression that every race was an exercise in almost complete torment.

Whatever the pros or cons of his running style, his improved results convinced him that what he was doing in the way of training was right. By this stage of his career he was reportedly doing daily workouts of 20x200m or 20x400m either on the track, or on forest paths.

While his fifth place in the European Championships may have come as a surprise, his 1947 season proved that it was certainly no fluke. His very first race was a new personal best time over 3000 metres, his 8:13.6 making him the eighth fastest ever for the distance. While that may have come as a shock to many, it was nothing compared to what followed a few days later. In Prague on June 25, he ignored the opposition and the windy conditions to win over 5000 metres in a time that supplanted Wooderson as the second fastest ever over the distance

– 14:08.2. Five days later he was in Helsinki to run against the local hero – Heino, over the same distance. After a punishing early pace, Zatopek managed to edge ahead in the final straight to win in 14:15.2, a mere 0.2 ahead of the Finn.

Later in the year he ran (and won) both the 1500 and 5000 metres at the World Student Games in Paris. His winning 1500 metre time of 3:52.8 would remain a career personal best, no doubt partly because he never again ran the distance in serious competition. 1947 was the turning point for Zatopek. He had begun the year as a promising newcomer, and ended it as one of the best in the world. With his ungainly style, fierce competitive instinct, and fast times, he was definitely a man to watch the following year.

1948 was an Olympic year, and Emil had made the decision to try for both the 5000 and 10,000 metres at London. The fact that he had not yet run the longer race on a track did not seem an issue. His training, which by this stage had progressed to sessions of up to 60x400 metres, convinced him that he was capable of performances on a par with his efforts over the shorter distance.

In late May, in Budapest, he tried the longer distance for the first time. Although his time of 30:28.4 would have ranked him behind only five others the year before, he knew he was capable of much better. As if to justify this conviction, less than two weeks later he reduced his 3000 metre best to an impressive 8:07.8.

In Prague on June 17, he decided to try and atone for what he had seen as a mediocre debut over 10,000 metres. Winning by over six minutes, he missed Heino's world mark by a scant 1.6 seconds as he improved dramatically to 29:37.0. Five days later, his time of 14:10.0 for 5000 metres would be the fastest of the year. On the eve of the London Games, Zatopek had the fastest times for the year in both the five and ten thousand metres, and was the justifiable favourite for both.

His daily training during the year had been to run 5x200m., 20x400m., 5x200m., with each followed by a 200m. jog. During his final build up, however, he reported doing 60x400m. ten days in succession. On times for 10,000 metres, Heino and Zatopek were over thirty seconds ahead of the next best, and the form guide seemed to indicate a two man race. The day was hot as Heino went to the lead, setting a pace considerably faster than world record schedule. Zatopek ran at a much more even tempo, and gradually threaded his way through the other twenty six starters until taking the lead before the half way mark. Briefly Heino resumed the lead, and led at 5000 metres in 14:57.0. However, the heat, along with Zatopek's pace proved too much, and Heino retired after sixteen laps. Zatopek went on to win by over forty seven seconds in 29:59.6. Second was the French – Algerian Alain Mimoun, who would become one of Emil's great rivals over the next few years.

Whilst it had been unpleasantly hot for the 10,000 metres, three days later conditions were almost the exact opposite for the shorter race. Rain had fallen steadily and the track was sodden. Undeterred by the conditions, Zatopek went to the front and led until 3000 metres, reached in 8:33. In his wake were Gaston Reiff of Belgium and Wim Slykhuis of Holland. Two hundred metres later Reiff went to the front and drew away. With a lap to go, Slykhuis was twenty metres behind the Belgian, with Zatopek another twenty further back in a seemingly hopeless position. It was only then that he seemed to sense the seriousness of the situation. Mounting a frantic last lap sprint, he raced past Slykhuis, and in the final straight looked as if he would catch the tiring Reiff. Just in time the Belgian realized how quickly Zatopek was coming, and managed to raise his pace over the last few metres just enough to hold him off.

Being beaten by Reiff was certainly no disgrace. He was obviously in excellent form, as demonstrated by a new world 2000 metre record (5:07.0) only a few weeks after the Games. He also had a much faster 1500 metre time than Zatopek. Later in the season, Reiff agreed to a re-match against Zatopek over 5000 metres, and the result was the same as in London (Reiff 14:19.0 to Zatopek 14:21.2). This was a significant defeat for Emil. He did not suffer another loss over the distance for almost four years.

The 1948 Olympic 5,000m final. Zatopek leads from Ahlden (Sweden) and eventual winner Gaston Reiff.

Zatopek's 1948 season established him as the world's premier distance runner. In addition to his Olympic gold and silver medals, he had run seven of the fastest twelve times of the year over 5000 metres, and four of the six fastest over 10,000 metres. To cap his year, in October he married the javelin thrower with whom he would share his life for over fifty years – Dana Ingrova. The two coincidentally shared the same birthdates.

Emil began his 1949 season with two 5000 metre races, the second in a good 14:10.2. Realizing he was in good form, he set out on June 11 to try for the 10,000 metre world mark. The event was the army championship and the venue was the Ostrava track. Ahead of Heino's record pace the entire way, Emil passed the half way mark in 14:39.5, and went on to record a new time of 29:28.2 for the distance – 7.2 seconds faster than Heino.

Only a week later he was back on the same track, running the same distance. His time on this occasion was an almost routine 29:49.6, but he was still one of only three to have ever broken thirty minutes for the distance. Three weeks later in Helsinki he crushed Heino with a winning time of 29:58.4, returning the next day to win the 5000 metres in 14:20.0.

After his effort in London and his recent defeat by Zatopek, Heino appeared to be a spent force. His Olympic disappointment was felt keenly by many of his countrymen and he was determined to redeem himself in their eyes. During his winter preparations his wife died, leaving him to raise their four children alone. With these setbacks and his early season loss to Zatopek, it came as a shock when he reclaimed the 10,000 metre world record for Finland. In the town of Kouvola on September 1, he had enough in reserve to make the last kilometre his fastest, and break Zatopek's mark by one second in 29:27.2.

Not to be outdone, back at Ostrava sixteen days later Emil ran another 10,000 metres. His time of 29:38.2 convinced him that with a few more weeks of hard training he could get the record back. By October 22 he was ready. Running yet again on the Ostrava track he was six seconds ahead of Heino's time at half way, and held that advantage to the end to finish in 29:21.2. That was his final word for 1949. Undefeated, and now with a world record to go with his Olympic medals, had there been any doubts about who was number one at the start of the year, there were certainly none at the end.

While 1949 was the real start of the "Zatopek era", 1950 could in many ways be seen as his "golden year". All things considered, it may even have been better than his 1952 Olympic year. Being both a national hero and a member of the armed forces, Emil now had almost unlimited time to train, even if he did have to bow to the state sometimes when it came to his competition schedule.

Training had progressed to the stage where he was now undertaking sessions of up to 80x400 metres with his customary 200 metre jog for recovery. After a low key start to the new season, any doubts about his fitness were put to rest after three days in Finland. In Helsinki on August 2 he ran a new personal best for 5000 metres, his 14:06.2 replacing his own time as the second fastest ever. Two days later, in Nurmi's hometown of Turku he took the 10,000 metre record to a new level. His time of 29:02.6 took 18.6 seconds from his own mark and brought the twenty nine minute barrier well within reach. With Heino and Wooderson now retired, he was in a league of his own.

The European Championships in 1950 were held in Brussels in late August. It had rained heavily prior to the 10,000 metres, and sections of the track were covered by water. Seemingly oblivious to the conditions, Zatopek ran like a metronome as the field dropped steadily further back with each lap. Considering the conditions, his winning time of 29:12.0 was almost certainly superior to his world mark for the distance. Mimoun was next over the line in 30:21.0.

The 5000 metre heats were the next evening. Emil qualified in an easy 14:56.0, saving his energy for the final two days later. The final was a rematch of the London Olympic race. Reiff, the local hero, expected to run close to the world record and led for most of the race. Zatopek, despite dropping up to ten metres behind never lost contact. He took the lead with just under four laps remaining, only to have Reiff reclaim it again. With a lap to go, the Belgian led with Zatopek on his heels. At this point, Zatopek made his move and the race was over. Reiff crumbled as Zatopek sprinted away to an easy win. Despite being together at the bell, the winning margin ended up at twenty three seconds, as Reiff lost second place to Mimoun. The winning time of 14:03.0 was a new personal best and less than five seconds from Hagg's world mark of 13:58.2.

It is doubtful if any runner has had a more dominant season than Zatopek in 1950. In addition to his overwhelming victories in the European Championships (against the world's best), he also recorded the seven fastest times of the year over both five and ten thousand metres. In addition, in the shorter race he had run the second, third, and fourth fastest times ever, while over the 10,000 metres he had recorded both the world record and the second fastest ever. In the longer race, while he was within a few strides of the twenty nine minute barrier, no one else had broken thirty minutes during the year. Clearly he was a class above his contemporaries.

With the huge volume of training that Zatopek was undertaking, it was probably to be expected that the longer the race, the better he would perform. Also, the fact that he had trouble breaking two minutes for 800 metres, and his 1500 metre best would remain at 3:52.8 was ample evidence that he was very much a strength runner. His most common tactic was to grind opponents into submission, and such was his superiority that for the great majority of his races there was little need to vary it. However, he was able to demonstrate a blazing sprint at the end of races when required, indicating that with some specialization he may well have improved his shorter distance times by a considerable amount.

While the 1950 season demonstrated Zatopek's superiority over his opposition, a single race in 1951 would reinforce just how great the gulf was between Emil and his pursuers. In 1945, Heino completed 19,339 metres in an hour, and four years later had run 20,000 metres in 62:40.0. Both world records had been previously held by Nurmi.

In Prague on September 15, an attempt was organized for Zatopek to try for both records in the one race. In reality it was more a time trial than a race. Running the first half in 31:05, he increased his pace to 30:10.8 for the second half. His time for the second half would have been good enough to rank third over 10,000 metres for the preceding year. His distance for the hour was 19,558 metres, while his 20,000 metre time was 61:15.8 – both new world records.

Realizing how much he had in reserve after this effort, he decided to try again a fortnight later. In perhaps his greatest run he set new records for the ten miles (48:12.0), 20,000 metres (59:51.8), and completed 20,052 metres in one hour. To put this into perspective, the previous

The final bend of the 1952 Olympic 5,000m. Zatopek leads from Mimoun and Schade, Chataway having fallen.

year no one apart from Zatopek had broken thirty minutes for 10,000 metres, and he had done it twice in one race. In 1951, only two runners would have been able to keep pace with Zatopek for half the race, based on their best 10,000 metre times for the year. This race, probably more than any other demonstrated his superiority over the rest of the distance running world.

After such a run in 1951, Zatopek should have been the overwhelming favourite for any race that he entered in the Helsinki Olympics the following year. However, in the weeks leading up to Helsinki, it was obvious that times had changed. This change was the result of three main factors. The first was that the motivation of an Olympic year invariably gives rise to new talent. Athletes are prepared to work harder, and the incentive of fierce competition will often bring forth results not otherwise seen. The second factor was that the rest of the running fraternity had seen Zatopek's results and the training that had made them possible. They realized that they too could follow a similar path to success. By 1952 a number of his rivals had been training along similar lines long enough for the fruits of their labours to be realized. The third factor was that Zatopek himself did not seem to be the same runner in 1952 that he had been the previous year.

Illness early in the year resulted in missed training, and after resuming, his early season results were mediocre – not just by his standards, but also in comparison to other Olympic hopefuls. In his first races in late May, he failed to better 14:45 for 5000 metres or thirty minutes for the 10,000 metres. Two weeks later he was in Kiev for the USSR – Czechoslovakia meet. In the 5000 metres the unthinkable occurred when he was beaten convincingly by both Russian entries. His time of 14:22.0 was both well outside his best, as well as being almost nine seconds behind the new Russian national record of Kazantsev (14:13.2). It was also his first defeat at the distance since the London Olympics.

The next day in the 10,000 metres he was over 100 metres behind the leader after only five laps. Aleksandr Anufriyev had taken to Zatopek type training with great gusto and, by all accounts, was undertaking prodigious training sessions. He had barely managed to break thirty one minutes for the distance in 1951, but this year he was a different man. Eventually Zatopek reeled him in to win in 29:26.0, with Anufriyev demolishing both his previous best and the national record with 29:31.4. The Russian's career would be stymied by seemingly being overawed on the big occasion, along with a strong tendency to start nearly all his races at a frantic pace, only to pay for such exuberance near the end. This tactic almost certainly cost him the 5000 metre world mark later in his career, and Zatopek himself was of the opinion that with more prudent pace judgment the Russian may well have broken some of his records.

As the season progressed, Zatopek did improve, but so did others. Mimoun improved to 29:38.2 over 10,000 metres, while at the shorter distance the German Herbert Schade had run 14:06.6, while Kazantsev had improved his national record to 14:08.8. There were many who did not expect Zatopek to do as well as he had in London four years earlier.

The 10,000 metres was the first of the distance events, and there were thirty three starters. As to be expected, Anufriyev went to the lead, but after five laps Zatopek assumed his rightful place at the front of the field. After that, it became a contest to see who could hang on the longest. One by one his rivals dropped away. The last to go was Mimoun who managed to cling to Zatopek for twenty two of the twenty five laps. He eventually lost over fifteen seconds in the last three laps, but still managed to comfortably hold second position. Zatopek's winning time of 29:17.0 broke his own Olympic record, while Mimoun finished in 29:32.8 (a personal best), with Anufriyev next in 29:48.2. That the first six all broke thirty minutes was an indication of what was happening to distance running standards.

Two days later were the heats of the 5000 metres. All of the favourites survived to take part in the most anticipated race of the Games. Schade, Reiff (the defending champion), Mimoun, and the young British pair of Chataway and Pirie were all seen as potential challengers to Zatopek. Another two day break saw the fifteen finalists face the starter on the afternoon of July 24.

Schade went straight to the front, and set a pace that was faster than the existing world record. Gradually however, the pace slowed. Despite leading stints by both Zatopek and Pirie, the great bulk of the front running was done by the German. At the bell, any of four was still with a chance – Schade, Chataway, Mimoun and Zatopek. Approaching the back straight for the last time, Chataway had taken the lead, and looked like a possible winner. Into the last turn Zatopek made his final effort. With some 140 metres left, just as Mimoun went past Schade, Zatopek hit the front. Chataway, suffering from exhaustion rather than interference, tripped and fell. Zatopek, all his legendary fighting qualities on full display, pulled away to win from Mimoun (again!) in 14:06.6. His last lap had taken just 57.9 seconds. Mimoun finished in a new personal best of 14:07.4, with Schade third in 14:08.6. The crowd had expected a great race and they were not disappointed. The last lap was a fitting finale in which veterans were pitted against new comers. In this case, the veterans in the form of Zatopek and Mimoun prevailed. Pirie and Chataway (fourth and fifth respectively) would both have to wait a little longer for their time in the sun.

To cap a great day for the Zatopeks, Emil's wife Dana won the gold medal for the javelin. Having returned to the Olympic village after his race, Emil had to be satisfied with following the event via the radio coverage.

Not content with his double victory, three days later Zatopek was lining up for the start of his first ever marathon. Despite never having completed the forty two kilometre distance under race conditions, there would have been any number of days when he would have exceeded the distance in training.

Zatopek's entry in the marathon was not a spur of the moment decision as sometimes described. He had decided some time before to enter. While he was something of an unknown quantity in this event, the English runner Jim Peters – seen by many as the favourite – was not. Peters had run against Zatopek in the 10,000 metres four years before in London, and after his eighth place finish had retired. Talked out of retirement by his coach Albert "Johnny" Johnston, he decided to concentrate on the marathon in his comeback. Unlike Zatopek, he did little interval training, concentrating on fast continuous runs at close to the pace he hoped to maintain for the full race distance. It was not long before he was running a considerable weekly mileage, most of it at a fast pace.

Clearly his training was working. In 1951 in his first race over the distance, he won the AAA championship in a new national record of 2:29:24. Noteworthy as that was it did little to prepare the running fraternity for what was to happen in the same race the following year. Setting a pace no one had before attempted, he set a best ever time for the distance – 2:20:42.2. Such was the shock, that officials had the course re-measured. It was found to be slightly longer than the official distance. With six weeks before the Olympic event, British hopes were high.

Peters however, had a most unpleasant plane trip to the Finnish capital and was not at his best come race day. Undeterred, he led the field of sixty six out of the stadium and reached the five kilometre check point in 15:43. Such a pace would have broken his world best by over eight minutes. By ten kilometres (passed by Peters in 31:55), the pace had slackened somewhat, with Zatopek seventeen seconds behind in third place. By fifteen kilometres the Swede Jansson had caught Peters, with Zatopek only a few strides behind. Shortly after nineteen kilometres, the three were together, with a gap of over a minute to the fourth runner. At this stage, Zatopek asked Peters if the pace was too fast. Despite Peters tiring badly, he claimed it was too slow.

At this point, Zatopek moved ahead of Peters and the race was virtually over. By twenty kilometres Peters had lost ten seconds to Zatopek and Jansson, and over the next ten kilometres Jansson lost twenty six seconds to Zatopek. While the five and ten kilometre winner strode to a third victory, Peters dropped out at thirty two kilometres, while Jansson was overtaken by the Argentine Reinaldo Gorno at thirty nine kilometres.

Zatopek's winning time of 2:23:02.2 was a new Olympic record, with Gorno second (2:25:25.0) and Jansson third (2:26:07.0). If ever a seal on his greatness was required, it was provided by his exploits in Helsinki. It is doubtful if his feat will ever be repeated. Interestingly, despite his years of training at volumes and intensities never before seen, after his marathon win he was unable to do more than hobble for the next week.

As a postscript, the following year Jim Peters became the first to run under 2:20 for the marathon, and in 1954 improved yet again to 2:17:39.4. It is sad that he is perhaps best remembered for collapsing due to heatstroke within a few metres of the finish in the 1954 British Empire and Commonwealth Games marathon while leading by over five kilometres.

Although there was no doubt that Zatopek was still number one, it was obvious that the rest of the world was catching up. Nowhere was this better illustrated than in the ten thousand metres, where there were twenty five times run below thirty minutes in 1952. His perpetual shadow, Mimoun, was one of two who had achieved the feat four times in the year. Zatopek had done it "only" three, but he was still over twenty three seconds clear of the next best.

That the rest of the world was catching up to the Czech master was even more evident the following year. Zatopek began the year with some physical problems (notably sciatica and tonsillitis), which led to a slow start to his competitive programme. Others did not wait. In early June, the Russian Anufriyev completed a double that could best be described as Zatopek like. In the 5000 metres he raced through the first kilometre in 2:39, and then got progressively slower for each succeeding kilometre. Despite this, his 13:58.8 missed Hagg's world mark by only 0.6 second. With better pacing, it would have surely fallen. The next day, his 29:23.2 for 10,000 metres made him second only to Zatopek on the all time list.

Leading into the International World Youth Games in Bucharest in early August, Zatopek had improved his best times to 14:11.4 and 29:48.6 – good, but still far from his best. His first event was the 5000 metres, and here he met the up and coming Russian, Vladimir Kuts. Using the same tactical ploy as his countryman Anufriyev, Kuts set off at a seemingly suicidal pace. In the end it took all of Zatopek's renowned fighting qualities to run him down over the last two laps. His winning time of 14:03.0 equaled his personal best, while Kuts finished in 14:04.0, with the Hungarian Kovacs just 0.2 further back in third place.

In the 10,000 metres, Kuts was again second to Zatopek (29:25.8 to 29:41.4), while Anufriyev failed to break thirty minutes in third place. To further stress how quickly the opposition was improving, by the end of September Kovacs had run 14:01.6, Kuts 14:02.2, and Pirie 14:02.6.

Pirie had also become the second fastest ever over 10,000 metres with a time of 29:17.2.

However, Zatopek was not yet prepared to concede to his younger opponents. In mid October he faced an in form Josef Kovacs over 5000 metres. In less than ideal conditions he was some twenty metres down on his opponent with a lap to go, but quickly made up the deficit to win by the same margin in 14:09.0. Heartened by this return to form he decided on an attempt at his 10,000 metre record on November 1 in Prague. Despite cold conditions and a heavy track, he ran a remarkably even paced race to finish in 29:01.6, taking exactly one second from his previous time.

He finished the year clearly on top over 10,000 metres, but on the all time list for 5000 metres he had slipped to sixth. With the exception of the retired world record holder Hagg, the others in front of him were improving, and it looked as if his chances of claiming the record were rapidly slipping away. After all, his best for the distance was his 14:03.0 from 1950, and while he had managed to equal it three years later in beating Kuts, it had taken everything he had to beat the fast improving Russian.

Certainly Zatopek himself was under no illusions about his vulnerability to the younger brigade. He saw that Kuts and Pirie in particular were both capable of re-writing his records.

While a lesser man may have conceded, that was not the Zatopek style. Over the winter of 1953-54, he put in more kilometres than ever. In a great start to the new season, his first race was over 5000 metres. His winning time of 14:04.0 was just one second from his best ever. Clearly in great form, he went firstly to Paris to run 5000 metres on May 30, and followed it with 10,000 metres in Brussels two days later.

In the Paris race, he went to the front before the first lap was over and continued to draw away from the field. His last kilometre was easily his fastest as he finally claimed the record, his 13:57.2 taking a second from Hagg's long standing mark. His winning margin was over forty five seconds.

Not one to rest on his laurels, his Brussels effort was even more noteworthy. While he was the third runner to break fourteen minutes for the shorter race, he was the first to go below twenty nine minutes for the longer race. Apart from a faster first and last kilometre, the rest of the race was run at a remarkably even pace as he finished in 28:54.2. Those two races said as much about Zatopek's desire and spirit as any. It was yet another example of his ability to rise to the challenge when required.

Despite these two great runs, it was obvious from a race in Budapest in early July that the rest of the world was catching up. In the Czechoslovakia versus Hungary dual meet, the slightly built Josef Kovacs out sprinted Zatopek over the last lap to win the 10,000 metres in a fast 29:09.0 to 29:09.8. Amazingly, this was his first ever defeat over the distance since his debut in 1948. He had gone undefeated in thirty seven consecutive races. The good form of Kovacs was a prelude to the Hungarian record breaking onslaught that followed in 1955.

The major event for 1954 was the European Championships held in Berne in late August. After his defeat at the hands of Kovacs, Zatopek made it clear from the opening lap of the 10,000 metres that he did not intend to leave the result dependent on a last lap dash. Steadily drawing away from the opposition, he went through the first half in 14:26.0 to finish in 28:58.0. He had the triple satisfaction of the title, the second fastest time ever, and beating Kovacs by almost twenty eight seconds.

The 5000 metre final four days later presented a different scenario. Although Zatopek was the newly crowned world record holder over the distance, there were five within a few seconds of his best. This race had all the makings of a genuine contest where the result would most likely be in doubt until the very end. That might have been the theory – the practice was very different.

There was nothing subtle in the way Vladimir Kuts ran. Almost from the gun he went to the lead and proceeded to set a pace that none could, or would, follow. The opposition either believed he would collapse, or else was running at a pace they could not hope to emulate. Either way, it was obvious well before the finish that he was not coming back to the field, and the only real race was for the minor medals. The previously little known Ukrainian won by the length of the straight in a new world record time of 13:56.6. Chataway won the sprint for second over Zatopek 14:08.8 to 14:10.2.

Determined to prove that he was better than his third place effort showed, four days later in Stockholm Zatopek made an all out effort to reclaim the record. The first kilometre took just 2:43 0 (13:35 pace!). At three kilometres he was still well under record pace, but was gradually slowing. A fourth kilometre in 2:52 did the damage. Despite a great effort over the last kilometre and a new personal best, he missed the record by just 0.4 second.

A few weeks later (October 13) in an epic race in London, Chataway won from Kuts by the narrowest of margins. His 13:51.6 was a new world mark with Kuts also well under his old time with 13:51.7. Despite the exhausting nature of the race, only ten days later Kuts was ready to try again in Prague, this time with Zatopek in the field. Displaying his customary style he went through the first lap in under sixty seconds and the first kilometre in 2:38.4. Zatopek was outclassed by his younger opponent. The best he could do was 14:19.0 while Kuts broke the record yet again with 13:51.2. A new era – at least for 5000 metre running – had arrived.

The new order that had been ushered in during 1954, gathered pace the following year. There were runners with more natural speed than Zatopek training harder than ever. By the end of the year the Hungarian Iharos had brought the 5000 metre record down to 13:40.6, and with a last kilometre in 2:33.6 it was doubtful if that would be the last word. Also, Kuts had joined Zatopek as a member of the sub twenty nine minute 10,000 metre club.

Zatopek responded by training as much as ever. Running up to three hundred kilometres weekly in his fast slow fashion, he seemed to be as keen as he was years earlier. Despite running 14:04.0 for 5000 metres (in a losing effort to Gordon Pirie), the event was almost certainly now too short for him.

The highlight of his year came on October 29 when he set new world marks for both fifteen miles (1:14:01.0) and 25,000 metres (1:16:36.4). They would be his last records. He was no longer the invincible runner of previous years. For the first time in over a decade he lost to one of his country men over 5000 metres, while over 10,000 metres others were getting close to his record. In addition to Kuts's sub twenty nine minute run, Anufriyev had got down to 29:10.6, while Kovacs had run 29:02.6, beating Zatopek convincingly in the process. By the end of the year, his personal best over 5000 metres from the previous year was good enough for only sixth on the all time list, and while he still led the all time list at 10,000 metres, there were now nine others who had run below 29:25.

While the bell had been tolling on the Zatopek era in 1955, it reached a deafening crescendo the following year. In one of the more dramatic years for distance running, a combination of athletes from Great Britain, Hungary and Russia re-wrote the record books. While Iharos looked to have what was required to further reduce the 5000 metre record, it was Gordon Pirie who did the trick with his 13:36.8 in Sweden. Politics and injury saw to it that Iharos never really got to have another genuine attempt. The Hungarian did however get Zatopek's record over 10,000 metres. In July he ran 28:42.8, only to have that time beaten by Kuts in September with his 28:30.4.

The Olympics, being held in the southern hemisphere, took place at the end of the year – a novelty for the Europeans. Zatopek entered only the marathon, and many expected him to defend the title he had won in Helsinki. However Mimoun, despite being now thirty five, had improved his 10,000 metre best to 29:13.4. This, coupled with a running style that seemed ideally suited to the event, saw him win by over one and a half minutes. His time of 2:25:00 was outside Zatopek's Olympic record, no doubt in part because of the warm conditions.

The winner had decided to run the event only after his dismal showing in the 10,000 metres. Being lapped and finishing twelfth made up his mind. Zatopek finished a gallant sixth in 2:29:34. Mimoun had at last stepped out of Zatopek's shadow, and a more deserving winner would have been hard to find. The winner waited for his great friend and rival to finish before the two embraced. It was a fitting end to what had been a great era.

Despite time passing him by, Zatopek continued to race with his usual enthusiasm the following year. His times of 14:06.4 and 29:25.8 were not far removed from his bests, but as an indication of progress in his events, these times would have ranked him second and first respectively on the all time lists at the start of his career. Now they were good for just twenty fourth and eleventh on the annual list.

1958 was Zatopek's last year of competition. His last international race was the prestigious San Sebastian cross country event. Among his opposition was the Great Britain runner George Knight, fastest in the world over 10,000 metres the previous year. As a conclusion to a magnificent career, Zatopek ran away from the field over the final lap to win convincingly.

In no small way, Zatopek was responsible for his own demise. He made no secret of his training, and proved just what could be achieved by steadily increasing the volume and intensity of such work. Those that followed adopted and improved on his regime. Runners such as Pirie, Kuts and Iharos applied intensity to their training that Zatopek had largely ignored, believing that increased volume was the key to success. While he would run up to eighty or even one hundred repeats over four hundred metres in a day, Kuts might run twenty five such repeats, but much faster and with a very short rest. Also, those that followed would vary their training much more than had Zatopek. Such training included everything from short sprints to longer repeats over perhaps 1200 to 2000 metres. If there was one constant however, it was the recognition that year round training, at a level largely not accepted before Zatopek, was the key to success in endurance events.

Zatopek – either directly or indirectly – had a marked influence on the entire distance running world. The influence he had on Australian running serves as a good example. Prior to the 1952 Olympics, distance running standards in Australia were far removed from world class. Two athletes on the Australian team, however, realized after their European experience and witnessing Zatopek and his training, what was required to make the quantum leap into world class. Those two athletes were John Landy and Les Perry.

While Landy would become the better known on an international level, both would influence the next generation of runners. Another Australian Zatopek devotee was Dave Stephens who met up with Zatopek on a European trip in 1953. The highlight of his career was breaking Zatopek's world six mile record and would have also taken his 10,000 metre record had the race been over the metric distance. Athletes such as these served to inspire a young Ron Clarke, among others, to put his energies into running.

It is no coincidence that the most eagerly contested distance race in Australia each year is the "Zatopek 10,000" held each year in Melbourne.

Long before his retirement from competition Zatopek was a national icon in his homeland, and a revered figure abroad. Humble, multi lingual, and friendly to all he met, he was always happy to accommodate even seemingly outrageous demands on his time. As good an example as any was when the eccentric Australian coach Percy Cerutty tracked the great man down in the Olympic village in 1952. Preparing for his events and no doubt wishing for a good nights sleep, he was happy to give up his bed to the interloper while he slept on the floor. Years later, when Ron Clarke visited him in his hometown, his parting gift was one of his Olympic gold medals. Such gestures were typical of the man.

During his career he was as renowned for his fierce competitive spirit on the track, as he was for his friendship and encouragement off it. It is doubtful if any of his rivals spoke ill of him. For much of the time they seemed in awe of him. It is fitting that there are two statues outside the Olympic museum in Switzerland, one of Paavo Nurmi, the other of Emil Zatopek. He dabbled in coaching briefly after retirement, but found it hard to handle athletes whose work ethic did not match his own.

After retiring from his competitive career, Zatopek (by now a colonel in the army) was something of an unofficial ambassador for his country. Although a member of the Communist party, he with many others became increasingly disillusioned with the heavy hand of Russian domination. In 1968 the issue came to a head with the so called Prague Spring. Alexander Dubcek became party secretary and promised a move towards greater freedom. Reminiscent of the Hungarian revolution twelve years before, Russian troops moved in to re-establish their authority. Zatopek was one of those to publicly criticize the Soviet response. For his effort he was dismissed both from the Communist Party and the army. For several years he was given a series of menial laboring jobs, not unlike Dubcek who was sent to work in a timber yard for the next eighteen years.

While this was the official response, the reaction of the normal man in the street was far different. He was still treated with the respect afforded a national hero. After his work as a manual laborer for seven years, his language skills were put to use translating foreign sporting publications in the Ministry of Sport.

By the late eighties, with the introduction of the Perestroika policy by Soviet leader Mikhail Gorbachev, the writing was on the wall for European Communism. In line with other Communist states, in 1989 the Czechoslovakian communist government collapsed and Dubcek was elected chairman of the Federal Assembly.

With the establishment of the new government, Zatopek received an official apology for his dismissal from the army twenty years earlier and had his full rank restored.

He retired from work aged sixty. A back problem left him with a pinched nerve in his neck, resulting in a permanent limp. In 1998 he was awarded the Order of the White Lion by President Vaclav Havel.

The last year of his life saw an increasingly frail Emil admitted to hospital for firstly pneumonia and then a broken hip. He suffered a stroke on October 30 and was admitted to the Prague Military Hospital. He died on November 22, 2000 at age 78. Thousands attended his funeral in a fitting tribute to a man who, besides being a true patriot, was unsurprisingly voted Czechoslovakia's greatest ever athlete.

As an athlete, Zatopek showed just what hard training could achieve. There were almost certainly many more physically gifted athletes than he, but it is doubtful if any had his combination of perseverance, competitiveness, and perhaps most importantly his unbridled joy of running and competing. His legacy lives on not just in distance running, but in almost all sports. That the records of today were once deemed impossible, is in no small way due to the influence he had on training. He showed by example what could be done, and eventually the rest of the world followed.

SÁNDOR IHAROS

"A great runner, a beautiful runner."

IN MANY WAYS THE early nineteen fifties were the golden years of Hungarian sport. Their national football team largely revolutionized the way the game was played, and was generally considered the best in the world – almost certainly the best never to win the World Cup. For an all too brief period, their runners were also the very best in the world.

In the season leading up to the 1956 Melbourne Olympics, Hungary could boast a group of four runners that were expected to be among the medalists come the time of the Olympiad. That group comprised Sándor Iharos (holder of five world records from 1,500 to 5,000 metres), Istvan Rózsavölgyi (the 2,000 metre record holder), Laszlo Tábori (co-holder of the world 1,500 mark with Iharos), and Jozsef Kovacs (one of the best over both 5 and 10,000 metres). Great things were expected with such a talented lineup, but sadly politics in the form of the 1956 Hungarian uprising put paid to such expectation. Following Melbourne, defections led to the breakup of the national team, and the dream of what could have been Olympic glory was all that remained.

Of the above mentioned quartet, the names Iharos, Tábori, and Rózsavölgyi were so strongly linked with that of their coach, that it is difficult to write about one without the other. That coach was Mihály Iglói. Without the advent of Iglói, there would almost certainly have been no Iharos warranting a chapter as one of the five and ten kilometre record holders. As such, this is as much a story about a coach as about an athlete.

One of the unique aspects of Iglói's coaching career was that he achieved success over a number of years in three different countries. Until 1956 he was based in his homeland of Hungary. Following his defection after the Melbourne Olympics he settled in America and after achieving great success there, he finished his coaching career in Greece. All told, Iglói coached athletes broke some 49 Hungarian records, 25 European records, 21 world records, 45 American records, and 157 Greek records. While in the US, his athletes at one stage had run more sub four minute miles than the combined total of all other US runners combined.

Iglói himself first made his mark as an athlete not as a runner, but as a pole vaulter. As a nineteen year old he became national junior champion – only two years after his introduction to the sport. Between 1929 and 1933 he studied physical education at Budapest University. It was during this period that three events coincided that would have a profound effect on world distance running.

The first was that Iglói himself forsook the pole vault for distance events, recording times of 2:01 for 800 metres and 4:18 for 1500 metres. The second was the influence of Dr. Misagi, one of his university lecturers. From him he came to appreciate the importance of gradual adaptation over a long period of time to ever more severe training. His third notable experience was being able to witness first hand the training of the Polish champion Janis Kusocinski. The slightly built Pole was competing at a time of almost absolute Finnish dominance in distance running. Not to be deterred, he embarked upon a systematic form of training that would much later be embraced by much of the sporting world – interval training. By the time Iglói saw him he had broken the world 3000 metre record, and stunned the Finnish fraternity by running away with the ten kilometre gold medal at the 1932 Olympics.

In February 1933, Kusocinski visited Budapest and Iglói took the opportunity to train with him. After an hour's run together, Iglói's training for the day was over. Kusocinski, however, proceeded to undertake the second part of his session while Iglói looked on. What Iglói saw was Kusocinski undertaking fifteen 200 metre runs, separated by relatively short recoveries. Both the volume and intensity of his training was a revelation to Iglói. Deciding to try similar training himself, he progressed steadily, became an Olympian at Berlin in 1936, and finished his career with the very respectable times of 1:53.9 (800 metres), 3:52.2 (1500 metres), 5:29.0 (2000 metres), and 8:28.8 (3000 metres).

In the late thirties he began to put his ideas into practice with others, and after two years one of his athletes, (and one he had earlier competed against), Andras Csaplar, started to reap the rewards of his methods. The first notable event was his world leading time for 10,000 metres in 1941 (albeit with much of the athletics world more concerned with weightier matters), followed by a world mark over 20,000 metres some three months later. Shortly after, the widening of war caused athletic competition to be put on hold.

Not long after the cessation of hostilities in 1945, an unsuspecting Iglói was picked up on the streets of Budapest and sent to a labor camp – a not uncommon event in the Stalinist dominated regimes of the time. It would be almost three years before his family would see him again. Upon his return in late 1947, Iglói resumed his chosen profession as a physical education teacher, while also coaching. This entailed long hours, as he was a firm believer that the coach should be on hand for every training session (a belief that he lived up to for his entire coaching career). Csaplar meanwhile had resumed his athletic pursuits, notably with a third placing in the 1946 European Championships 10,000 metres behind the Finnish pair Heino and Perala. He himself later began coaching; his best known charge being Joszef Kovacs, who would go on to take second place to Kuts in the ten kilometre event at the Melbourne Olympics. Iglói's double job as both teacher and coach continued until 1951 when he won the position as professional coach at the Budapest athletic club.

Introducing a regime of training based heavily on the interval principle, Iglói was able to instill in the athletes under his care a belief that almost anything was possible. This belief was based on a foundation of hard and ever increasing workloads, surrounded by something of an aura that the coach possessed a secret formula for success that he alone knew. Iglói's approach was very much of the "old school" where the coach was in command and knew what was best for his charges. While this may have had an element of truth, probably just as important was the personality, enthusiasm, and consistency of the man.

Almost every interview given by athletes whom he coached refer to him in almost reverential terms. He was admired, respected, and held in such regard that when he later moved to North America, athletes would relocate their families to receive his coaching – at a time where athletics was still very much an amateur affair.

The workloads undertaken by his athletes – both in quality and quantity – were the stuff of legend. In Hungary this was largely possible because the big three (Iharos, Tábori and Rózsavölgyi) were all members of the armed forces. In reality, they were essentially full time athletes, a situation not uncommon in eastern European countries during this period.

One of the incentives of being in the forces was that high profile athletes received privileges not available to the general populace. This was definitely an advantage in a country such as post war Hungary where conditions remained harsh after the cessation of hostilities. It was estimated that post war reparations alone cost the country about a fifth of its annual national income. Also, being within the Soviet sphere of influence prevented it from trading with the West, or receiving Marshall Plan aid that benefited so much of post war Western Europe.

Throughout his coaching career, Iglói was always the first to arrive and the last to leave training, treated all his charges equally (be they beginners or world record holders), and had individual programmes for each athlete. No two days were ever the same. Although he did have a sense of humor, for the most part Iglói was very serious. He was also extremely dogmatic, and determined that everything should revolve around achieving the best possible results for the athletes in his care. This frequently brought him into conflict with officials and meet promoters who did not always share similar ideals.

This became more of an issue after he left Hungary. In his homeland, money for his athletes could be relied on from the government, whereas after leaving he was more dependent on promoters. Not that Iglói himself was motivated by money. For most of his life he lived a frugal existence, but was never heard to complain about the long hours or the level of compensation he received for such a demanding schedule.

Although his training was shrouded in secrecy, in reality it was based mainly on large volumes of frequently intense short repetitions separated by short recovery periods. The intensity could be maintained by dividing a single session into a series of sets.

Iglói himself never published details regarding his coaching, but over the years, former athletes and observers have given examples of training undertaken by various athletes under his care. To say there was a set system or plan would be somewhat misleading. Rather, the coach would watch each runner, and then ascertain the format of the training session. Training was always twice daily, with the exception of a single session on Sundays. Morning sessions were no mere warm-up for the evening sessions, but rather intense sessions, not unlike the main later session of the day. On days of competition, there was still morning training.

Certain key elements do seem to recur in the training of Iglói coached runners. The first was the emphasis on large numbers of short repetitions – usually between 100 and 400 metres. For example, in the week leading up to his world two mile record, Bob Schul (who had been coached by Iglói, and continued to use his approach), did no fast runs beyond 300 metres. Also, prior to his 1964 Olympic triumph over 5,000 metres, he concentrated almost entirely on short repetitive training, to the exclusion of longer continuous runs. An example of a day's training in the week leading up to his two mile record was 60x100m in the morning, followed in the evening by sets of 10x100m, 10x150m, 20x200m, and 10x100m. The starting and ending of training sessions with a set of 10x100 was commonplace, as it was to use such sets between more arduous parts of the training session.

Another example has been given of a typical session done by Rózsavölgyi (the 2,000 metre record holder) in 1955. The main session of the day included: 10x100m in 20 seconds (50m recovery jog), plus 10x300m in 45-48 seconds (100m recovery), plus 5x600m in 1.40 (200m recovery), plus 10x100m (50m recovery), plus 10x300m (100m recovery), plus 10x100m (50m recovery).

On another occasion, 1956 Olympic 800 metre winner, Tom Courtney, reported that he once saw part of a session undertaken by Iharos, Tábori, and Rózsavölgyi. The three ran 5x400m (400m jog recovery after each), 5x400m (200m recovery), and 5x400m (100m recovery). Each 400m was completed in 55 seconds.

Although training stressed short repeats, often done at intense speeds with short recoveries, at times longer distances were also covered. As part of a session, in 1955 (his best year), Iharos was reported as completing a workout that included 2x1200m in 2:57.6 and 3:01, with a 400m walk between each. The volume and intensity of some of the training sessions undertaken by the Hungarians was both a tribute to the belief they had in Iglói, as well as a demonstration of what the human body could endure with the correct preparation.

The story of Iharos is a sad one in many ways. He never knew his father; while at the peak of his powers he was denied the chance of Olympic glory; and he died alone and embittered at the relatively young age of sixty-five. However, during his golden year of 1955, and all too briefly in 1956, he compiled a series of races that compared favorably with any runner before or since.

Born as Sándor Izrael in Budapest on March 10, 1930 the identity of his father was unknown to him, and he was raised by his mother and other relatives. During 1948 he became an apprentice at the Gamma factory (a large Hungarian corporation), and at age nineteen started running after being given a pair of sport shoes as a gift.

In 1951, like all young men his age, Iharos embarked upon a period of compulsory military service. It was here that he met up with Iglói, who by this time was the national distance running coach. Although he coached the armed forces runners, (a position he took up in 1950) Iglói himself was not a member of the forces.

Although Iharos had been training and competing before coming into contact with Iglói and life in the army, there was certainly little evidence of what would eventuate. With a 1500 metre time of 4:06, and a 400 metre best of just under 58 seconds, only the most optimistic would have seen a future world record holder. Certainly a great deal of persuasion was needed on the part of Iglói to convince Iharos and others that his methods would work. Later that year, however, his 1500 metre best had improved to 3:54.2, sufficient for second place in the national championships.

From his earliest days as a serious runner, the exceedingly thin Iharos – he was 1.81m tall, but weighed just 62 kilos – showed a greater ability against the clock than against opponents in major competitions. In important meets he was invariably nervous and easily distracted, but in low-key meets or planned record attempts, he was often in a class of his own.

By 1952 Iharos was good enough to earn Olympic selection, his 1500 metre time having improved to 3:49.4. However, he was eliminated in his heat. That same year, in a very early prelude of what was to come later in his career, he also finished a ten kilometre race in 33:04.4. The following year his most noteworthy performance was probably his third placing in the World Student Games 1500m behind Stanislav Jungwirth (who would later break the world record), and fellow Hungarian Erno Beres. His time of 3:48.8 was some 2.6 seconds behind the winner.

1953-4 saw two further athletes join the Iglói stable as a result of compulsory military service; firstly Istvan Rózsavölgyi, and then a month or two later Laszlo Tábori. The group of runners under Iglói 's care was small – only five or six. In a way, the latter two were able to benefit from joining the group later, as Iglói had been refining his training methods with Iharos. In many ways, Iharos was a test bed for Iglói's ideas. As a result, they were able to progress more quickly than had been the case with Iharos.

The three, although very different in temperament, trained together, sometimes doing the same parts of workouts as one, at other times quite separate. The one common factor was the ever watchful eye of Iglói, who never formulated training more than a day in advance, and was always prepared to modify sessions according to how he assessed the runner's condition to be at the time. Three to four hours of training per day were the norm, split over two daily sessions (with the exception of the single Sunday session).

Quickly adapting to the type of work being administered by Iglói, the two newcomers improved rapidly. The different attributes of the three probably complemented each other – Rózsavölgyi with his considerable natural speed, Tábori with his strength and competitiveness, and Iharos with his ability to absorb great training loads. While many outside the Iglói coached group were skeptical about his methods, those within could see the marked improvement they were making and usually held no such reservations.

That the system was working was amply shown during the summer of 1954. By this stage, Iharos had been promoted in rank within the army, and was married with a young son. In quick succession, he began with 1500 metres in 3:49.0 on June 13, and then followed with a 3:48.2 on June 19. On July 3, he improved once more, running 3:46.4 to win narrowly against Stanislav Jungwirth. Shortly after, he improved yet

The coach and his runners. 4x1500m world record,
July 1955. L to R.Mikes, Iharos, Iglói, Rózsavölgyi, Tábori.

again, this time to 3:46.0 in the meet against Sweden (losing, however, to the Swede Ingvar Ericsson who ran 3:45.0). In addition to his individual efforts, on July 14, he, along with Rózsavölgyi, Tábori, and former rower Ferenc Mikes, set a new world mark for the 4x1500m relay. Iglói, incidentally, was of the opinion that Mikes may well have been the most talented of the group.

Although Iharos was obviously improving, his results did little to prepare the athletic world for what was to happen on August 3. Running on the famed Bislett track in Oslo, in a Norway – Hungary dual meet, the now twenty four year old Hungarian followed the leaders as laps went by in 56, 63, and 62 seconds. By 1000 metres, the Norwegian Audun Boysen had taken the lead, passing 1200 metres in 3:01, with Iharos close behind. It was assumed by most that Boysen (with bests of 1:48.1 and 3:46.0) would win. However, in a shock to most, Iharos began to sprint, and moved away to win by over ten metres in a surprising new European 1500 metre record (3:42.4). Boysen was second in 3:44.2.

Despite the European record, his relatively poor showing in the European titles of that year probably led most to believe that his record was perhaps a feat never to be repeated. Although making the 1500 metre final, he was left well in arrears as Roger Bannister won comfortably in 3:43.8. Iharos was left languishing in sixth place in 3:47.0. Certainly such a result gave little indication of what was to follow. However, perhaps as an indication of future promise, after his 1500 metre record, he had also run the second fastest 3000 metres of all time (7:59.6).

While the 1954 season gave a glimpse that better things might follow from the Hungarians (and Iharos in particular), it certainly did not prepare the athletic world for the record onslaught that was to eventuate the following year.

While Iharos had been primarily a 1500 metre runner, in 1955 he moved to the longer distances and immediately made a dramatic impact. At Budapest on May 14 he opened his season with a new 3000 metre world mark, his 7:55.6 eclipsing the six year old mark of Gaston Reiff by 3.2 seconds. A week later on the same track, he came close to equaling his

European 1500 metre record, running 3:42.6. His team mate Rózsavölgyi improved dramatically to finish a close second in 3:43.2.

His next major race was at the British Games at White City Stadium a fortnight later. Although meant to run the mile, he withdrew as a result of sickness, leaving Tábori as the sole Hungarian entry against the Englishmen Chataway and Hewson. Tábori, incensed at hearing one of the officials bemoaning the fact that the 40,000 spectators were only getting to see the "second string" Hungarian, proceeded to run away from his more fancied rivals, winning in 3:59.0. In the process, he not only became the third man to beat four minutes for the distance, but also dragged the minor place-getters under the once insurmountable barrier – the first time three runners had been under four minutes in the one race. In light of his last lap (56.3 seconds), a more evenly run race may well have brought a new record.

The following holiday Monday saw the second day of competition and another crowd of 40,000 in attendance. They were not to be disappointed. Iharos, recovered from his sickness, was set to tackle the two mile world mark in a planned attempt. Tábori, fresh from his great mile victory forty-eight hours earlier, agreed to be the pace-maker for the first six laps. This he did, and then stepped off the track, leaving Iharos in the lead. Surprisingly, however, he was closely followed by the Sheffield born Ken Wood. The result was fought out over the last half lap, with Iharos winning in a new world mark of 8:33.4, exactly seven seconds under Reiff's old time. Wood finished second in 8:34.8; amazing running for someone who had never before been under nine minutes for the distance.

In Belgrade, on June 16, Iharos lost his European 1500m mark to his rapidly improving colleague Rózsavölgyi. Following a 3:42.8 effort on June 4, Rozsa did even better twelve days later. Following a first lap of 55 seconds, he held on to pass 1200 metres in 3:00.0, and still finish in 3:42.2.

Reverting to his original distance of 1500 metres for his next major race, Iharos and Rózsavölgyi were to be partners in the match against

Finland in Helsinki. As was often the case, the Hungarians cooperated to achieve the best result possible. The newly crowned European record holder for the distance led the first lap in 56.9, before Iharos took over to lead at 800 metres in an unheard of 1:55.7. Despite keeping up the pressure, Rózsavölgyi was forced to drop back as Iharos went through 1200 metres in 2:57.2. He held on gamely to win in 3:40.8, reducing John Landy's world standard by exactly a second.

A few weeks later, (September 6), both Tábori and the Dane Gunnar Nielsen equaled Iharos's mark in an Oslo meet. To round out the year of metric miling, four days later Rózsavölgyi ran 3:41.2 – the fourth fastest time ever. Thus, at the end of 1955, the three Iglói coached Hungarians had recorded three of the four fastest times ever run, with two of them equaling the world record. Rózsavölgyi would have to wait until the following year to have his turn as a record holder at the distance.

As the 1955 season neared its end, Iharos turned his attention to longer distances. The Iglói system of training was designed to improve both speed and stamina, and most importantly the time an athlete could run at a given speed. Given both the volume and speed of the training being undertaken by Iharos, plus his times at shorter distances, records in longer races were not exactly unexpected.

At the start of the season, his best five kilometre time stood at 14:12.2. However in early August, he improved this to 13:56.6 at the World Student Games, albeit in losing to the Pole Jerzy Chromik (13:55.2). Missing Kuts's world mark by less than six seconds was more than enough encouragement to have a more serious attempt. On September 10, again on his home track in Budapest, and as part of the Hungary – Czechoslovakia dual meet, he won comfortably in 13:50.8, a new world mark. Miklos Szabo, the second string Hungarian, was second in 14:11.4. With the final kilometre being the fastest (2:41.2), there was promise of perhaps more to come.

More was to come, but initially it was not from Iharos. Only eight days later, Kuts reclaimed his record with a front running 13:46.8. For Iharos, one final competition remained – the national championships

Three of the greats. Iharos, Chataway
and Tábori. White City, May 1955.

on October 23. As was often the case, it was a planned attempt on the
record. Tábori (who had run 3:43.0 for 1500 metres the day before) was
with Iharos until just over a kilometre remained. At this point, Iharos
changed to another gear, flying over the final kilometre in 2:33.6, with a
last lap of 59.6. His final time of 13:40.6 was over six seconds inside the
old mark. En route, his three mile time of 13:14.2 was also a new record.

At the start of the season, the only world record that belonged to
the Hungarians was the 4x1500m relay. By the end of the season the only
record between one and five kilos that had eluded them was the mile
record of John Landy. Iharos held world marks for the 1500m (joint record
holder with Tábori), 3000m, 2 miles, 3 miles, 5000m, plus membership
of the 4x1500m relay team that had broken their own record.

Because of his remarkable season, Iharos was voted the world's top
sportsman for 1955. This was a first (and last at time of writing), for any
Hungarian to achieve.

After the conclusion of the European season, the trio of Iharos, Tábori, and Rózsavölgyi made a trip to Australia. After such a long and arduous year, coupled with the long flight to an Australian summer, it would have been unrealistic to have expected great things. As if that were not enough, they would be competing against a rapidly rising new star in Dave Stephens – the so-called "flying milko".

After a defeat at the hands of Tábori and Iharos over two miles in their first encounter, the next two races over 5,000 metres and then three miles saw Stephens finish over Iharos on both occasions. As a spectator at the second race, a young Ron Clarke would have his interest in athletics aroused to the extent that he decided to give up cricket as a summer sport in preference to running. While the defeat of the Hungarians may have come as a shock, shortly after their departure, Stephens went on to break the world six mile record.

With the amazing year that had been 1955, the Olympic year of 1956 held great promise for the Hungarians. However, as is often the case, Olympic years bring new faces to the fore, and this was certainly the situation in 1956. In June, Iharos lost his world 5000 metre mark to Gordon Pirie, with Vladimir Kuts also under the old mark. Not to be outdone, less than a month later Iharos removed one of Emil Zatopek's revered records from the books. At the national championships on July 15, he completed 10,000 metres in 28:42.8, some 11.4 seconds under the old mark (also passing six miles en route in

Athlete and coach. Iharos and Iglói after breaking the world 10,000m record, his last record. Budapest, July 15, 1956

27:43.8, another world mark). In doing so, he became only the second athlete ever (after Paavo Nurmi), to have held 1,500, 5,000, and 10,000 metre world records.

Later in the season, on September 4 in the Swedish city of Malmo, the Hungarian trio took on Gordon Pirie over 3,000 metres. Pirie had earlier equaled Iharos's world mark over the distance, and was obviously in great form. The aim of the Hungarians was to run as a team, with Rózsavölgyi – being the fastest of the group – to out sprint Pirie at the end. The plan very nearly worked, with Rózsavölgyi running under the old world mark. However, Pirie was unstoppable. Running what he would later describe as his greatest race, he reduced Iharos's world mark down to 7:52.8. Rózsavölgyi finished in 7:53.4, with Iharos a disappointing third almost fourteen seconds behind (8:06.6). Despite this result, Pirie still considered many years later, that had the political situation in Hungary been different, Iharos may well have beaten Kuts in Melbourne.

Some three days later, still in Sweden, Iharos ran a fast 13:46.6 to defeat fellow countryman Miklos Szabo (13:54.4). With the Olympics fast approaching, expectations among the Hungarians were high. Such expectations were soon to be crushed.

From a sporting viewpoint, the weeks leading up to the Hungarian team's departure for Melbourne were a disaster. For most, interest in the forthcoming Olympics was overshadowed by the dire political situation at home.

Following the conclusion of the Second World War, Hungary had been absorbed into the Eastern Bloc, with a Stalinist government imposed. With Stalin's death in 1953, there followed a period of liberalization. In Hungary, this took the form of the hard-line Stalinist Matyas Rakosi, being replaced by the more liberal Imre Nagy as Prime Minister. However, Rakosi retained the position of Party General Secretary, and in this capacity undermined many of Nagy's moves towards liberalization. By early 1955, he manoeuvred to have Nagy removed from office.

Early the following year, Krushchev delivered his "secret speech", in which he denounced the Stalinist personality cult, along with those who had benefited by such policies. As a consequence, Rakosi was replaced as General Secretary in July. This move led to a much greater degree of political activism and criticism, especially from students, writers, and journalists.

The final flashpoint came on October 23. What began as a demonstration by some 20,000 demanding greater freedom in the afternoon had grown to ten times that number by evening. What had been a peaceful demonstration turned ugly, as demonstrators attempted to broadcast their demands from the radio Budapest building. The secret police guarding the building fired on protesters, with many being killed. Hungarian soldiers, called in as reinforcements, sided with the protesters.

Four days later, former Prime Minister Nagy convened a new national government that abolished both the secret police and the one party system. By October 28, a ceasefire with the Soviet troops had been arranged, and by the end of the month, the Russians had left Budapest for the nearby countryside. For many Hungarians, there was a belief that their aims had been achieved. For a very short time, their belief was justified.

On October 30, the Russian Presidium decided it could live with the newly installed government, only to reverse their decision twenty-four hours later. The over-riding reasons for such a change of heart appeared to be the Hungarian desire for neutrality (and hence leaving the Warsaw Pact), along with the perception that recognizing the new government would be seen as a sign of Russian weakness.

Early on the morning of November 4, Russian troops entered Budapest with overwhelming force. Within six days the resistance had been quelled. In addition to the 2,500 Hungarians killed, many times that number were injured, while some 13,000 were imprisoned and approximately 350 executed.

The Hungarian Olympic team left Budapest on October 28. Because of the risks associated with flying into Budapest, airlines were only prepared to take the team from Prague. Hence it was decided to travel by train from Budapest to Prague. As an example of just how tense the situation was, on the way to the station in Rózsavölgyi's car, he, Iglói, and the two other occupants were ordered from the car and lined up against a wall. Only after convincing the troops who they were could they proceed. At the very last minute a change of plans meant that the team went to Prague not by train, but by bus.

Of the Iglói coached runners, both Rózsavölgyi and Tábori went to Melbourne, but were only shadows of their former selves. Tábori had not trained for six weeks. That he was still able to finish fourth in the 1500m and sixth in the 5000m was little short of amazing.

Rózsavölgyi had finished 1955 as joint world record holder in the 1000 metres (2:19.0), and the sole holder of the 2000 metre mark (5:02.2). In 1956 he was even better, running 3:40.6 to succeed Iharos as the 1500 metre world record holder. In Melbourne he could not get through the heats, being run out in 3:49.5.

Iharos did not even get to Melbourne. In the weeks leading up to the team departure he had injured an ankle, and had also left his wife and young son for another lover – something of a scandal at the time. With the outbreak of hostilities, they (along with some 200,000 others) fled the country, returning some months later.

At the time of the team leaving for Melbourne, it appeared that the Soviets might succumb to the will of the Hungarian people. It was only during the stop in Czechoslovakia that the team heard the news of the Soviet change of heart and subsequent invasion.

Following the Games, the decision of whether to return home or seek asylum elsewhere, was the main topic of conversation among team members. Quite independently, both Iglói and Tábori decided to try their luck in America. Rózsavölgyi went home.

Iglói's decision was no doubt influenced by the fact that he had been elected to a dissident committee representing sporting organizations shortly before the team's departure. Upon his failure to return, the government accused him of inducing others to defect. This was almost certainly not true. Even Tábori had no inkling of what his coach was doing until he later met up with him, by accident, in America. Iglói's family would not see him again until they were given permission to leave Hungary in 1963.

Following his defection to the US after Melbourne, Iglói would forge a successful coaching career in his newly adopted country. Based in California, he attracted a group of runners who would take American distance running standards to new heights. His two most notable charges were Jim Beatty and Bob Schul. Beatty would break the world two mile record and become the first runner to break the four minute barrier indoors, in addition to setting a number of US records. Schul would also break the world two mile mark, set a US record over 5,000 metres, and crown his career with a victory in the Tokyo Olympics over that distance. Although he was not training with Iglói by that stage, he gave him credit for the success he achieved.

Iglói remained in the US until late 1969, when he took a contract in Greece to help prepare athletes for the 1972 Munich Olympics. He remained in Greece until he finished his coaching career, before returning to the land of his birth. He died in Budapest on January 4, 1998, aged eighty-nine.

After leaving Hungary in 1956, Iharos returned the following year. He resumed his athletic career, but things would never be the same again. Without the guiding light of Iglói, Hungarian distance running largely slid back to where it had been before he appeared on the coaching scene. While he continued to run well on occasions, Iharos was never able to repeat the magic of 1955 and 1956.

In 1958 he made the final of the European Championships over 5,000 metres, but finished a disappointing sixth in 14:07.2, well behind the Pole Krzyszkowiak (13:53.4). Iharos continued to be world ranked for the rest of the decade (apart from 1957), and ran both the five and ten kilometre events at the Rome Olympics, finishing tenth and eleventh respectively. He also continued to win national titles, still being good enough in 1961 to win over 5,000 metres in 13:51.8. However, it was obvious his glory days were over.

He competed until 1962. Following his return to Hungary he was no longer in the army, but worked as a sports trainer. Following his retirement he worked for a manufacturer of building materials, as a salesman, barman, and service station attendant. However, his life was slowly unraveling. His situation was not unlike that of his Russian contemporary, Vladimir Kuts. Without the structure that the training of an elite athlete could provide, it appeared that his life lost much of its purpose.

Sadly, he began finding solace in alcohol, and became increasingly reclusive. In his later years he rarely left his apartment other than to buy drink. By this stage he had given away his various awards, and was leading a lonely and embittered existence. It was a sad way for such a great runner to end his days. He finally died in Budapest on January 24, 1996, aged sixty five.

His national records at five and ten thousand metres would stand until 1965, when both were broken by Lajos Mecser.

Perhaps the best epitaph for Iharos came from his coach. Interviewed after the death of Iharos, Jim Beatty said how proud Iglói had been of his Hungarian runners, often reminiscing about their exploits. Of Iharos, Iglói's comment was that he was, "A great runner: a beautiful runner."

VLADIMIR KUTS

The all or nothing man

OF ALL THE DUAL 5 and 10 kilometre record holders, probably none had a career that featured so many classic races in such a short space of time as Vladimir Kuts. His career, his physique, and his sad subsequent decline all marked him as anything but the typical distance runner. His life, along with his running, seemed to epitomize an all or nothing approach, and his career needs to be viewed through the prism of this approach, along with that of the Cold War era during which he lived and competed.

One of the key factors that set Kuts apart from all other runners was his method of competing, i.e. the tactics he used. The plural form is really wasted as he had only one – as fast as possible, and always at the front. For Kuts, there were no "easy" races. After he achieved international prominence, rivals knew that any competition in which he was involved would entail simply trying to hang on to a relentless, frequently changing pace for as long as possible, with the (usually vain) hope of out sprinting him at the end. When he was at his best, this really only happened on two occasions, and both times it required a world record to do the trick. On both occasions, it should be noted that shortly after such a loss, the natural order was quickly put right in the form of re-writing the record or winning a most significant victory on the biggest stage of all.

Considering the era in which Kuts was born and lived his early life, that he not only survived, but went on to become the figure he did, says as much about fate and coincidence, as it does about his personality and physical talent. To say that Kuts had humble beginnings would probably be something of an over-statement. He was born on February 7, 1927 in the village of Aleksin, in the Ukraine. Both parents worked in a sugar factory. Being Ukrainian, Kuts's first name was either the more commonly known Vladimir, or the Ukrainian alternative Volodymyr. Growing up when he did, his formative years were thus dominated by the Stalinist regime, the Nazi invasion of the Second World War, and later the Cold War.

In a way, it could be said that were it not for the invasion of Russia, the world may never have heard of Vladimir Kuts. In 1943, the Red Army had reached Alexin, and Kuts, despite being only sixteen, enlisted. The small detail of putting his age up two years was required for this to occur. Not long after enlisting, he was sent to the Artillery School in Kursk. He never arrived, due to the road train in which he was traveling being hit by enemy bombs. Having lost all his personal documents, he was returned to Aleksin, by which time those who knew him assumed he was dead. In autumn 1945, he left to serve in the Baltic Fleet, initially as a simple gunner, but promotion soon followed. It was as a member of the navy that he had his first main track race, a competition held to commemorate Victory Day, in 1950. With little formal training, (although he had done some boxing, skiing and rowing) he won impressively.

A time of 15:34.8, while good for a novice (even a 23 year old one), gave only a vague hint of the potential of the powerfully built Ukrainian. In the spring of 1951 he teamed up with noted coach Leonid Homenkovyn in the city of Sochi. Progress was relatively rapid, no doubt in part due to the conditioning he had undergone as a result of his interest in other sports.

Yearly training was split into three main seasons. The first three months of the year stressed strength training, the second three months emphasized continuous daily runs, building up from a starting distance of ten kilometres, and gradually increasing the distance, and finally six months of Zatopek style interval training.

He first came to national attention in 1952, with times of 14:32.2 (5,000m), and 31:02.4 (10,000 metres), along with a sixth place finish in the national championships in 14:56.0. It was in 1953 however, that the world got its first real glimpse as to what the Ukrainian's capabilities might be. Until that time, Zatopek was the undisputed master, although there were ominous signs that his days at the top were probably numbered.

The first real sign came in early June, and while it involved the muscular Ukrainian, it was only in a minor supporting role. The scene was a match between the cities of Moscow, Leningrad, and Kiev. In a preview of what was to become Kuts's trademark approach to competition,

Aleksandr Anufriyev took off at breakneck speed in the 5000 meters, covering the first kilometre in an unheard of 2:39 – 13:15 pace, when the world record stood at 13:58.2. Although inevitably slowing, at the 4000 meter mark he was still three seconds up on Gundar Hagg's world record time. Despite what must have seemed like an endless final kilometre, he missed the record by just 0.6 of a second. Finishing exactly 30 seconds behind, Kuts still recorded a personal best. While an improvement, it was merely a prelude to what was to follow later in the year. This came in the form of the so-called World Youth Games, held in Bucharest in early August. Despite the grandiose title, it was in reality largely an Eastern Block sports festival.

The 5000m was held on the first day of competition and featured Anufriyev, Zatopek, the Hungarian Jozsef Kovacs, and Kuts, who by this stage had improved his best to 14:14.6. As was to become his trademark, he took off at a seemingly suicidal pace and quickly built up a sizeable lead. Shortly after the two kilometre mark, Zatopek and Kovacs managed to reel in the Russian, whereupon he raised his effort and quickly gained a thirty metre lead on his pursuers. The gap remained constant until the final kilometre, when Zatopek, drawing on all his reserves, managed to gradually overhaul the startling newcomer to world-class distance running. The quality of Kuts's effort was highlighted by the fact that it required Zatopek to record his equal best time for the distance, and was only able to take the lead in the final straight. Kuts had improved dramatically to 14:04.0 in finishing just one second behind the great Czech. Kovacs, incidentally, finished a bare 0.2 second astern of Kuts.

The 10,000 metres, held four days later in very hot conditions, saw another personal best from Kuts. Despite being soundly beaten by Zatopek, finishing second (29:41.4 to 29:25.8) was certainly no disgrace and clearly marked him as a man of the future. As if to allay any doubts about his credentials, less that three weeks after his return from Bucharest, Kuts revised his 5,000 metre best yet again with a 14:02.2 effort in Moscow on August 27. By years end he was ranked fourth in the world over 5000 metres, and ninth over the longer distance.

The winter of 1954 saw Kuts come into contact with a new coach in the form of Grigoriem Nikiforovym, who recognized a rare talent when he saw one, and set about transforming a talented newcomer into an irresistible force in world distance running. By all accounts, Nikiforovym had almost a complete control not only of Kuts's training, but also his life in general, covering such aspects as a strictly controlled diet. Training by this stage was severe, both in volume and intensity.

Whereas the Zatopek model of interval training had relied on a large number of repetitions at a frequently modest speed (usually involving just 200 and 400 metre distances), training under Nikiforovym involved a wide variety distances at generally very intense efforts. In this respect, training could be seen as something of a combination of the old Zatopek school and the Hungarian methods of Mihály Iglói, soon to make such an impact on the international scene.

Typically, training sessions would involve a lengthy warm up, some sprints or acceleration runs, then sets of different distances (anything from 200 to 2000 metres), usually at intense speeds with short recoveries. Most training was carried out at race pace or faster. It was not unusual for even 1200 or 1600 metre repeats to be separated by only 100 metre jog recoveries or less. He was reported to have completed such sessions as 6 x 1200 metre repetitions in 3:15 with very short jog recoveries. This combination of both volume and intensity obviously had its limits, and was only able to be accomplished with the aid of regular massages to aid recovery, and very light training usually twice weekly.

Although training differed somewhat depending on the time of year and proximity to competitions, the basis was firmly rooted in both varied pace running and the above mentioned intense interval training. From the earliest stages of his career, Kuts had been able to demonstrate an ability to push himself to the limit both in training and competition. Although this may not have been a unique quality, his physique may have been in some way responsible for him being able to absorb the large volume of intense training that led him to so quickly move on to the world stage. At 1.72m. he was probably about average height for his chosen events, but at 72kg, he had the physique more of a wrestler, boxer, or even weight-lifter than an endurance specialist. His muscular frame was further enhanced by his frequent use of gymnastics and strength training as an integral part of his training, as was common for Soviet runners of the time.

If 1953 had seen the introduction of Kuts to the international stage, the following year would firmly cement his position as one of the very best. Considering his dramatic improvement that year, one could perhaps have forgiven his opponents for thinking that such progress could not be sustained. How wrong they were, as the European Championships were to prove.

Held in Berne in late August, the 5,000 metres was one of the most eagerly anticipated events. The standout performers were Zatopek (fresh from a world record of 13:57.2 earlier in the year, and the 10,000 winner four days before), the diminutive Jozsef Kovacs of Hungary (with a best of 14:01.2), Chataway and Green of Great Britain (both with 3 mile best times of 13:32.2), and Kuts, whose best remained his 14:02.2 from the previous year, but arrived in Berne with a seasonal best nine seconds slower. However, he had recorded a fast 3000 metres in the month before the championships (8:05.8 – the third fastest ever). Alarm bells perhaps should have sounded louder for his rivals as he completed his heat in a fast 14:18.8.

The final was run in warm, humid conditions and the Englishman Green assumed the early lead – but not for long. After barely half a lap, Kuts went to the front and proceeded to steadily draw away. By the end of the first lap, his lead was only some three metres, but after two laps it had grown to twenty, and the first kilometre went by in 2:44.0 – well under world record pace. A somewhat slower second kilometre, coupled with an effort by Zatopek to bridge the gap, cut his lead somewhat, but a faster third kilometre saw his lead grow to some 120 metres and put the issue beyond doubt. His final kilo was almost as fast as his first, and it was only a frantic last lap by Chataway to claim the silver medal that reduced his lead somewhat. As it was, he won by a huge margin in 13:56.6, a new world record and 12.2 seconds ahead of his closest pursuer. It is always easy to be wise in hindsight, but it should not have come as a complete shock to see Kuts achieve what he did, bearing in mind his previous best times and his modus operandi as demonstrated the previous year. Certainly any element of surprise would not be there for future encounters.

The next major test came just a few weeks later and would prove to be one of the greatest races of all time. The setting was London, and the occasion was a match between London and Moscow. The date was October 13, and the venue White City stadium. There were 40,000 spectators on hand to witness the epic dual, and an estimated further 15 million watching on the new sporting medium of television – something of a captive audience, as there was only the single television station operating in England at the time. Chataway claimed to have been ignorant of Kuts at the European championships. While that may have been true in August, it most certainly was not in October.

The inter-city match was itself almost a sideshow to this, the main event. The race was seen very much as a match race between not just two rivals, but the representatives of two political systems and two widely differing approaches to life. Chataway had been instrumental in Roger Bannister's successful attempt on the four minute mile earlier in the year, and where Kuts was seen as the full time "state professional", he was a representative of the "gifted amateur" school. Appearances counted for much, and one could not be seen to be training too hard, or taking sport too seriously. In reality, Chataway did train quite hard (certainly more than was frequently admitted at the time), and in the build up to a race like this, how could one not take it seriously?

Following the European Championships, he went for a family holiday, partly to relax, partly to train in a different environment. After a week away, he returned to London and resumed his more formal track training. While quite hard, it was the sort of work that for Kuts would probably have represented an easy day. Not dissimilar to the training that had worked so well for Bannister, it included such sessions as ten or twelve repeat quarter miles in 59-60 with a lap jogging between, or longer repeats such as four repetition miles in 4:25 – 4:30 with a ten minute rest between each.

A further contrast between the two was the apparent dour and serious approach of the Russian compared with the easy-going attitude of the Britton. Again, things were not always as they may have seemed. While Chataway saw Kuts as something of an automaton, others, notably Zatopek and some of the Australians he came in contact with later at the Melbourne Olympics, found him quite a pleasant character. Certainly he got quite nervous before big races, and was known to sing to himself to try and calm his nerves on such occasions. One other human frailty was the matter of his health. Although apparently indestructible, he did in fact have some significant health problems, most notably stomach ulcers that caused him quite some concern both during and after his running career.

There were only four runners in the race, Chataway, Kuts, and the second strings Peter Driver and Vladimir Okorokov. Had Chataway any doubts about what Kuts's tactics might be, they were dispelled at the start. He dashed to the front immediately, running the first half lap in under thirty seconds, and the first lap in 62.8 seconds. The first mile went by in 4:24.4, some 5 seconds below world record pace. Fast as the pace was, it should be remembered that, as was the Russian's trademark, it was not achieved via the most efficient method of even pace running, but rather via constant surging in an effort to break the spirit of his English pursuer. After the seemingly ridiculous first four laps, Kuts then ran faster still – a lap in 62.4. If ever Chataway was going to be broken, this was the time. The gap stretched to some ten metres, but Chataway did not panic, and slowly closed the distance between them. Two miles was passed in 8:54.6 both runners separated by only a stride. The drama of the event was made greater by a spotlight picking out the two protagonists in a near dark arena. As the pace and constant surging took its toll, the speed inevitably lessened, with both ninth and tenth laps just under 70 seconds. With two laps remaining Kuts made what was perhaps his last effort to get rid of his pursuer. As Chataway was to say later, one more burst and he probably would have been forced to concede. As it was, he was able to remain in contact and finally hit the front only metres from the tape. With a last lap of 60.4, the world record was dramatically reduced to 13:51.6; with Kuts also well under his old record only 0.2 behind. Almost as an aside, Moscow soundly won the inter-city match 103 points to 56.

Not only did this prove to be perhaps the greatest race ever run on British soil, it would also prove to be something of a landmark in the coming together of sport and television. The direct telecast of the event was perhaps a major reason why Chataway was voted the inaugural BBC sporting personality of the year for 1954 – no mean feat considering Roger Bannister's epic breaking of the four minute mile earlier in the year, coupled with his win over John Landy in the "mile of the century" at the Vancouver Commonwealth games later in the year. Chataway would later go on to break four minutes for the mile himself, play an important role in the early days of British television, and forge an impressive public career that included becoming minister in a conservative government.

While there can be absolutely no doubt that both runners gave their all that night, Kuts was able to repeat the dose a mere ten days later. The setting was Prague in front of 50,000 spectators for the USSR – Czechoslovakia match. As was the norm, the red vested Russian took off at a furious pace and essentially the race was over by the end of the first lap. Hardly surprising, since it took him only 59.4 seconds, his lead growing to forty metres. The first kilometre went by in 2:38.4, and despite slowing somewhat (particularly in the second and third kilo-metres), he still had enough in reserve to run the final kilo in 2:43.6. Despite his last lap being some eight seconds slower than Chataway's effort, he still managed to run 13:51.2, some 0.4 under the recent record. Zatopek finished a long way behind in 14:19.0.

Within the space of only sixteen months, Kuts had progressed from the status of promising national class runner, to multiple world record-breaker. On each occasion he had done it the hard way, from the front, and never at an even pace. Clearly, he was capable of better, but as is so often the case, once the standard has been raised, others also rise to the new challenge.

The first such example in this case was given by the Hungarian Sándor Iharos. Prior to 1955 he had been primarily a 1500 metre exponent, but all that was about to change. Following world records at 3000 meters, 2 miles and 1500 metres, he took aim at the 5000 metre mark on September 10 at Budapest in the Hungary - Czechoslovakia match. Winning by over 20 seconds, he achieved his target by a mere 0.4 of a second, recording 13:50.8.

Not to be upstaged, Kuts resumed his place at the top of the rankings only eight days later. In Belgrade on September 18, in a virtual time trial (second place was over 30 seconds behind), he reduced the record to 13:46.8. Significantly, the fastest kilometre was his last (2:40.8), and there was considerable variation in pace during the race; the slowest kilometre (the fourth), taking almost ten seconds longer than the fastest.

In what was to prove a portent of things to come, Kuts completed ten kilometres at Bucharest on October 3, winning easily in 28:59.2 to become only the second man under twenty nine minutes for the distance. Normally that may have been expected as the final stanza in the athletic year, but 1955 was anything but normal. In one last hurrah, Iharos, running in the Hungarian championships, finished with an amazing final kilometre of 2:33.6 (last lap 59.6) to reduce the record to 13:40.6. En route the three mile record was also revised downward to 13:14.2. In just on twelve calendar months, the record had been reduced by some sixteen seconds by three different runners in five different installments, and the following year was an Olympic year!

For Kuts, the new year brought new challenges, most notably in the form of Englishman Gordon Pirie. Tall and thin (1.88m and 65kg), Pirie had devoted his life to getting the greatest performance possible out of his seemingly frail body. From an early age he had progressively increased both the volume and intensity of his training, until by 1956 (at 25 years of age) it is doubtful if anyone trained as assiduously – Kuts included. A firm disciple of interval training, and great admirer of Zatopek, his confidence, self-belief, and outspoken comments were frequently too much for the staid British administration – a problem often compounded by his ability to back up his words with action. Pirie had teamed up with Waldemar Gerschler from Freiburg University, who had given interval training a scientific basis. Where others had warned the young Pirie about the possibility of over-doing his training, such problems did not seem to concern Gerschler. While Zatopek had popularized interval training, it was Gerschler who had really put it on a firm footing, and the successes of Rudolph Harbig (pre-war 400 and 800 metre world record holder), and Josy Barthel (shock 1500 metre winner at the 1952 Olympics) served to confirm his approach.

Pirie had gradually increased his training load until he was able to complete such sessions as 80 x 200 metres in 29 seconds with a 30 second jog, and 54 x 400 metres in 64 seconds with a 45 second jog. With Pirie, sessions always began with a warm-up of approximately an hour, and finished with another 20 minutes or so of easy running. It was not unusual for training to take five hours a day. By 1956 Pirie was ready to show the fruits of his prodigious labours. On June 19 he met Kuts over 5000 metres at Bergen in Norway. Ostensibly in the country for a fishing holiday, fish were probably the last thing on his mind as he prepared for what would prove another epic Russia – England battle. Pirie had been tipped off by a Norwegian friend that Kuts would be competing there, and was determined to meet him before the Melbourne Olympics. Training, as was usual, took up a good part of his day. Undertaking three sessions a day, examples of the type of work he did were as follows:

Day 1

7.30 a.m. 30 minutes easy run

12.00 p.m. 4 x alternate 800 / 1200 (2:08, 3:11, 2:08, 3:11, 2:09, 3:12, 2:08, 3:13) Plus 60 minute warm-up, 20 minute easy at end.

6 p.m. repeat noon training.

Day 2

7.30 a.m. 30 minutes easy running

12.00 p.m. 8 x 800 metres in 1:58 -1:59, five minute jog between each.

6 p.m. 10 x 400metres in 57 – 58 seconds, four minute jog between each.

The race itself was run in cool, wet conditions, hardly surprising for Bergen, one of the wettest cities in Norway. Pirie had intended to lead, but Kuts would have none of it. The first lap was run in 60 seconds, and the first kilometre went by in 2:36 – even pace for a time some 40 seconds under the world record. In some ways the race was a repeat of the earlier duel with Chataway, but Pirie was obviously fitter and more confident than his compatriot had been. He kept challenging Kuts, not letting him slow down sufficiently to gather his resources for the brutal changes of pace that he normally used so effectively. Pirie went by with just under three hundred metres left, and there was no response. Kuts had run well, but Pirie was in a class of his own, finishing the last lap in 55 seconds, and bringing the world record down to 13:36.8. Kuts finished in 13:39.6, a time he would replicate later in the year on a much grander stage. Bearing in mind his finishing speed and the ease of his win, there is little doubt that Pirie was capable of better, but despite years of trying, that Norwegian run would remain his best. Going through a purple patch, Pirie later both equaled and then broke the world mark for 3000 metres, both with very fast last laps.

For the up-coming Olympics, he looked like the man to beat. However, it was an Olympic year, and being in Melbourne there was still much time for northern hemisphere contestants to show their wares. The most notable efforts came over 10,000 metres. The first to strike was Iharos. Running in the national championships at Budapest on July 15 he sliced over 11 seconds from Zatopek's record with a time of 28:42.8. He went through the first half in 14:14.2 and won easily from Kovacs (29:25.6).

Not to be outdone, Kuts made his attempt on September 11. The venue was Moscow's vast Lenin Stadium, with an audience of 100,000 in attendance. His attempt at the world mark followed an earlier national record of 28:57.8 in August. After an opening kilometre in 2:42.5 (27:05 pace!), he ran more steadily, but still covered the first half in 14:08. However, he still had enough in reserve to make the last kilometre the second fastest of the race (2:47.9). His final time of 28:30.4 established him as at least equal favourite (with Pirie) for the longer event in Melbourne.

The Melbourne Olympics were the first conducted in the southern hemisphere, and as a consequence, Europeans were competing "out of season" as the games began in November. Athletic events, along with the opening and closing ceremonies were held at the Melbourne Cricket Ground, with a track laid just for the duration of the games (as soon as the games finished, it was relocated to a suburban oval).

Following his defeat in Bergen, Kuts and his coach realized that in order to achieve success in Melbourne, some changes would be required. His training emphasis switched to shorter, more intense efforts (but retaining the short recoveries), in an attempt to improve his speed. As evidenced by his new 10,000 metre best, the training appeared to be working, but only some two weeks before the start of the Games severe problems arose. Either as a consequence of his severe training programme, his underlying health problems, or a combination of the two, his resting pulse rate rose dramatically. This, accompanied by a rise in blood pressure was a real cause for concern. For the Russians to be without one of their genuine stars at the Olympics would have been almost unthinkable. At the height of the Cold War, and following their appearance at the Helsinki Olympics where they had not won a single event, the propaganda effect could have been devastating to say the least.

Kuts travelled to Melbourne by liner, and the relaxed atmosphere, coupled with some rich food and cognac, seemed to be just the tonic he needed. The team doctors gave him the all clear to compete. Training in Melbourne followed largely the Zatopek formula of brisk 400 metre runs separated by short jog recoveries. Dave Stephens, the world six mile record holder at the time recounts how he trained most days with Kuts in his lead up to the games. On one particular occasion, some ten days prior to the 10,000 metres, they (and some other Australians) were running repeat 400 metre runs on Caulfield race course. Despite a relatively slow pace, Kuts was not able to keep up. Rather than persevere, he finished the session after only eight kilometres, and went home. The next day he rested. The following day, Stephens took Kuts to a grass oval with a track marked. After a warm up, they began running repeat laps in 63-67 seconds with only a brisk 100 metre jog after each. Stephens could only keep up for twelve such repeats, Kuts completed twenty five. For Stephens, it was the best training session he had ever seen in his life.

The 10,000m was the first distance race on the programme (run on November 23), and would go down as one of the most memorable in Olympic history. Iharos, as a consequence of the Hungarian uprising, had not made the trip to Melbourne, and it was obvious from pre-Olympic competition, that the 5,000 and 10,000 metre events largely shaped as match races between Kuts and Pirie.

In retrospect, Pirie probably erred in running the longer event as his best was a long way behind that of his Russian rival, and in fact he would never approach it during the rest of his career. There had also been criticism of the number and quality of races he had undertaken leading up to the games. Had he stuck to the shorter race things may well have been different.

While Pirie had been very pleased with his pre-Olympic training, he had also seen Kuts doing some of his best workouts, and was fully aware of the task that awaited him. On a very soft track Kuts took the lead as usual and proceeded to run at well under world record pace while injecting almost full speed sprints before slowing just as suddenly. The first half went by in a phenomenal 14:06.8, with Pirie hanging on, convinced that if he could stay in contact until the last lap or so, victory would be his. From the earliest stages it had become a two man race. Just when Pirie thought the worst was over, Kuts slowed almost to a walk, forcing his pursuer into the lead. One look told the Russian all he needed

Kuts finishing the 10,000m in Melbourne after his epic battle with Pirie.

to know. He sprinted one last time, and Pirie was gone. While he ran on to victory, Pirie struggled over the last three laps to finish eighth in 29:49, over a minute behind the winning time of 28:45. Russian coaches later admitted, that had Pirie not buckled when he did, it could well have been Kuts and not Pirie that succumbed.

Considering the state of the track and the manner in which the race was run, there can be little doubt that it was a performance that far exceeded the existing world record. That Kuts was also exhausted by his efforts was indicated by the much slower second half of the race, and the fact that the minor place getters (Kovacs and Lawrence) were gaining on him quite rapidly at the end.

Apart from the great strength of mind and body shown by the winner, probably just as important an element in his victory was that Kuts had trained for the type of race he ran, i.e. fast sprints with very short recoveries. While the others had trained hard, they had not trained to withstand the extreme varied - pace running that had been inflicted on them. The great physical toll on both of the main protagonists was perhaps best demonstrated by the fact that following the race, Pirie slept for a full 48 hours, while Kuts's medical examination showed blood in his urine and initially prompted his decision not to contest the 5,000 metres.

After some not inconsiderable pressure, this decision was reversed and only three days later both Pirie and Kuts lined up for the heats. Both got through comfortably and the race looked like it could well be one between the lone Russian and the British team of Pirie, Chataway, and Ibbotson. Teamwork was not the British way however, and it was every man for himself. The three clung to the front running Kuts, until he got away over the last four laps, going on to win convincingly in 13:39.6, the same time as his Bergen loss to Pirie earlier in the year. Pirie was second in 13:50.6.

Once again, bearing in mind the conditions, this was almost certainly superior to the existing world record. It speaks volumes for both Kuts and Pirie that they were able to run so well such a short time after their titanic battle over the twenty-five lap distance. However, in Kuts's case, things were not as good as they appeared. Checked by the Russian medical staff following his second gold medal performance, they were shocked by his condition. Some time after the race, his face was ashen, his lips had a bluish tinge, and his pulse abnormally rapid. He was advised to take a rest – which he did.

Return to Russia after the Games was via ship. Apparently, conditions were basic to say the least, with even supplies of toilet paper being inadequate. Kuts's response to this slight on the heroes of Mother Russia was to go on a drinking binge. Arriving home, so the story goes, he was called before a disciplinary hearing to explain his behaviour. The hearing was abandoned when it became obvious that the subject was too intoxicated to stand, let alone explain himself.

After resuming training, Kuts was but a shadow of his former self. In training, he was routinely beaten by runners who normally would not hold a candle to the Olympic champion. Stomach ulcers caused more problems, which in 1957 caused him to curtail both his training and racing. At the national championships in Moscow he was narrowly out sprinted by future Olympic champion and dual world record holder Pyotr Bolotnikov in the ten kilometre event (29:10.0 to 29:09.8), but managed to retain his five kilometre title (his fifth straight) in 13:48.6.

There was still enough left for one last hurrah. In Prague on October 6, he narrowly missed Pirie's world record, running 13:38.0. Realizing his return to form, he made a final attempt on the record a week later in the Rome stadium that was to be the venue for the 1960 Olympics. In what was to be a virtual time trial he went straight to the front, reeling off the first kilometre in 2:37.8 (13:09 pace!). Despite the physical demands made by such a fast start, he managed to push himself to a new record, finishing in 13:35.0. Second place-getter Bolotnikov finished over 30 seconds behind in 14:06.5. Not for the first time, the effort completely exhausted Kuts, who was hospitalized after the event and advised never to run again. Although ignoring the advice, this proved to be his last major race.

In December, he went to Brazil and ran in the annual Sao Paulo San Silvestre race, finishing a disappointing eighth. The following year he attempted to regain form, but it was not to be. The reality became apparent when in July of that year he competed in Tallinn and finished last. He officially retired the following year, but for all intents and purposes, his career had really come to an end about eighteen months before.

Following retirement, he enrolled at the Leningrad Institute of Physical Education, with a view to becoming a sports trainer – a course of study he completed in 1961. He became a trainer of runners at the Central Army Sports Club. While the life of a runner had been hard work for Kuts, the life of a non-runner proved to be even harder. While stomach ulcers had caused problems during his running career, matters became much worse in retirement, not helped by his now severe drinking problem. His taste for vodka, coupled with his sedentary life-style, caused his weight to balloon to well over 100 kilogrammes. It reached the stage where the authorities would not permit photographs of the former champion to be published. Kuts himself, by all accounts, felt very self-conscious about what he had become, but seemed power-less to do anything about it. For one who had shown such iron discipline during his competitive career, it was a sad turn of events.

Besides his problem with ulcers, Kuts also developed a heart condition, and despite his relatively young age, suffered more than one heart attack. On the eve of August 17, 1975, after quarreling with his former wife, he returned home, drank heavily, and took some pills. Next morning, he was found dead at the age of forty-eight. The official reason for his demise was given as a heart attack.

In any discussion of great athletes, Kuts has to be considered as one of the greatest. Despite his relatively short career, he broke the 5,000 metre record four times, and on two other occasions finished below the old record in coming second, in both cases being responsible for setting the pace virtually the whole way. He also broke the ten kilometre record, and of course was a dual Olympic champion.

Kuts was the first Russian to record an athletics Olympic victory. When he entered the scene, the five kilometre record stood at 13:58.2, when he left, it was 13:35. Considering the way he ran, there is no doubt that he was capable of much faster times than he actually recorded.

Whether he was competing in a major meet or against fields of lower quality, his methodology of very fast starts certainly did not make for the fastest times possible. With the form he was in at Melbourne, under good conditions, and with a more judicious pace, there is little doubt that both records could have been dramatically reduced. Certainly, as a competitor able to push himself to the limit, he had no peer.

RON CLARKE

"The hardest step for a runner to take
is the first one out the door."

One of Clarke's great
breakthrough runs in1965.
The first man to run under
thirteen minutes for three miles.

PROBABLY MORE THAN ANY other runner, Ron Clarke was responsible for revolutionizing standards in the distance events. At his best, there would invariably be a fast time in any race he entered. The way he attacked races, meant that others in the field knew that if they hung on long enough, they would be dragged to a time that, in many cases, they could normally only dream about. It would probably be no exaggeration to say that more runners ran fast times because of Ron Clarke than any other single athlete in the history of the sport.

From a record point of view, he has few peers. During his career he set records at all distances from two miles through to the one hour run. In many cases, he broke records for the same distance on multiple occasions. For example, the 5,000 metre record fell to him four times, the 10,000 metre time three, and even the two-mile record (an event really too short for him), twice.

However, facts and figures do not really do justice to Clarke's career. What they do not spell out is the way he raced, and the frequency of his racing. He would race almost anyone, at any time, and under any conditions. A prima donna he most definitely was not! Invariably it was he who set the race up, setting as fast a pace as he could handle. At his best, and if conditions were good, that would as often as not mean a world record.

During his competitive career, he probably competed more than any world-class athlete before or since. A typical year included the Australian track season over summer, and during the winter either cross country at home, along with track races in Europe and North America. There were also indoor competitions in America during the southern hemisphere summer.

If ever an athlete gave his rivals a chance to win, it was Ron Clarke. Whilst he exhausted himself with a punishing schedule of races and travelling, his rivals tended to be far more selective with their choice of competitions. They knew that they could almost always rely on a fast, front running effort from the multiple world record-holder. In this day and age tracks are synthetic, and non-championship races usually have designated pace makers. Clarke, for most of his athletic career, had neither.

When he began the record-breaking assault that was the hallmark of his career, the three-mile record stood at 13:10.0, the 5,000 metre mark was 13:35.0, the six-mile mark 27:43.8, and the 10,000 metre mark was 28:18.2. With the exception of the six-mile time, all were considered strong marks. In just over two years he reduced those times to 12:50.4, 13:16.6, 26:47.0, and 27:39.4. Clearly, he had ushered in a new era in distance running.

That Ron Clarke became a runner was fairly simple – he was not good enough to be a footballer (at least not at the highest level). Football in this case, meant Australian Rules, something akin to a religion in sports mad Melbourne where Ron grew up. Not making the top grade as a footballer was initially disappointing, given that he grew up in a family environment dominated by football. His father played 103 games for the Essendon club in the years 1927-34, was twice selected in Victorian state teams, and after retirement served as a club committee member for another thirty years.

As if that were not enough, Ron's older brother Jack, would develop into one of the true legends of the game. Playing for the same team as his father, he was a gifted all-round sportsman who could have excelled at any of a variety of sports. Choosing football, he would play his first senior game in 1951, at just eighteen, and played in the grand final later in the year. He would go on to earn state honors twenty-seven times, be selected in the first ever All Australian team, and captained Essendon between 1958 and 1964. His crowning moment came when he led the club to the premiership in 1962 with a best on ground performance. Three years later he played in another premiership, and later coached the club. With a brother like that, maybe it was a wise move to try and excel at something other than football!

Such was the esteem in which Jack was held, for a long while (despite his international reputation), Ron was probably just as well known in Victoria as Jack Clarke's brother.

The active lives that the Clarke boys lived while growing up in Melbourne, were probably not far removed from the norm for many boys their age. In an era before the advent of television, computers, and other inactive pastimes, sport and physical activity in general played a far more important role in the life of young Australians than is the case now. Sport, however, was fairly traditional. Football was played in winter, and cricket, tennis, and swimming in summer.

Athletics was a regular fixture on most school sporting programmes, however, it was in a minor way compared to the more traditional sports. Ron competed in the regular sports, but from his earliest time in high school showed that he had some real talent in running events. Athletics was normally something of a Cinderella sport in Australia. However, these were not normal times. Melbourne would be hosting the 1956 Olympic Games, and the race for the four-minute mile was on in earnest. John Landy was one of those most closely involved in this quest. Being a local Melbourne boy, this raised interest in athletics to heights not seen before or since.

Huge crowds would flock to see Landy's attempts to break through the barrier on home soil. Due largely to poor conditions and lack of competition, it was not to be. It would not be until he journeyed to Finland in mid 1954 that his aim would be achieved. Bannister, however, had beaten him by six weeks in achieving the feat. Landy, incidentally, would years later be appointed governor of Victoria.

Clarke's running career during this period flourished. As a sixteen-year-old (in 1953) he had run the mile in 4:31.1, improving to 4:27.2 the following year. Embracing interval training, in 1955, he set a series of personal bests and national junior records, culminating with a mile best of 4:15.6. However, at the national junior championships in Adelaide, he was beaten in both the half mile and mile by another rising star – a young West Australian by the name of Herb Elliott.

The following year – the Olympic year – saw a new spate of national, and then world junior records from Clarke; culminating with a junior world mile record of 4:06.8. That year had both highlights and lowlights for Clarke. One notable highlight was being chosen as the final torch-bearer for the Melbourne games. As probably the worlds best junior, it could have been seen as a vote of confidence in what the future might hold for him. If that was the basis for the decision, the next few years hardly seemed to justify the choice.

If lighting the Olympic flame was a highlight, a lowlight was his time in compulsory national service. In a way, this was the start of the end for Clarke's running career (or so it seemed at the time). Difficulty in finding the time to train, putting on weight, and contracting a sinus infection made life difficult. Although he continued to train and compete, a combination of study, work, and marriage led to more important priorities and less time.

Although he continued to race and train, it appeared as if his time had passed. The new prodigy was no longer Ron Clarke, but the now world beating Herb Elliott. Married in 1959, Ron played golf and football in addition to the occasional athletic competition. His fitness, enthusiasm, and times were a shadow of his former self. It seemed that he had become just another example of a talented junior not making the grade as a senior competitor.

However, a confluence of circumstances made things different in his case. By late 1960, Ron had finished his accountancy studies and had moved house to a suburb much closer to his place of employment. As a consequence, he had much more leisure time. He, along with the blessing of his wife Helen, decided to give athletics one more go. At the time, his ambition did not extend beyond the hope that he may improve enough to gain state representation.

Initially, his training was done with Les Perry, who lived nearby. Les was a true running enthusiast. Short and slightly built, he had been good enough to earn selection for the 1952 Helsinki Olympics. This experience, coupled with meeting and watching games hero Emil Zatopek, only served to further his enthusiasm for the sport.

Training with his much shorter and older partner took the form of continuous road runs. The initial runs were an ordeal for the relatively unfit Clarke, and led him to question the wisdom of his proposed return to serious competition. The enthusiastic Les, however, decided that after some sessions the time was right to introduce Ron to a group that trained regularly at Caulfield race-course. Unlike some countries, race-courses in Australia are made of soft grass – a most forgiving surface both for horses and their two-legged counterparts. Conveniently for human runners, most equine training is done in the early hours – often being completed before sunrise. The decision to join this training group proved pivotal; not only for Ron, but for the future of world distance running.

The key figures that were to provide a constant in the training of Ron were Tony Cook and Trevor Vincent. Both were excellent State and national calibre athletes, with Tony probably at his best over ten kilometres, while Trevor had greatest success in the steeplechase (his greatest triumph being the 1962 Commonwealth Games title). Training was not complicated. It involved just plain running – usually ten miles (about sixteen kilometres) each evening after work. Regular weekend competitions were either road, track, or cross-country depending on the season. Ron's progress was rapid, and after one winter of regular training, the resurgent Clarke was narrowly beaten by his training partner Cook to finish second in the 1961 Victorian State three-mile title.

At this stage, he was still playing football, but a badly broken finger proved sufficient inducement to put all his sporting energies into running. If ever there was a wise sporting choice made, that would have been it.

In addition to the regular evening training runs, there was also a regular longer run on Sunday mornings. These were run over hilly courses in the Dandenong Ranges on the outskirts of suburban Melbourne. There were two main courses, covering either approximately twenty-seven or thirty-seven kilometres, but both involving severe uphill sections.

Later in 1961, Ron tried his first marathon. Despite his steady training and obvious improvement in fitness, it was to prove a chastening experience. Despite finding the early going comfortable, and building a sizeable lead, the last few kilometres were seemingly never ending. Eventually finishing in 2:53:09, it would not be the last time that he would be humbled by the forty-two-kilometre event.

After the marathon effort came a series of personal best performances during the 1961-62 track season. Finishing third in the state titles over one, three, and six miles was sufficient to gain selection for the nationals. Running in the three-mile event in Sydney, he was good enough to hang on for fourth – no mean feat considering that the first two positions went to Dave Power (1960 Olympic bronze medalist over 10,000 metres), and Alby Thomas (former world record holder over two and three miles). Ron's time was yet another personal best, 13:42.0.

Some four months later, turning his hand to longer distances, Ron broke his first senior records. His ten-mile time of 50:02.0, and 19,355.2 metres (12 miles, 47 yards) for the hour, were both national records.

More personal bests followed, leading to the selection trials for the 1962 Commonwealth Games. Held in Melbourne in late October, Ron entered more in hope than expectation. His results were better than he could have ever expected. Finishing second in the three and six miles, he was selected for both races.

Just over a month later the Commonwealth Games were held in Perth. On a typical Perth summer day – temperature in the high thirties – the six miles was Ron's first event. Obviously feeling the effects of the heat, he dropped out after some eight laps, deciding that to continue would put any chance he had for the shorter race in jeopardy. The race was eventually won by the precocious young Canadian Bruce Kidd, with Dave Power showing his best form for the year taking second.

Two days later the three-mile event was held. It was one of the highest quality fields of the Games. Favourite was Murray Halberg. The New Zealander was both the world record holder for the distance as well as the Olympic champion over the metric equivalent. In addition, there was Bruce Tulloh (the European champion), Alby Thomas (the former world record holder for the distance), Derek Ibbotson (former mile world record holder), and the recently crowned six-mile champion, Bruce Kidd.

The early going was slow, with no one really prepared to take the lead. It was not until Bruce Kidd made a move with three laps remaining that the racing really began. However, after this initial move (covered by both Halberg and Clarke), the pace slowed again, such that virtually the whole field was bunched with a lap to go. In a frantic last lap sprint, Halberg went home a clear winner, while the surprising Clarke went past firstly Tulloh, and then Kidd to take second place. His run was as much a surprise to himself as it was for most athletic observers. His time of 13:36.0, while not a personal best, showed obvious promise for the future. In his first international competition, he had shown that he could hold his own against the best.

The training group of which Ron was a member returned from Perth with a gold medal (Trevor Vincent in the steeplechase), a silver (Ron in the three miles), and a bronze (Rod Bonella in the marathon).

The 1962-63 track season was somewhat of a letdown following his Commonwealth Games performance. He did run personal best times for both the mile (4:03.4), and two miles (8:44.4) in New Zealand in late January and early February, but failed to improve at other distances during the Australian summer. Perhaps a more accurate guide to his increased training and fitness level came during the following winter, with a vastly improved marathon time of 2:24:38 in July, followed by a win in the national cross country in August.

Clearly Ron was improving rapidly, as the start of the 1963-4 track season was to show. In quick succession, he reeled off new national records for both the ten miles (48:25.2) and one hour (19,758.4 metres), 2,000 metres (5:09.2), and 3,000 metres (8:00.0). There were also new personal best times for three miles (13:29.3, and then 13:27.5), two miles (8:35.2), and 5,000 metres in 13:51.6 (albeit in losing to Alby Thomas). Clearly things were looking good, but just how good was a shock not just to Ron, but to just about the entire distance running fraternity both nationally and internationally.

His 5,000 metres personal best was treated as a trial run for the 10,000 metres he was to run three days later. Although beaten, he knew he was running well – well enough to contemplate an attempt on a world record. At the time, the 10,000 metre mark belonged to the 1960 Olympic champion Pyotr Bolotnikov at 28:18.2. He had also held the previous record, just 0.6 second slower. Experts considered the record one of the strongest on the books. Certainly no one had come close to breaking it. The six miles (then officially recognized for world record purposes), was a different story however. That had been held by the Hungarian Iharos (at 27:43.8) since 1956. Despite the world record times at 10,000 metres of both Kuts and Bolotnikov being notably superior, no interim times had been taken en route for the shorter distance in any of their record attempts.

Clarke's aim was to attempt the six-mile mark; the longer distance he considered well beyond his reach. Confiding only to one friend and his brother Jack of his intention, Ron worked a normal day at the office before making his way to Olympic Park for the race. Summer conditions for track events in Australia can be something of a lottery. On this occasion the weather was favorable – reasonably cool and not too windy. There was a field of twenty-four – not the one-man time trial as described in some international reports.

From the gun Clarke made his intentions clear. He went straight to the lead and proceeded to push the pace. His intention had been to run 68 second laps for the first eight laps, and then gradually slow as fatigue set in. The reality was that the first lap took only 64 seconds, before slowing to laps of 67 and 66. After the first four laps he was some seven seconds ahead of his intended time. Although slowing somewhat, his time at three miles (13:32) was only a few seconds from his best ever for the distance. Continuing to push, it was obvious well before the end that the world mark would fall. Picking up the pace over the last few laps Ron managed a final lap of 64 seconds to come home in 27:17.6. Stopping to recover, it was only then that a friend exhorted him to try for the longer record as well. Taking off again, he finished the race in 28:15.6.

Two world marks in the one race. The transition from promising junior to world-class athlete had been achieved, and from an athletic point of view, life would never be the same again.

One of the big changes resulting from his world record was the request by promoters to run at their meets. The first of these was an invitation to run indoors in America. Prior to leaving Australia, Ron ran two excellent 5,000 metre times, the first a national record of 13:41.6 in Melbourne and a few days later 13:45.8 in Sydney. Clearly, he was in good form.

His first US race was in Los Angeles in early February. Unaccustomed to the short, steeply banked track, it was not as straight-forward as it might have seemed before the event. In the end, he was out-sprinted by a little known American, Bob Schul. It might have been just another race to Clarke, but it was the start of a great year for Schul.

Ron's second US race was another two-mile event, this time at the famed Madison Square Garden in New York. Facing up to both Schul and the Canadian Kidd proved too much, and he finished a close third, Kidd taking the honors.

His next race was again over two miles, this time against a new opponent. Gerry Lindgren was a high school runner from the state of Washington. Although seventeen, his looks and demeanor were more akin to someone two or three years younger. It seemed hard to believe that he could seriously challenge someone of Clarke's caliber. Coming into the race, his best for the distance was 8:46 (in itself a dramatic improvement from his 9:17 the year before), but at the start he dashed to the lead. For much of the race he refused to let his much more senior opponent pass, and even after Clarke did get by, refused to concede. While Ron won in 8:36.9, the real story was Lindgren's high school record of 8:40.0. Later that year he would run 5,000 metres in 13:44.0, become an Olympian, and the following year while still a teenager, break the world mark for six miles. Despite his amazing early career, aspects of his life off the track probably prevented him from fulfilling his truly amazing potential.

Clarke's next race of the trip was the US indoor three-mile title, again in New York. This was to prove his best race of the tour, culminating in victory in a new indoor world mark of 13:18.4. Lindgren, who finished third, very nearly did not make it to the start line, as an official manning the entry gate refused to believe that he was old enough to be in the field.

The final race of the tour was another over two miles, again in New York. Again, Bruce Kidd prevailed – but only just (8:39.0 to 8:39.2). The tour proved to Ron that when fully fit, he could race frequently, and at a high level.

Some few weeks after returning from his American tour, Ron was on a plane again, this time to Europe. In the interim, he had changed employment. His new job (still as an accountant) had the dual benefit of both being able to train more (sometimes thrice daily), as well as planning ahead so that he could take trips to compete without jeopardizing his work output.

It is worth noting that Ron, along with other Australian world-class runners of the time such as Kerry O'Brien and Derek Clayton, had a full-time job. Training and competition fitted in around the job, not vice versa. Thus, training would be done either before or after work, and any trips taken would usually be as part of their annual holiday entitlement - certainly a far cry from the full-time athletes of today.

Ron's last competitive outing before leaving was another national record over ten miles, this time in 48:21.6. Twenty-four hours after touching down for his first European trip, he was on the track for a 5,000 metre event in Zurich. After leading for almost the whole race, he was out sprinted by the Russian Bolotnikov. This result did not really surprise Clarke as he was tired from both the trip and a long run the day before. What did surprise him was the time. While the winner ran 13:38.6, Clarke was a mere 0.4 behind in 13:39.0. Under the conditions, to miss the long-standing world record of Kuts by only four seconds was amazing. In quick succession he ran another four races. His final two races were over 5,000 metres, winning firstly against Harald Norpoth (13:41.0 to 13:48.4), and then Michel Jazy (13:45.2 to 13:49.2). He returned home having won three of his five races over a fifteen-day period.

With the Olympics to be held in Tokyo in October, the focus was now on preparing for both the five- and ten-kilometre events. Local races leading up to his departure showed that the good form from his European trip was continuing. These included three miles in 13:18.0 and ten kilometres in 28:36.4.

With a time much faster than any of the other serious contenders, Ron went to Tokyo as favorite for the longer of the two track events. His final effort, some five days before the race, was a three-mile time trial in 13:23. His lead up races and training seemed to justify his favoritism.

The ten thousand metres saw no fewer than thirty-eight starters. The track was damp from morning rain, but conditions were good – cloudy and just over eighteen degrees. From the start, the race basically revolved around the world record holder. The first four laps went by in 4:21.5, eight in 8:55.0, with the half way mark being passed in 14:04.6. At this point the little known American Billy Mills was leading, but since it was within seven seconds of his best for the distance it was reasonable to assume that he would soon drop back rapidly. The main US hope, the precocious Gerry Lindgren was suffering from both an ankle injury and an infection, and was never really a factor.

Some six hundred metres after half-way, the contenders had been reduced to four. Before the race one would have got very long odds if betting that three of those four would be from Tunisia, Ethiopia, and the US. Except for Clarke, all the big names had gone, and the four remaining alternated the lead at a steady pace. Even so, most assumed it was only a matter of time before the others would drop back, allowing the Australian to coast to victory. The problem was, with three laps to go they were still there.

Finish of the 10,000m in Tokyo. Shock winner Billy Mills from Gammoudi, with Clarke third, passing lapped runners.

Another lap, and the Ethiopian (Mamo Wolde) had dropped back ten metres. The last lap was chaotic, with lapped runners clogging the track. The leaders passed no fewer than twelve – some on the inside, some on the outside. On the back straight for the last time Mills led. After Clarke edged him out to prevent a collision with a lapped runner, the Tunisian Gammoudi sprinted between the two. Mills seemed out of contention as Clarke gradually reeled in Gammoudi. And then it happened. Mills stormed down the home straight, hitting the front with some fifty metres remaining. It was all over. The American, whose best time for the distance the previous year was 30:08, was the winner in

28:24.4. He was the third fastest ever, with Gammoudi now the fourth best only 0.4 second behind, with Clarke another second further back.

Mills's win would have to go down as one of the greatest upsets in Olympic history. However, closer inspection of both Mills and Gammoudi would perhaps indicate that their results were not necessarily the huge surprises they first appeared. Both were obviously very talented runners whose careers were just taking off. Mills had qualified for the US team both in the marathon and the ten thousand metres and a few days before his gold medal performance he had run a 220 yard trial in training in 23.4 seconds, giving him confidence that if he could hang on long enough, no one would out sprint him. Within a few months of their gold and silver medals respectively, Mills would set new world figures for six miles (27:11.6), while Gammoudi would win the always hotly contested British six mile title in 27:38.2. While the gold medal effort of Mills was undoubtedly the highlight of his career, Gammoudi would go on to win gold and silver over five thousand metres at the next two Olympics (gold in Mexico City, silver in Munich).

If the ten thousand metre event was a disappointment for Ron, the five thousand was a disaster. Of all the races in his career, this was perhaps the only time he really ran well below his capability. The pre-race favorite was justifiably the American Bob Schul. A product of the training system developed by Mihály Iglói , 1964 would see him achieve something like his true potential. He arrived in Tokyo as the newly crowned world record holder over two miles, and the fastest in the world for the year over the five kilometre distance. The latter was a 13:38.0 effort in the hotly contested Compton Invitational. Just as impressive as the time (a new US record) however, was the manner in which it was achieved. With apparent ease, he sprinted the last lap in fifty-four seconds, giving the impression that with a faster pace the world record would have almost certainly fallen.

The five thousand metre final was run four days after the ten. It was cold and wet, and as a consequence the cinder track (this would be the last non synthetic track used in Olympic competition), was sodden. The pace was largely dictated by Clarke, who decided that running from the front and surging would be the best way to break up the field. With fast finishers such as Jazy, Norpoth of Germany, and Schul in the field, there was probably little real alternative. The problem was that the surges were not sustained enough to shake off his main rivals and the longer the race went, the less effective the surges became.

With six hundred metres remaining, there were still nine in contention, with all the renowned big finishers in with a chance. With a lap to go, the Frenchman Jazy took off and quickly gained a ten metre lead. With three hundred metres to go, he looked the likely winner. And then Schul began his final sprint. On a muddy track, he covered the last three hundred metres in 38.7 seconds. He was unstoppable, and went home a clear winner in 13:48.8, while Jazy faded to fourth a second behind. While Schul ran his last full lap in 54.8, Clarke ran his in 64.0 to finish a disappointing ninth in 13:58.0.

Three days later Ron was at the starting line for the marathon. Remembering his previous efforts over the distance, he was realistic about his chances, but nevertheless pushed the early pace. Leading the field at five kilometres, by ten he had been joined by the Irishman Jim Hogan, and the defending champion, Abebe Bikila. At the fifteen kilometre mark the three were still together and running at well below world record pace. First Clarke, and then Hogan slipped off the pace as Bikila went on to complete probably the most dominant performance ever seen in a high level marathon. He went on to win by over four minutes in a time (2:12:11.2) that took marathon running to a new level.

Meanwhile Clarke, despite suffering badly over the last few kilometres, finished a creditable ninth in 2:20:26.8 – a best ever time for an Australian. Mills finished some five places and over two minutes further back. Despite the agony of his marathon effort, only four days later Ron was back on the track in Osaka, winning easily over five kilometres in 13:48.0. Obviously in good form, he had failed to do himself justice at Tokyo. Just how good was soon to be shown.

Returning to Australia, his first race was a loss to Bob Schul over two kilometres in Sydney. Then followed a series of races in quick succession highlighted by a new three mile world mark (13:07.6 in Melbourne in early December), a new world five kilometre best (13:34.8 in Hobart in mid January), another five kilometre best (13:33.6 in Auckland in early February), a national record for ten miles (47:45.8 in Melbourne in mid February), and finally a new world ten mile mark (47:12.8 in Melbourne in early March).

As if this was not enough, there were numerous other local races, and even a brief American trip to run indoors (two races, two wins – both over two miles). As hectic as the Australian summer had been, it was really only a prelude for what was to follow.

Arriving in the US at the end of May, Ron ran three races before moving over to Europe. As if to prove that his southern hemisphere efforts were genuine, he firstly ran a personal best two miles (8:32.0 to win easily over the American Ron Larrieu), then followed it up with a great new world mark of 13:25.8 in the Compton 5,000 metres, winning by over thirty seconds. En route he brought his three-mile time down to 13:00.4. His final North American effort was over three miles in Toronto. The result was the second fastest time ever, his 13:03.4 leaving his Tokyo conqueror Mills almost nine seconds behind in second place.

In any year, for almost any athlete, this would have been considered more than enough; but it was 1965, and Ron was only just getting started.

His first European race was over 10,000 metres in the southern Finnish city of Turku. More like a time trial than a race, Ron won by over two minutes in a new world mark of 28:14.0. He followed this less than forty-eight hours later with 5,000 metres in 13:40.8 in Tampere. From Finland, it was on to France to race Michel Jazy over two miles. Despite the distance being well short of his best, he agreed to assist with pace making chores. The result was a world record 8:22.6 by Jazy, with Ron also under the old mark in 8:24.8.

From France it was back to Finland for another 5,000 metres (13:33.0), and a losing effort over three kilometres in 8:00.4. Next up were the World Games in Helsinki, with the feature event being the five thousand metres. Besides the Australian, there were two other main draw cards – one well known (Jazy), the other (Keino), not quite as well known, at least not yet.

Fresh from his two-mile world mark, Jazy had also twice set European records for the twelve and a half lap event (13:34.4, and then 13:29.0), and only two days before the Helsinki encounter broke the world mile mark (3:53.6). Kipchoge Keino was a Kenyan, which at that time did not mean very much in athletic circles. True, he had run in the 1962 Commonwealth Games, and made the five thousand metre final in Tokyo. However, neither event really provided any indication of what was to follow. This would all change after just one week in Europe.

The Helsinki event was run on June 30. As was normal, Clarke did most of the work at the front at close to world record pace. Try as he may, he could not shake Jazy, who began his final drive for home with just over a lap remaining. The surprising Keino also went with the Frenchman but could not close the gap on him. The result was Jazy (13:27.6), Keino (13:28.2), and Clarke (13:29.4).

Only two days later, Clarke and Keino met again over 5,000 metres, this time at Turku on a wet track. Feeling tired from his busy schedule, Clarke was more than happy for Keino to assume the front running role for a good part of the race. Going to the front after some nine laps, Clarke attacked but Keino was obviously still fresh. Taking the lead with some three hundred metres remaining he sprinted home in a great 13:26.2 – the second fastest ever, and a mere 0.4 off the world record. Clarke followed him home in 13:29.0.

After a four day break, the two were at it again, this time in Stockholm. Keino had announced his intention of going for both the three mile and five thousand metre records, and clearly with this in mind set off at a pace well under what was required for the records. For a change Clarke was the follower, as the kilometre mark was passed in a swift 2:37.5, and the two kilometre mark in 5:19.0. The pace drifted somewhat after that, but Clarke found his unaccustomed role of follower much easier than that of leader. With only the straight remaining, he went past Keino to win in 13:26.4 to 13:30.4 for the Kenyan. Despite this effort, only twenty four hours later in Oslo he out-sprinted a strong field over three thousand metres in 7:56.8 on a rain soaked track.

After such an exhausting schedule, with so many fast races and so little rest between, it would have been entirely reasonable to have packed up and come home. However, Clarke was really saving his best for last, as his three races before leaving Europe put his previous efforts in the shade.

Travelling to London after his Oslo effort, he lined up for the British three mile championship on July 10. It was a strong field of local runners plus the notable inclusion of Gerry Lindgren, who had earlier in the year tied the world six-mile record with Billy Mills.

The race was not a planned record attempt, but the presence of Lindgren and a fast early pace ensured not just a competitive race, but one of the great breakthroughs in athletics history. The two world record holders were on their own after a little more than three laps, and by two miles (reached in 8:36.4), a new world record seemed inevitable. It was one of those rare occasions when all present realized they were watching history being made, even if they did not know by whom at this stage of the race. Slowly but surely however, Clarke's surges were beginning to take effect, as his younger opponent gradually dropped back. Despite running one of the fastest times ever for the distance (13:04.2), Lindgren finished nearly twelve seconds behind. The thirteen-minute barrier was demolished by Clarke. Taking a full eight seconds from his own record, he finished in 12:52.4. The Australian and the American then took a victory lap together.

Four days later, again in Oslo at the famed Bislett stadium, Ron was lining up for the start of the ten thousand metres. Unlike the earlier three-mile race, this was a record attempt, but not like modern day affairs with pace makers. Rather, it was a time trial – Ron against the clock. Initially, the meet promoter (Arne Haukvik), tried to dissuade

Ron from the race, preferring that he run three thousand metres, since Billy Mills had opted out of the longer race (probably a wise move as it transpired). Adamant that he should have one last attempt in Europe at his best distance, only two others made up the field – the Irishman Jim Hogan, and Claus Boersen of Denmark. Clarke himself was largely responsible for getting the rest of the "field" to run, thus satisfying the requirement (a minimum of three runners in the race) for any resultant record to be ratified. Notable amongst the spectators were Billy Mills and Bob Schul, the gold medalists from Tokyo.

While most would have believed that Clarke's three-mile effort would have to be the highlight of an amazing year of record breaking, it was really just an entrée to the main course. His confidence was high, and he virtually assured promoter Haukvik of a new record. The only question was how fast. Making his intentions clear from the first stride, Ron went through the first half in 13:45.0 (a new stadium record for that distance), and finished in 27:39.4 (six miles having been passed in 26:47.0). His own world mark had fallen by 34.6 seconds, while Mills recent six mile time fell by 24.6 seconds. Clearly, standards of distance running had been raised to a new level. After watching the run, no less than Billy Mills said: "Watching Clarke set his record in Oslo makes one understand that there is a revolution going on."

All that remained to complete his tour was a five thousand metre event in Paris. This he won in a now almost routine time of 13:32.4, to win by the length of the straight from the man who finished ahead of him in Tokyo, Mohamed Gammoudi.

Rounding out the year was yet another marathon attempt, failing to finish in the prestigious Fukuoka event in Japan. He went on to set new world marks for both the twenty kilometres (59:22.8), and one hour run (20,231 metres). Later, Keino visited Australia, and defeated Clarke over five thousand metres (13:40.6 to 13:47.2). This defeat at the hands of one of his great rivals highlighted Ron's approach to competition. Despite being below his best, he was still prepared to race against someone who was obviously in great form after a world record breaking run in New Zealand. Most others in a similar situation would almost certainly have opted out.

Sandwiched in between these races was a visit to Mexico City. Ominously, the best he could achieve over five thousand metres was a second place to Gammoudi (14:41.2 to 14:40.6), while Mills failed to better 15:10.

In retrospect, 1965 proved to be a watershed year in distance running. At the start of the year, the five thousand metre record stood at 13:35.0, and had withstood all challengers for just on eight years. During the year, Ron bettered the old record on no fewer than eight occasions. If we also include races where his three mile times were obviously better than the metric equivalent, the count rises to ten.

In his better event, he brought the ten thousand record (his own), down from 28:15.6 to the above mentioned 27:39.4. By the end of the year he had broken every world mark from two miles to the one hour run, some on a number of occasions. It came as no surprise that he was named athlete of the year for 1965.

By the end of 1965, every distance record from the mile to the ten thousand metres had been re-written, in many cases more than once. As a sign of things to come, Keino had made a return trip to Europe where he ran the third fastest mile of all time (3:54.2), and also obliterated the 3,000 metre standard with 7:39.6. He also made a trip to New Zealand (prior to his Australian sojourn), where he took Clarke's 5,000 metre time down to 13:24.2. The first of the great Kenyan runners had arrived on the international athletic stage.

The following year saw more of the same from Clarke - frequent races over a variety of distances in Australia, two indoor trips to the US (that included a new world indoor mark over two miles in 8:28.8), and trips to the US and Europe during the Australian winter. The highlight this year was reclaiming his 5,000 metre record from Keino in Stockholm. Winning by almost forty seconds from Bill Baillie of New Zealand, he

Ron Clarke 5th July 1966 Stockholm – world 5,000m record: 13:16.6 – the last of his 5000m records. European 1500m champion Bodo Tummler leading.

ran 13:16.6, taking 7.6 seconds off the Kenyans' time. His three mile time of 12:50.4 en route was another record. A week later he ran the second sub 28 minute time ever for ten thousand metres when he recorded 27:54.0 in Oslo. Typical of his schedule; in the thirty two days of his European tour he raced fourteen times, and was defeated twice (once by Keino in a fast 13:26.6 to 13:28.4), the other finishing fourth in a mediocre (by his standards) 13:37.0 in London.

After Europe, and a quick return trip to America, it was off to Kingston, Jamaica, for the British Commonwealth Games. First up was the six miles. Despite being run in the evening, the tropical climate assured that the humidity was high. In such conditions, physiology dictates that a good little man will have a decided advantage over a

Ron Clarke 5th July 1966 Stockholm. Alone at the front again, later in the race.

good big man, due to the relative advantage in dissipating heat. In this case, the good little man was the diminutive Kenyan newcomer, Naftali Temu. Running at a level he had never before approached, he cleared out over the last laps to win easily in a fast 27:14.6, Clarke finishing second (ironically in the same time as his ten thousand metre record).

Two days later he lined up against Keino over three miles. Despite pushing the pace and running under thirteen minutes, he was out sprinted by the Kenyan (12:57.4 to 12:59.2). Keino also won the mile in a most impressive display, while Clarke, a true glutton for punishment entered the marathon – retiring after seventeen miles.

After Kingston, Clarke's Australian season saw easy wins against Temu, and the second fastest six miles ever (26:52.0).

The following year (1967) Clarke undertook a European tour that included a new world mark over two miles (albeit inferior to Keino's 3,000 metre mark), and a narrow miss at lowering his 5,000 metre time in Stockholm. Passing three miles in 12:54.8, he finished in 13:18.8 – the second fastest ever. Shortly after, he ran under thirteen minutes for three miles twice in three days – no mean feat considering that only one other runner (Keino) had ever bettered such a time once.

After returning to Australia he again entered another marathon, this time the national championship race in South Australia. A newcomer to the event was just making his way, and the two ran together for much of the journey, before Clarke was forced to concede, retiring at the twenty mile mark, as Derek Clayton went on to win in 2:21:58. The world was to hear a lot more of Clayton the marathon runner, as a few months later he would take over two minutes off the world's best time for the distance, running 2:09:36 in the Fukuoka event in Japan.

1968 was an Olympic year, and following his disappointment in Tokyo, Clarke was determined to give it his best shot. Whereas in Tokyo he had been very much a newcomer to international athletics, he was now a veteran of that scene. There was one major problem however – the venue.

Mexico City, at an altitude of two thousand two hundred and forty metres, would have to be one of the most ill considered choices for a sporting venue in history. It became apparent in the various meetings held at similar altitudes leading up to the Games that endurance athletes from sea level were at a huge disadvantage compared to their altitude based counterparts. The latter came mainly from Kenya, Ethiopia, and

Photo to a friend. A lean, tanned Clarke training at Lake Tahoe before his ill-fated Mexico Olympic races.

the host country. It was clear that while lengthy periods of acclimatization would help, it was virtually impossible to completely redress the imbalance.

In hindsight, Clarke's build up to Mexico and his performances there were a bit like the unfolding of a Shakespearian tragedy. Wishing to give himself every chance, he took time off work, and spent some five months training at altitude, notably at Font Romeu in France and Lake Tahoe in America. His training was much as it normally was, the only difference being the inclusion of more tempo runs in order to better gauge his pace when competing at altitude.

Whatever he was doing, it seemed to be working. During his Olympic build up he ran a personal best for the mile, and later revised his world two-mile record down to 8:19.6. However, without doubt, his best effort was in London on August 29 at Crystal Palace. Running in gale force winds, he ran 10,000 metres in 27:49.4. Clarke believes that this run was the best of his career – by a considerable margin. He was in the form of his life.

As if the inappropriateness of Mexico City as an Olympic venue needed any emphasizing, it was provided just days before the opening of the Games. The right wing government of President Diaz Ordaz quelled in a most brutal fashion a student gathering in the housing estate of Tlatelolco, just a few kilometres from the Olympic stadium. In what had the appearance of a carefully orchestrated undertaking, the army fired on protesters. Official figures were never given, but it is believed that perhaps three hundred were killed, with another thousand taken into custody by the army and police. Many fled the country. Needless to say, there was little unrest during the Games. The government largely managed to suppress knowledge of the event, and for most of the international media, the Olympic Games was the only story in town.

The 10,000 metres was the first of the distance finals. On times, Clarke was head and shoulders over the rest of the field, but times at sea level meant little in the oxygen thin environment of Mexico City. The field went through the first half in 14:55, and by six thousand metres there were still twenty in the leading group. With four laps remaining the pace increased and the real race began. The tiny Ethiopian Mamo Wolde went to the front with a lap of 68.4 seconds; a marked increase over the 71-73 second pace it had been to that point. The next lap was at a similar pace. Despite it being a 69 second lap, Ron was clearly in trouble. While the first three (Wolde, Temu, and for a while Gammoudi) dueled for the lead, he lost over seventeen seconds on the leaders over the last two laps.

Fading from fourth to sixth, he collapsed at the end. Administered oxygen by Brian Corrigan, the Australian team doctor, it was ten minutes before he regained consciousness. His time of 29:44.8 was over two minutes outside his best. The following day a picture of Clarke in the national dailies said it all. Unconscious, an oxygen mask on his face, being attended by a doctor in tears; his Olympic dream was over.

Despite such an ordeal, only two days later he lined up for a heat of the 5,000 metres. Despite qualifying easily in 14:20.8 (0.4 second behind Temu) in the second of three heats, it was with more than a little trepidation that he faced the final two days later. After a slow early pace, the real racing began in the ninth lap. In many ways it was a replay of the longer race. With just over a kilometre left, Clarke was in the lead, followed by Gammoudi, Temu, and Keino. However, with over a lap to go, it was obvious the winner would be one of the latter three. In a frantic last lap sprint, which both Gammoudi and Keino covered in 54.8 seconds, the Tunisian finished a scant 0.2 ahead of the Kenyan – 14:05.0 to 14:05.2. Clarke held up better than in the 10,000, finishing fifth in 14:12.4. With the exception of the winner (who had spent probably more time training at altitude than any of the sea level runners), Ron was the highest placed of the non-altitude competitors.

Although he ran well after his Mexico experience (including an indoor record over three miles in January the following year), he was never again at his superlative best. He had thoughts about continuing on to Munich in 1972, but gradually those ambitions evaporated. At the 1970 Commonwealth Games in Edinburgh, he was out-sprinted in the 10,000 metres by local hero Lachie Stewart, and then faded to fifth in a high quality 5,000 metre field a week later. After three more races in Europe, he announced his retirement. His last official race was over ten kilometres in Oslo on August 5 – his sixth place in 29:00.4 sufficient to convince him that his decision to retire was the right one.

Following Mexico, Ron found it very difficult to reproduce his previous efforts. In light of subsequent events, speculation was rife that his Olympic effort was the cause of long-term physical problems. Despite finding exertion harder than previously, a series of stress tests at the Royal Melbourne Hospital cardio unit did not detect any problem.

However, following a comprehensive heart test in 1972, a heart murmur was detected and subsequently monitored. Some eleven years later (1983), he suffered severe heart fibrillation while training and was promptly admitted to hospital for surgery to correct a faulty heart valve. A successful operation saw Ron return to his normal active lifestyle.

Following his retirement from competitive running, Ron had more than enough to fill in his time. As previously mentioned, he had always put in a full days work, with training fitting in around the normal working day. Overseas trips were undertaken as part of annual holidays, the only real exception being the lead up to Mexico. As such, running was really only a part of his life, certainly not his whole life.

During most of his competitive career, Ron had been the accountant for a business form printing company, before being appointed general manager of Adidas in Australia. He then started his own sports consultancy business in 1972. In 1983, with his wife Helen, he made the shift to London as a result of purchasing a sporting club that had been placed in receivership. After reviving its fortunes and greatly boosting membership, he sold out ten years later. During his thirteen years in England, he was also a member of a consortium that developed the highly successful Combe Grove Manor, a Country Club Hotel.

Returning to Australia in 1996, Ron relocated to the Gold Coast in southern Queensland, and was instrumental in the building of the Couran Cove Resort. His next project was an integrated fitness / hotel complex at Runaway Bay. Both resorts were state of the art undertakings and in their design and construction reflected Ron's concern that they should be as environmentally friendly as possible.

As if that were not enough to keep him occupied, in 2000 he was instrumental in setting up CEPA – the Council for the Encouragement of Philanthropy in Australia. The aim of this organization is to encourage private and business donations to aid worthy causes. It has been responsible for the allocation of millions of dollars to such ventures.

In addition, Ron has authored and co-authored a number of books. Two of these – The Lonely Breed (with Norman Harris), and The

Unforgiving Minute (with Alan Trengove), are recognized as excellent sporting books, the latter one covering his career until the end of his great 1965 season.

In 2004 he successfully ran for the position of mayor of the Gold Coast Council. He was re-elected for a further four-year term when he stood again in 2008. Active all his life, he died of kidney failure after a short illness on June 17, 2015 in his adopted state of Queensland.

In the federal parliament, both the Prime Minister and Opposition Leader paid tribute to Clarke as a great Australian. Herb Elliott remembered him as a "great man", whose "contribution to athletics was enormous". Friend, former world mile record holder and governor of Victoria, John Landy, said of Ron: "… by his running feats….in a world sense, demonstrated the potential athletic achievement possible." The American Frank Shorter spoke of Clarke being his idol when beginning his athletic career, referring to him as, "the symbol of running."

Much has been made of Ron's failure to win any of the major championship races he entered. Looking back over Ron's athletic career, it is too easy to focus on his "failure" to ever win a gold medal at either Commonwealth or Olympic Games. It is also easy to focus on the number of races he lost. What this over-looks to a great extent is the approach he took to competition. Virtually unique to world-class performers, he was prepared to compete against any rival under any conditions, almost always as the front runner. The travesty of holding the Olympics at high altitude deprived Ron from showing what he was truly capable of on the greatest sporting stage of all. At sea level, it would have been a brave man indeed to bet against him in the longer race.

His true legacy to athletics was the manner in which he revolutionized the sport. Almost single handedly, he raised distance running standards to new levels – not just in the times he ran, but also in the frequency.

Had he never run a step, his story would be well worth telling. After all, running was only one part of it, but that part made him one of the truly great runners of all time.

LASSE VIREN

The lone wolf of Myrskyla

Finish of the Munich 5,000m. Viren
winning from Gammoudi and a fast
finishing Ian Stewart.

Following the conclusion of the Second World War, it appeared at first glance as if the natural order of distance running had been restored. At the 1946 European Championships, held in Oslo's famed Bislett Stadium, Finns finished first and second in the 10,000 metres, and due to a scheduling mistake, were on the track when their countrymen were also filling the first two places in the marathon. Viljo Heino was the new record holder over the ten kilometre distance, having earlier reduced Mäki's time down to a most impressive 29:35.4 at Helsinki on August 25, 1944.

True, other countries had won the remaining distance events at the first championship event after the war, (Strand of Sweden in the 1,500 metres and Wooderson of Great Britain in the 5,000 metres), but with Heino, Finland appeared to have the future of distance running. Appearances, however, can be deceiving.

Had anyone the audacity to suggest that it would be another twenty six years before Finland would win their next Olympic gold medal in a distance event, they would have been ridiculed for their lack of judgement. However, the ending of global conflict resulted in not just a new political order, but also a vast change in world distance running. That change would result in the emergence of countries never before known for their distance running prowess, along with a rising of standards to heights unimaginable before the war. The days of Finnish domination in endurance events were over.

The first rumblings that the end of Finnish dominance was nigh came in the form of Emil Zatopek. The amazing Czech single-handedly took over the distance running mantle from Finland, who in turn was supplanted by Russians, Hungarians, New Zealanders, Australians, and even Americans. Also present was the first stirring of an African movement. It would not be until the early seventies, some twenty-five years on, that Finland would be heard from again on the world stage of distance running.

That presence would initially be the somewhat eccentric Juha Vaatainen. Outspoken, the fount of numerous running quotes, and

The master and the apprentice – but not for long. Vaatainen leads from Viren in a domestic race prior to Viren taking over his mantle as the pre-eminent Finnish runner.

seeming to revel in the nick-name, "Juha the Cruel", it was he who first put Finland back on the distance running map.

Born on July 12, 1941, he began his athletic career as a sprinter – he had bests of 10.9, 22.1 and 48.9 for the 100, 200, and 400 metres respectively. He gradually added endurance to his obvious speed. This was done mainly via long runs, often with bursts of speed thrown in. Weeks of over three hundred kilometres were not unusual. He seemed to revel in training harder than any of his competitors, most of his training being done in natural surroundings, with the track being largely reserved for competitions.

By 1963 he had recorded 1:52.3 for 800 metres, and two years later was good enough to win his national title over that distance. By 1967, he had reduced his two lap best to 1:48.4, and the following year ran 1,500 metres in 3:43.7. It was not until 1969 that he turned seriously to the longer distances. Recording five and ten thousand metre times of 13:50 and 28:53 was certainly promising, but in 1970 he began to realize his true potential over the longer distance with a national record of 28:19.6. With the 1971 European championships being held in Helsinki, Vaatainen's aim was to compete in both distance events. He very nearly did not make it. Partly because of injury concerns, he did not post qualifying times until just a month before the major meet of the year. At the national championships in his hometown of Oulu, he gave an indication of what the future might hold, with a new national record over 10,000 metres, winning in 28:12.8.

In the European meet, the longer race was first on the programme. It would later be remembered as one of the greatest distance races of all time. In ideal conditions before a crowd of 40,000, the bulk of the pace-making was done by the new European record holder, Dave Bedford. Despite the fast pace (the half way mark came up in 13:54.4), at the bell Bedford was shadowed by no fewer than five runners. The last lap was one of the most exciting ever. It was certainly one of the fastest. Drawing on his early career as a sprinter, Vaatainen ran the last lap in an amazing 53.8 seconds, to finish in 27:52.8. The rare feat of achieving a sub twenty-eight minute time was done by no fewer than five runners. Prior to this, there had been not a single race where more than one runner had dipped below that time. Such was the quality of the event that no fewer than ten national records were set in the one race.

Four days later, the 5,000 metres saw a similar result. The last kilometre took only 2:28, but Vaatainen only really began sprinting over the last three hundred metres. His last lap, faster even than in the 10,000 metres, was variously timed at between 52.8 and 53.4, as he went home in 13:32.8.

With the Munich Olympics only twelve months away, Finns believed they had found their next Olympic gold medalist. They had, but it was not the man they anticipated.

While the man of the moment was undoubtedly Vaatainen, another Finn was also running well. Despite finishing in 28:33.2 for the longer race, it was good enough for only seventeenth place, while in the shorter race his time of 13:38.6 saw him come home in seventh place. The name of this slightly built, quietly spoken, bearded runner was Lasse Viren. Unlikely as it might have seemed in August of 1971 after the euphoria of Vaatainen's triumphs, it would be he, and not his older compatriot, who would revive Finland's Olympic distance running fortunes. Although obviously improving, and seen as a man of the future, it would have been a brave person to have predicted what would happen to Viren over the next year.

Born on July 22, 1949, Viren grew up in the southern Finnish town of Myrskyla (population about 2,000). Like many boys his age he took part in a variety of sports, but by age sixteen running was his main interest. From the very start it was obvious that he had ability. His hometown, like nearly all in Finland, could boast its own track. Once the winter snows had melted, regular athletic meets were the norm over the summer months.

Training with his local club, by 1965 he was running a kilometre in 2:49.2, and 3,000 metres in 9:33.8. Besides his running in summer, he was also cross country skiing in winter. The following year he improved his 3,000 metre time to 9:17.0 (good enough to be the thirteenth fastest youth time in Finland for the year). By 1967, he was the Finnish under 18 record holder at both 3,000 metres(8:32.8), and 5,000 metres(14:59.4), as well as finishing second in the national youth cross country.

The following year he undertook a year of military service – compulsory for all Finns his age. Despite increasing his training considerably, his results were not great. He improved his times, but only at distances he had not run very much, finishing the year with bests of 2:02.8 (800 metres), 4:06.8 (1500 metres), and 32:18.8 (10,000 metres).

While 1968 was something of a lost year (as far as improving his times at his best distances were concerned), the situation changed dramatically in 1969. He reduced the national junior 5,000 metre record on no fewer than five occasions, finishing with a best of 13:55.0. He also finished the season with a junior national record over 3,000 metres in 8:05.2, as well as winning the national senior title over 5,000 metres in 14:10.2.

From his earliest time in the sport, it was obvious that he had both great natural talent, along with an ability to push himself more than most – both in training and racing. Toward the end of his breakthrough year of 1969, he accepted a scholarship to Brigham Young University, in the American state of Utah. The experiment did not work. After a few disappointing races and being homesick, he returned to Finland a few months later. His first race after returning was a lacklustre 14:51 for 5,000 metres. It was at this stage that he asked former runner Rolf Haikkola to be his coach.

Haikkola had been a 14:14 5,000 metre runner, and had listened to what the famed New Zealand coach Arthur Lydiard had to say while he was in Finland as part of a two year coaching contract. What Lydiard was preaching was that firstly, Finnish dominance of distance running had passed because their runners were not prepared to work hard enough. Secondly, he pushed his idea that long, continuous runs were a large part of the solution. With athletes like Viren and others, his ideas found a receptive audience. Although heavily influenced by Lydiard, Haikkola was also influenced by the ideas of Percy Cerutty, Mihály Iglói , and Paavo Nurmi.

Increasing his mileage under the guidance of Haikkola, Viren showed rapid improvement over the Finnish summer of 1970. He finished the season with bests of 13:43 for 5,000 metres (finishing second to Mikko Ala-Leppilampi's national record of 13:40.2) and 29:15.8 for 10,000 metres. For the first time, thoughts of the Olympics two years hence began to surface.

The following year saw new best times in his build up to the European Championships. In succession there was a new national record over 5,000 metres (13:35.2), a 10,000 metre best of 28:16.8, along with other bests of 7:54.0 (3,000 metres), and 3:47.3 (1,500 metres).

As previously mentioned, in the championships Viren finished seventeenth in the 10,000 and seventh in the 5,000, with times of 28:33.2 and 13:38.6 respectively. Although commendable, they were over-shadowed by the brilliance of Vaatainen. However, as a portent of things to come, a week after the championships Viren broke Vaatainen's national 5,000 metre record. Running 13:29.8 was good enough to rank as the fifth fastest time for the year.

Following the 1971 season, the aim for the following year was purely on the Munich Olympics. Everything else was of secondary importance. Both Viren and Haikkola could see the need to improve Lasse's finishing speed. While he was fast, he would never be in the same league as a Vaatainen if it came to an all out sprint over the last two or three hundred metres. Clearly greater endurance would be required to make a run for home from further out, rather than waiting purely for the last lap.

Beginning in October of 1971, the volume of training was increased, the great bulk of it being in the form of continuous running. Although the volume of training was considerably greater than he had done before, it never approached that of his better-known countryman. The largest volume totaled about eight hundred kilometres per month, but this was really only achieved on three or four occasions in the twelve month period leading up to Munich. At other times it was often considerably less. All told, Viren covered a little less than 7,500 kilometres in his year-long lead up to the Olympics. By contrast, Vaatainen was reported to have covered almost 11,000 kilometres in an equivalent time in the lead up to his European Championship victories.

By this stage of his life, Viren was working as a policeman in his home-town. Although not overly taxing, he was expected to put in a full days work. He would normally run for up to an hour in the forest, before starting work at eight. His duties would finish by four, when it was time for the second session of the day. On winter days, if it had been snowing too heavily, he had a treadmill at home on which to train.

Earmarked as one of the Olympic hopefuls by the Finnish authorities, Viren received the maximum allowance of 10,000 marks to assist with training expenses in the lead up to Munich. In order to avoid the worst of the Finnish winter, training trips were undertaken outside the country, notably to South America. The only short-coming in Haikkola's planned preparation came with the proposed visit to Font Romeu, in France, for altitude training. When Viren arrived in April, there was too much snow to enable the proposed training to take place.

All training was carried out in a systematic and purposeful fashion, with the sole aim of being at his best for the Olympics. Likewise competitions; whose purpose was mainly to assess the effectiveness of training, try different tactics, and as a form of speed training.

Although the main foundation period leading up to the competitive season was characterized by steady runs, as the season approached the volume decreased, while the intensity of the work rose. Training was rarely done on a track, mainly to avoid the likelihood of injury. However, trial runs were done on a regular basis to test the effectiveness of the training. Examples of these were an eight kilometre timed road run (on the same regular course), and a tempo run over twenty five kilometres with every fifth kilometre being run at close to full speed. One of the infrequent track tests undertaken involved 2x10x200m with a brisk jog between each, and a five minute recovery between each set. In mid June Viren could average 30.6 for each 200 metre run. Within two months, his average was 27.3 (some eight days before the Olympics).

As was the norm for Viren, competitions were used in large part as training for the major upcoming competition, with results not considered to be of overly great importance. Thus, in his first eight competitions of the Finnish season, his ledger was: won two, lost six. It was not until just over a month before Munich that he began to show his true capabilities. In the space of four weeks, beginning on July 25, his last five races before the Olympics included three national records and one world record.

The first of the series was 5,000 metres at Helsinki. His time of 13:19 was the third fastest ever, but perhaps more notable was the way the race was run. In a fast race, the last two kilometres were 2:39 and 2:30. In what was to become his hallmark, Viren was showing his ability to produce a long acceleration over the last six hundred metres or so of a race. His next race, only two days later, was a 3,000 metre event in the northern city of Oulu. The result was a new national record of 7:43.2.

Following this, he ran the 10,000 metres at the Bislett Games in Oslo on August 3. Running the first half in 14:00.2, he increased his speed over the second half to come home in 27:52.4 (breaking Vaatainen's national record). It was this race that confirmed his decision to try for the double at Munich.

The final race that really stamped Viren as one of the main contenders in Munich was his world two-mile record, run in Stockholm on August 14. In a star-studded field, Viren ran the second mile in 4:04.6 to come home in 8:14.0. Former world record holder Emiel Puttemans was also under his old record in second place. This was really his first race of the year against top competition, and he had crushed them all. Despite this great run, the previous day he had won his national title over 1,500 metres (in 3:48.5). His final tune up was a 5,000 metre victory in Helsinki on August 20 in 13:33.0.

At Munich, the 10,000 metre heats (the first time there had been heats since 1920) were run on the first day of competition (August 31). There was no clear favorite. Partly because Viren had burst on the scene so suddenly, he was still considered something of an unknown quantity to most observers. There was considerable anticipation about what times would be required to make the final. With three heats to be run, the first four in each became automatic qualifiers, plus the next three fastest.

The capacity crowd did not have long to wait for the main players to put their cards on the table. In the very first heat, Englishman Dave Bedford (the European record holder at 27:47) set a pace that threatened the world record, only to be out sprinted at the end by the Belgian Emiel Puttemans in the fifth fastest time ever (27:53.4). The second heat was little slower with the defending Olympic 5,000 metre champion Mohamed Gammoudi leading the first three home in under twenty eight minutes (his time: 27:54.8). Some way back, but still well ahead of fifth place was Lasse Viren in 28:04.4. To those seeing him for the first time, his run did not look overly convincing. It was a warm day, and it did not seem as if he was comfortable in the conditions. The final heat was a more leisurely affair, at least until the last lap. It was then that the tiny Ethiopian Miruts Yifter finished with a 56 second lap to put the issue beyond doubt (his time: 28:18.2).

The final took place as the last event on the fourth day of competition. Many were wondering how the heats would affect the final. They need not have worried. What was to unfold was one of the great individual efforts of these or any games. As was his want, Bedford went straight to the lead. Pushing the pace at a suicidal 59.9 seconds for the first lap, the kilometre came up in 2:36.9, and two kilometres in 5:18.8. Even after three kilometres in 8:06.4 and four in 10:55.5, only five had been dropped, despite a pace well under the existing world record. A little over a lap later there was clash involving Viren and the future marathon victor, Frank Shorter. As a result, Shorter stumbled, but Viren fell. In the process of falling, he fell across the path of Mohamed Gammoudi, who in turn was brought down heavily. Viren lost about three seconds, but quickly regained his composure and set off after the field. Gammoudi was not so fortunate. Having fallen more heavily, he lay on the ground while the field gained a hundred metres before he gave chase. This lasted for a lap and a half before he realized his cause was lost, and retired from the race.

By the half way stage (reached in 13:43.9), the situation began to change, with Yifter briefly taking the lead, and Bedford no longer the dominant force he was earlier in the race. The pace was also dropping, until by 9,000 metres it was some 10.2 seconds slower than Ron Clarke's time when he set the world mark. By this stage the winner would obviously come from one of the group of five who had moved away from the rest of the field. Just who that would be was far from clear. With only the final kilometre left, something would have to happen. Firstly Yifter went into the lead, only to be passed by Viren, and then Puttemans. With two laps to go, the Spaniard Haro dashed to the lead, only to be headed by Viren with 600 metres left to run. Launching his final drive for home, he quickly dropped both Shorter and Haro.

The increase in pace was deceptive. Viren did not look as if he was running that much faster, but the change in pace was in fact dramatic. The penultimate lap was sixty seconds, but Puttemans was only three metres adrift, with Yifter another ten further back. Viren continued to raise the tempo, but could not gain on his two pursuers. On the final bend it appeared as if Puttemans may well close the gap, but Viren maintained his form to finish 1.2 seconds ahead, with Yifter another 1.4 seconds further back in third.

The time was a new world mark – 27:38.4. Although great running, the way it was achieved led most to believe that it could have been much faster. Not only had Viren fallen, but his acceleration over the final stages was of an order rarely before seen in a distance race. His final kilo had taken just 2:29.2, his last two laps 1:56.4, and his final lap only 56.4 seconds. Such was the quality of the field, the first five finishers all set national records, and all recorded the fastest place times ever. The glory of Finnish distance running had returned!

Four days later (September 7) the heats of the 5,000 metres were run. There were five heats, with the first two in each to qualify for the final, plus the next fastest four. All went as expected, with the favorites making it through. Vaatainen won heat four in a good 13:32.8, while Viren won the last in 13:38.4. The only unexpected casualty was the 10,000 metre bronze medalist. For reasons never fully explained, Yifter did not make it to the start line. Due to politics (a boycott by African nations in 1976), it would be eight years before the Ethiopian would again have his chance to compete as an Olympian.

The final was on September 10, and after his great run in the 10,000 metres Viren was seen as the favorite. However, with one of the best fields ever assembled for the distance, the winner could realistically have been any of the finalists. While the longer race had been run at a cracking pace from the start, the pace of this one was anything but. With no one really prepared to lead at a solid tempo, the bunched pack went through the first three kilometre marks in 2:46.3, 2:46.3, and 2:47.6. With four laps remaining, the whole field was still tightly packed. It was only then that the real racing began.

While the preceding four laps had been between 66 and 68.5 seconds, Steve Prefontaine, the brash young American, went to the front and the pace increased to 62.5. The next lap increased again, this time to 61.2. With two laps remaining, Viren was in fact marginally in front of the group comprising, beside the Finn and the American, Puttemans, Gammoudi, and Ian Stewart of Great Britain. With some six hundred metres remaining, Prefontaine again took the lead, with the penultimate lap taking just 60.3 seconds. The previous three laps had taken just 3:04, but both Gammoudi and Viren looked comfortable. By the start of the final back straight, Viren was in the lead, but Gammoudi managed to get slightly ahead. Prefontaine also came again, as the three were almost side by side with slightly over 200 metres to run. With just over a hundred metres remaining, Viren proceeded to put the issue beyond doubt. His was a long graceful stride rather than a sprint, as he pulled away to finish a full second ahead of Gammoudi in 13:26.4. In a frantic finish for third place, Stewart passed the exhausted Prefontaine with fifteen metres left, to finish just 0.2 seconds behind Gammoudi to claim the bronze medal. As if to emphasize the difference a year could make, the last to finish was Juha Vaatainen in 13:53.8.

Viren's closing speed over the final laps again set new standards. While his last lap was an impressive 55.8 seconds, his final 800 metres took just 1:56.1, and his last 1200 metres 2:57.3. His final 1500 metres took 3:44.7! Clearly he was in a class of his own. Just as clearly, he led those watching to believe that had the situation required it, he had yet more to give.

Returning home a hero, Viren had enough left after the heroics of Munich for one last great run. Only four days after his Munich five thousand metres, he was at it again on a cold night in the Helsinki Olympic stadium. His main competition was Dave Bedford, no doubt in search of some atonement following his disappointing Olympic showing. Bedford led for the greater part of the race, but was forced to concede during the fourth kilometre. Viren finished strongly over the last kilo in 2:33.7, to complete the journey in 13:16.4 (rounded up by 0.1 as IAAF rules then required), a new world mark. Bedford was second in 13:30.0, whilst the hero of just twelve months earlier, Vaatainen, was a distant third in 13:35.4.

After a season that included three world records and two Olympic gold medals, it was no surprise that Viren was named the world athlete of the year for 1972. However, only six days after his 5,000 metre world mark, the record would be broken again, this time by Emiel Puttemans. The Belgian, who had run such a great ten thousand behind Viren in Munich, ran 13:13.0 in Brussels, on September 20. In light of Viren's career, it is perhaps more than a little surprising that he would never again run as fast as he did in those seven weeks of 1972.

Following his world record effort, his season finished as it had started. With six more races, over distances between 1,500 and 5,000 metres, his record was three firsts, two seconds, and a fourth. However, with his Munich victories he established himself both as one of the great Olympic competitors, as well as one of the greatest "peakers" of all time. What he had done before or after counted for little. It was what he had done when it mattered that told the real story of his season.

The post Olympic year was (by his 1972 standards), something of a letdown. Realistically, how could it not be? Times of 13:28 and 28:17 were well below his best, and at the European Cup final in Edinburgh, he could manage only fifth in the five thousand metres. However, 1974

Munich 1972. Viren leads from Yifter, Haro and Puttemans in the closing stages of the Olympic 10,000m.

would see the European Championships, and hopefully the chance for a return to his Munich form.

The Finnish cross country championships for 1974 were held in Kalajoki, on a soft, sandy surface. Lasse finished second, but while running twisted his ankle. This caused him to favor his injured foot, thus placing abnormal stress on other parts of his leg. What had seemed like a minor irritant, turned into a long-term problem. He could run, but not without pain. Despite frequent treatment and examinations, the problem persisted.

Despite the injury, he ran both races at the European title meet. Considering his troubled preparation, his results were better than could have been reasonably expected. His 10,000m in 28:22.2 saw him seventh, while in the shorter race, his 13:24.6 was good enough for third, albeit well behind the winning time of 13:17.2 by Brendan Foster.

The pain persisted, and as a last resort it was decided to operate. The operation was carried out early in the new-year. On the operating table, it was found that the problem had been caused by restrictions to the hamstring muscles. Once rectified, the pain was gone, but so was a good deal of his preparation for the 1975 season. Returning to full training was a slow process, but at least it was now pain free. Despite his limited preparation, he still finished the year with bests of 13:34.6 and 28:11.4 – a good prelude to an Olympic year. The serious preparation for Montreal could now begin.

One of the keys in the lead up to Montreal was a block of altitude training at Thomson Falls in Kenya. Training up to three times daily, Viren was putting in more kilometres than ever before, mainly through a combination of steady runs, hill repetitions, and fartlek. The weekly volume got up to 250 kilometres. At the back of his mind there was the intention to try for the marathon in addition to his two track specialties.

In a sense of déjà vu, his lead up to the games were (for his opponents), eerily similar to Munich four years earlier. After an indifferent (by his standards) three years, he finally showed his true colors with a 27:43.0 effort over 10,000 metres at the World Games in Helsinki, along with a 13:24.8 for the shorter distance. As if that were not enough to install him as favorite, the last minute boycott by the African countries only served to enhance his status (at least for the longer race). The boycott, caused by the South African rugby tour of New Zealand and the refusal of the IOC to ban New Zealand from competing, led to the notable exclusion of Miruts Yifter and Henry Rono.

Typical of the thorough and systematic approach that he had followed throughout his preparation, Viren did a number of sessions at close to midnight in order to prepare for the time difference between Finland and Canada.

As was his custom, he again used minor competitions as a means of preparing for the Olympics. Beginning with his World Games ten thousand metres, Viren would race six times in eleven days prior to his departure to Montreal. Included in this sequence of races was a 1,500 metre personal best of 3:41.8.

His final two hard sessions before leaving for the Games involved a five kilometre run of hard fifty metre sprints, followed by a slower fifty to recover (total time: 13:50), and a session of 20x200 metres in 28 seconds, with a 45-50 second jog after each. He knew he was ready. In Montreal, most training involved easy running twice daily, with frequent sessions of 10x100 metre acceleration runs.

The first of his events was the 10,000 metres. Three heats were held on July 23, with four to qualify from each, plus the three fastest losers. Unlike Munich, it did not require a sub 28 minute time to make the final, no doubt in part due to the warm, humid conditions. In the last heat, Viren finished third in 28:15.0, well behind the winner, Tony Simmons of Great Britain (28:01.8).

The final shaped as a race between Brendan Foster of Great Britain, who had the fastest time for the distance in 1975, Carlos Lopes of Portugal who had improved dramatically to 27:45.8 in the Olympic year, and the defending Olympic champion. However, with the fastest time going into the race, and knowing his ability to finish off the big races, it would have been a brave man to bet against the Finn defending his title.

In the final, the early pace was comfortable, with the kilometres passing in 2:53.0, 5:44.1, 8:33.4, and 11:22.8. Lopes had led since the eighth lap, but with six kilometres remaining began what turned out to be a long run for home. The pace increased, but not dramatically so, with half way being reached in 14:08.9. The next kilometre saw the pace again increase, taking 2:43.4. By that stage, the whole field was strung out in single file, with only the first nine having a realistic chance of victory. By 7,000 metres, (reached in 19:36.3), the leading trio of Lopes, Viren, and Foster had moved ten metres clear of the Rumanian Floroiu in fourth place.

By 8,000 metres (22:20.2), Foster, who had been laid low by diarrhea while in Montreal, started to lose contact with the two leaders, and within a lap was some fifteen metres behind. Lopes, realizing that his only chance for victory lay in getting rid of his pursuer before the last lap, ran the next kilo in 2:39.8 (9,000 metres passing in 25:02.0). By this stage it seemed just a matter of time before the inevitable would happen. Lopes was giving his all; Viren gave the appearance of being on a comfortable training run.

With a little over a lap remaining, he went to the lead. As was his custom, it was not a dramatic last lap sprint, but rather just an easing away from the opposition. It all just looked too easy, as he built up a thirty metre lead to go home the winner in 27:40.4. The gallant Lopes finished in 27:45.2, while Foster held on to take third in 27:54.9. Lopes would have to wait until Los Angeles in 1984 (by which time he was 37), to achieve Olympic glory, this time in the marathon.

The manner in which Viren achieved his victory left people shaking their heads. The second half had taken only 13:31.5, with the last lap being run in 61.3. The apparent ease with which he had achieved his win left those in attendance wondering just what he could achieve in an even paced run for time, rather than doing just what he had to in order to win.

Two days later came the heats of the 5,000. As per the 10,000, there were three heats with four to qualify from each, plus the two fastest losers. Running in the first heat, Viren did just enough to qualify, finishing fourth in 13:33.4. There were no real surprises from the heats, with all those expected to be in the medal hunt getting to the final. The only real disappointment was the out of form world record holder Emiel Puttemans not finishing the first heat.

The final was run in cool conditions, and the main question to be answered was how Viren would deal with a number of runners who were ostensibly faster than he if it came to an all out sprint finish. Conventional wisdom would seem to have dictated as fast a pace as possible on his part to blunt the finish of his main rivals. Of those, the New Zealanders Dick Quax and Rod Dixon seemed the most dangerous. Both were obviously in good form, and both boasted excellent 1,500 metre speed. Anything less than a fast race would surely play into their hands.

Shortly after the start, Foster assumed the lead and set a steady pace, passing the first kilometre in 2:41.5. The second slowed to 2:45.0, at which point Viren went to the front. However, rather than increase the pace as expected, he slowed it down. Laps of 68.6 and 67.7 followed. At this point, Foster went to the front again, but only briefly. The third kilometre was slower again (2:49.0), but the relatively slow pace belied the frequent changes of speed. At this pace something had to happen. Although almost the whole field was still in contention, only the two New Zealanders and Viren looked comfortable with the speed of the race. At this point, a betting man would almost certainly have put money on either Dixon or Quax to claim the gold, as both had far superior 1,500 metre times compared to the Finn.

With a kilometre to go, Viren went to the lead again. The tenth lap had been faster (62.9), but not dramatically so. With two laps remaining, Foster went by Viren on the inside, but the defending champion responded immediately to control the race. With 600 metres remaining, the pack was beginning to string out, but all the fast finishing threats were still in contention. The final sprints began with three hundred metres remaining. First Ian Stewart of Great Britain, then Dixon, and finally Quax. While the others were sprinting, Viren appeared to be just striding a bit more purposefully. As the finishing line loomed, Quax got the closest, but could never quite get past, while the West German Hildenbrand made a last minute lunge to edge out Dixon for third.

Viren's time of 13:24.8 led Quax by only 0.4, with Hildenbrand another 0.2 further back. Although the time was not exceptional (a number in the field had times considerably faster), the way Viren finished after such an unevenly run race told the story. While his finish was not as fast as Munich four years earlier, it was impressive. The last three laps took just 3:01.3, the last two 1:57.5, and the last one 55.4. The runner with the slowest 400 metre time in the field had won in a sprint finish.

Not content with being the only runner to have ever won the five and ten double "back to back", the very next day (only twenty one hours after his epic 5,000 metres) he fronted for his marathon debut. Obviously feeling the effects of his previous few days exertions, he was with the leaders until 25 kilometres, when defending champion Frank Shorter made his move. Shorter went clear, but was then overtaken by the East German Waldemar Cierpinski, who went on to claim one of the great upset victories of the Games in 2:09:55. Viren held on to finish a gallant fifth in 2:13:11. All things considered, this may well have been a greater performance than any of his Olympic track races. As if that were not enough, only four days later he competed in the US over two miles. Although not winning, his time of 8:21.4 following his exertions in Montreal was little short of amazing.

In typical Viren fashion, most of his post Olympic running was ordinary. He raced six more times over 5,000 metres (all in his home-land), for a single victory. His best time was over twelve seconds outside his Olympic winning time. Coincidentally, his best of 13:24.8 for the distance – a time that he achieved twice (both at the Olympics, and to win his national title) – was only good enough to rank him as the twenty fourth fastest for the year. However, there was little doubt as to who was really the best over both this and the longer track distance for 1976.

The post Olympic year was something of a non-event for the now four time Olympic champion. While hunting for moose during the winter, he managed to break his ankle. Surgery was required, followed by a long and gradual process of rehabilitation. He was unable to do the requisite training to be anywhere near his best come summer. His most notable performance was in the annual Finland – Sweden dual meet, running 13:35.8 to finish second to his countryman Lasse Orimus

1980 Viren leads from Martti Vainio in a domestic race. Vainio won the 1978 European championship over 10,000m and broke Viren's Finnish record for the distance.

(13:32.4). Despite training well below his best, for the next two seasons he continued to compete frequently.

Nineteen seventy eight was more promising, with bests of 13:33 and 28:11.8, while the pre Olympic year of 1979 brought a 10,000 metre best of 28:04.7.

As per usual in the lead up to Olympic competition, altitude training was undertaken in late 1979, and 1980; firstly in Brazil, and later in Columbia. Training volume was well over two hundred kilometres per week, following his normal routine of steady running, fartlek, and hill repetitions. Upon returning to Finland, specific preparation began in earnest, however, it was apparent that he was not in the form that had brought him four previous Olympic gold medals. As an example, in his standard test of running 2x10x200 metres, with brisk jog recoveries, the best he could achieve was an average of 28.5 seconds.

By comparison, before Montreal he could do 28, and in the lead up to Munich, 27.3.

The 1980 Moscow Olympics was always going to be a difficult assignment for Viren. He had accumulated more than his share of injuries, he was no longer a star still on the rise (he turned thirty one shortly before the games), the weather promised to be warmer than usual, and his form going into the games was not promising. As if that were not enough, he would be confronting a team of Ethiopians determined to atone for their boycott induced absence from Montreal. Despite a partial boycott of these games (led by the US to protest the Soviet invasion of Afghanistan), there was never any doubt that the Ethiopians would be there, ruled as they were by a government strongly allied to the Soviet regime.

Whereas before both prior Olympics, Viren's final 10,000 metre race had shown what great form he was in, his final effort in this case was far from convincing. At the World Games in Helsinki, he could only finish fourth in 28:10.9 – a far cry from his impressive sub twenty-eight minute times before both Munich and Montreal. Although not the last event on the programme, probably about half of the near capacity crowd left the stadium once he had finished. They left hoping, rather than expecting, for the best.

Realising his limitations, the defending champion at both distances opted only for the longer of the two races. The heats were run on July 28 in hot, humid conditions. There were three heats, with the first three in each to qualify, along with the three fastest losers. Some three laps before the end of the first heat, Finnish supporters had their worst fears realized when Viren dropped off the pace of the leading group. Just when all seemed lost, however, the Irish runner John Treacy, collapsed just short of the final straight, allowing the obviously below par Finn to finish in fourth position. As an indication of the effect the conditions were having, the fifth placed runner was over a minute further back.

The weather for the final three days later was considerably cooler, with much lower humidity. From early on, it was obvious that the

Ethiopians were running as a team, with the race being set up for their tiny number one, Miruts Yifter. He was in great form, as evidenced by his comfortable heat win, as well as his 400 metre best of 48 seconds achieved as part of his games build up.

After much changing of pace and positions, at the business end of the race it came down to a contest between Finland (in the form of Viren and the relatively unknown Kaarlo Maanika), and Ethiopia (represented by Yifter, Mohammed Kedir, and Tolossa Kotu). With two laps to go Viren went to the lead, and with just over a lap to run it looked as if the old magic might return. After his heat run, it was little short of amazing that he was still in contention, let alone leading at this stage of the race.

And then it happened. The diminutive Ethiopian was not known as "Yifter the shifter" for nothing. He sprinted ahead to break the tape a clear winner in 27:42.7. Behind him, Maanika (later to admit to blood doping) charged home for second (27:44.3), with Kedir getting third place (27:44.7). Considering his preparation, Viren's fifth place in 27:50.5 would have to go down as one of his greatest efforts.

Eight days later, he lined up for his second Olympic marathon; no doubt more wishing than hoping for a favorable result. Although in the large lead group at twenty kilometres, he withdrew at the twenty-seven kilometre mark. His Olympic career was over.

Post Moscow, he ran three 10,000 races, with a fourth place in 29:15.8 his best result. His last effort over the distance for the year was a 29:48 effort in Italy. When in form, that would probably have been an average training session for one of the greatest Olympic competitors of all time. He continued to train, albeit at a reduced level, but retired from competing in 1981. He did keep open the possibility of one last effort in Los Angeles in 1984; however, that never eventuated.

Following his retirement, Viren began working for the Union Bank of Finland, but in the late eighties lost his position as part of the economic downturn in the country. After leaving that job, he worked for the best part of ten years in his brother's trucking company, mainly in adminis-tration, but occasionally as a driver. Becoming involved in local politics, he first stood as a parliamentary candidate in 1995. Initially unsuccessful, he stood again four years later and was elected as a member of the conservative Kokoomus Party – a position he held until March, 2007 when he failed to regain his seat.

He still lives in Myrskyla with his wife Paivi, and has raised his three boys there. In the centre of the town there is a statue of Myrskyla's most famous resident, and each year the town hosts the Lasse Viren Run.

Throughout his career, and after his retirement, there have been frequent accusations – never verified – that Viren had used the process of "blood doping" as an explanation for his Olympic successes. The process involves the removal of a quantity of the athlete's blood, and its later re-infusion at a time close to the time of an important competition. At one stage he was even offered a million dollars to tell his side of the story. However, as he said at the time, there was really no story to tell.

No doubt the origin of the rumors was due to two main factors. Firstly, there was the fact that the process of blood doping was initially developed in Scandinavia, and secondly, the often below par performances by Viren both before and after the Olympics. It is worth noting that the process was not illegal, and in fact was not banned until 1985. By that stage it had been used by a number of Olympic gold medalists in more than one sport.

The case against such a charge seems stronger than the case for. Certainly no one who may have been involved in implementing such a procedure has ever come forward to suggest its use by him. As we have seen, there were a number of occasions when injury caused him to be below par for quite long periods. During these times, he still often competed. Even in Olympic years, he frequently ran in small, local meetings against mainly local athletes. Such competitions were usually undertaken as part of the normal training regime, with little or no easing of training before a meet. Only when it really counted did he ease up in training to be ready for a major effort.

Consider also the times he spent training at altitude. The aim of such training is the same as the aim of "blood doping", namely, to increase the oxygen carrying capacity of the blood. There would surely seem little point in doing both! The fact that others have used the process to achieve success does not mean that he did. It is worth noting that a number of his most serious rivals of the time did not believe he used the process.

Almost certainly, the reasons for Viren's success were really quite simple. He was without doubt a sublimely gifted athlete, who was prepared to sacrifice any short-term success for the chance at victory on the biggest sporting stage of all. He and his coach never lost sight of the big picture.

There is no doubt that Viren's athletic career was defined by the Olympics. What he achieved in his four gold medal winning races would stamp him not only as one of greatest Olympians of all time, but as one of the very best ever distance runners. His Munich effort of falling, and then going on to win in world record time would have to rank as one of the greatest sporting achievements of all time Always one who believed that actions spoke louder than words, by his actions, Lasse Viren will forever be remembered as one of the truly great five and ten men.

HENRY RONO

"I don't train to absorb the pain, I train to break the pain."

September 9, 1978. Henry Rono wins over 10,000m as a guest runner in GB v Finland meet at Crystal Palace.

IN AN AGE OF distance running so dominated by Africans (principally Kenyans and Ethiopians), it seems hard to believe that their emergence has been relatively recent. To the wider sporting world, the victory by Abebe Bikila in the Rome Olympic marathon was as much a shock as it was a novelty. That a barefoot member of the emperor's bodyguard could take on and beat the best the world had to offer – at the marathon no less – was surely a case of truth being stranger than fiction. That he was able to replicate the feat four years later in Tokyo (in a much faster time) only served to add to the aura and sense of mystery surrounding his name. It was as if an untrained nobody from a country few could probably locate on a map had suddenly emerged to beat all comers.

However, if Bikila was the first African to make the world as a whole take note of what might be in store from Africa, he was not the first from that place to make an impact on the world of athletics.

Some six years before Bikila's Rome triumph, some other African runners were venturing outside their homeland to give a glimpse of what the future might hold. Although they may not have been noticed by the sporting world at large, they did make some who saw them sit up and take notice.

Although Ethiopian runners had competed at the 1956 Melbourne Olympics, Kenyan distance runners had made an international foray some two years prior. At the 1954 British AAA championships, two Kenyan runners competed for the first time. The two were Lazaro Chepkwony and Nyandika Maiyoro. Chepkwony was the first to compete, over six miles. Running a most uneven pace, he fought anyone who tried to take over the lead, but was forced to retire after fifteen laps. The race was won by Peter Driver in 28:34.8. While Chepkwony may have been the first Kenyan to compete at that level, the very next day was Maiyoro's turn – this time over three miles. Of the two, it was Maiyoro who made the greatest impression. Against top class opposition he went straight to the front. After a first mile (in 4:23.4) he was both some 45 yards ahead of the rest of the field and well under world record pace. By two miles (reached in 9:01.6) he was dueling for the lead with Chris Chataway and

Freddie Green, still on world record pace. While the two locals fought it out for the title, Maiyoro faded to third in a creditable Kenyan record of 13:54.8. Meanwhile, both Green and Chataway broke Hagg's world mark. Both ran 13:32.2, a scant 0.2 under the old mark, with Green claiming the win.

Maiyoro was undoubtedly one of the most beautiful movers seen on the track. He looked effortless despite the fast early pace, and some of those present realized that perhaps they had seen a portent of what might later follow. He would go on to compete in the Vancouver Empire Games later that year and, running a more even pace, finished fourth in a new personal best of 13:43.8. He would go on to finish seventh in the 1956 Olympic 5,000 metres (14:19), but undoubtedly the high point of his career was his 5,000 metre personal best of 13:52.8 – good enough for sixth at the Rome Olympics. Without a doubt, he had shown that Africans – in this instance Kenyans – could run with the best.

In addition to Chepkwony and Maiyoro, a third Kenyan could be rightfully categorized as a trailblazer. Arere Anentia competed in the 1956 Melbourne Olympics, but had finished only sixth in his 5,000 metre heat and did not progress to the final. However, two years later at the Cardiff Empire Games he showed great improvement to finish third over six miles. He was in a potential winning position with less than two laps to run, but just failed to stay with the Australian Dave Power and the British runner John Merriman as they made their final run for home. To finish a close third in such a race was indeed an achievement of note. His time of 28:51.2 was a new Kenyan record – less than four seconds behind Power's winning time.

After a disappointing run in the 1960 Rome Olympics (nineteenth in the 10,000 in 30:03), he returned in 1961 to break his Kenyan six-mile record in the British AAA event, recording 28:18 for fifth place. The following year (his last of competition) saw him break the national 10,000 metre record with a time of 29:14 in Helsinki.

Returning to Maiyoro. As with so many of his countrymen that followed, his athletic background began with his twice-daily runs of ten kilometres to and from school. In 1960 he was named Kenyan Sportsman of the Year by a national newspaper group, and in 1961 he received an MBE (Member of the British Empire) for his services to athletics. In 1987 he was awarded a Silver Star medal, and as late as 1995, a Distinguished Service award from Kenyatta University in recognition of his contribution to Kenyan athletics. As an old man, he still jogged each morning around his farm before starting his normal farm work. Clearly this was a man that others could look up to.

One that did was Kipchoge Keino. If Maiyoro was the trail-blazer, it was Keino who put beyond doubt that Kenyans could not only run with the best – they could be the best! Keino first came to notice in the 1964 Tokyo Olympics. In the 5,000 metres, run on a sodden track, he finished in fifth place, less than two seconds behind the winner, Bob Schul of the US. It may not have been apparent at the time, but not just a new star had emerged, but the start of a distance running dynasty. Keino would go on to break world records and win Olympic gold at both the 1968 and 1972 Games. For just on a decade he was one of the true global athletic stars.

Following the 1968 Mexico City Olympics, Kenyans realized that they could be as good, or better, distance runners than any other nation. No doubt greatly assisted by the altitude of Mexico City being similar to much of their homeland, gold medals in the 1500m, 10,000m and steeplechase, along with silver medals in the 800m and 5,000m saw Kenya emerge as the dominant distance running power of the games. While by this stage Kenya had many fine runners, it was Keino who was the real star.

If there was one single event that caught the imagination of the country and served as the inspiration for so many others to follow, it was Keino's victory over Jim Ryun in the 1500 metres. Starting at what many considered a suicidal early pace, Keino built up an insurmountable lead and held it to the end. His time of 3:34.9 was faster than most experts thought possible at such an altitude.

Just as Maiyoro had been an inspiration for Keino, so Keino proved to be an inspiration for the next generation. One of those was a young man by the name of Kipwambok Rono. He would become known to the athletic world as Henry Rono.

Born in 1952 in the hilly region of Nandi, that Rono could run at all was something of a surprise. When only two he suffered a serious ankle injury after having his right ankle caught in the spokes of a bicycle. It would be four years before he could walk normally. As if that were not enough of a setback for a young boy, Rono's father died as a result of falling onto a moving plough after trying to avoid a snake. The result was that young Henry was raised by his mother and grandmother, in what could only be described as poor circumstances.

Sixteen year old Henry Rono heard the news of Keino's victory in Mexico City over the radio. Like many his age, the news had a profound impact. Like many Kenyan boys, his sport of choice had been soccer. Not any more. From now on, running was the sport that would shape his future.

Three years later (in 1971), Keino came to speak at a nearby town. Rono made a point of attending, and if there had been any doubt about where his future lay, it was dispelled that day. He decided that the best avenue for him to achieve his aim of being a great runner was to join the Kenyan army. The armed forces had a policy of recruiting top runners, and being in the army meant that there would be both time and support to achieve his aim. By this stage his best effort had been running 3,000 metres in 8:30 – promising, but by no means any indication of what the future held.

Joining the army in 1973 meant that for the first time Rono was able to undertake formal training, with the additional benefit of adequate time for rest and recovery, along with adequate (if basic) meals. Accomodation and facilities may have been basic, but they were more than adequate for an aspiring world-class runner – certainly better than he had been accustomed to until that time in his life. The altitude (about 7,000 feet), the hilly terrain, and the supportive environment would lay the foundation for what was to follow. After twelve months of such training, Rono was the army record holder for the five and ten thousand metres, along with the steeplechase. For those with an eye for such things, he was seen as the heir apparent to Kip Keino.

If 1974 was the real start of his athletic career, 1975 was the year when he experienced for the first time what it meant to be an international athlete. After qualifying for a tour of New Zealand, Australia and Canada, Rono competed seven times in nineteen days. Coupled with the long flights and associated jet lag, it was not an easy introduction. Although winning only one of his six races in New Zealand and Australia, he did run a series of personal bests and managed to finish ahead of a number of world-class performers. He finished the tour with best times of 13:37.0 for 5,000 metres, 28:58.0 for 10,000, and 8:34.4 for the steeplechase.

The overseas experience made Rono realize that with more training, a place on the national team for next years Montreal Olympics was definitely within reach. One of the strategies he began using was to train in army boots – partly from necessity after wearing out so many pairs of running shoes, and partly due to the belief that normal shoes would feel so much lighter after wearing the heavy boots for training. Theory does not always relate well into practice. The boots caused an injury to the ankle he had injured all those years ago, and as a consequence he missed virtually all of the domestic season.

Discarding the boots, coupled with rest did the trick. After his recovery, he was determined to make up for lost time. One of the first things he did in the Olympic year was to transfer his training base from the army barracks to the town of Nyahururu. Whereas the area surrounding the barracks at Gilgil had been largely dry and uninviting, the area around Nyahururu had the benefits of altitude, a cooler climate, and much more pleasant vegetation. These factors, coupled with the fact that the area had become something of a Mecca for some of the world's best runners, made it an ideal place in which to prepare for the coming Olympics. If any further motivation was needed, seeing the double defending Olympic champion Lasse Viren on morning runs would no doubt have provided it.

During this period Rono trained very hard. There is among many the belief that African success at the distances is almost solely due to some innate genetic advantage. While this may well be part of the explanation, it is only a part. Added to his obvious natural talent, Rono was usually training three times a day in the lead up to Montreal. A typical day would see him rise early for a twenty kilometre run, followed by interval training / speedwork late morning, and finishing with an eight to ten kilometre run in the afternoon. Remember also, this was all done at 7 -8,000 feet, not sea level.

Training went well, and some keen observers were happy to predict that Rono could be a real surprise in Montreal, with a genuine chance of challenging for a medal. The only problem was that he had to first qualify. What should have been little more than a formality proved quite difficult. Due to a combination of poor conditions and lack of genuine opposition, he was only able to qualify for the Games at the last moment. Some three weeks before the Kenyan team left for Montreal, Rono managed to run a steeplechase in the port city of Mombassa in 8:29.0, thus booking his place on the team.

In a pre-Games meeting in Montreal, Rono ran a 5,000 metre personal best (13:30.8). Although four others finished ahead of him, it was a sign that he was rounding into form nicely. As a result, he was added to the list for that event as well as the steeplechase. All the pieces seemed to falling into place. And then (from Rono's point of view) the unthinkable happened.

The very night before the opening ceremony the Kenyan team was ordered to leave Montreal and return home. They, along with twenty-seven other mainly African countries decided to boycott the Olympics. The reason was the New Zealand rugby tour of South Africa – then under the apartheid regime. The African nations wanted New Zealand barred from the games because of their involvement. The IOC argued that since rugby was not an Olympic sport, they had no control over the administrators of that sport. They also took the view that in banning both South Africa and Rhodesia from Olympic competition they had done all they reasonably could to cut ties with those countries.

From the Kenyan athletes viewpoint, there was no discussion, just an order to leave. Instead of marching in the opening ceremony the next day, Henry and his team-mates would be marching off the plane in Nairobi.

The Kenyan boycott struck Rono like a hammer. He felt like little more than a pawn in a much larger game. He had done all he could to realize his Olympic dream, only to have it taken away at the last minute. He had no say in the matter. He decided that there had to be a better way of realizing his ambition to be a top runner.

One of the better ways was to move to the United States and take advantage of the collegiate scholarship system. For years, this system had provided an education and top competition for athletes from all corners of the globe in a wide variety of sports. Ironically, the first Kenyan runner to be noticed in the US college system was not there because of his athletic ability, but rather because of his academic prowess.

Stephen Machooka was born in 1936 and, unlike many in Kenya at the time, did well enough to qualify for secondary school. While there he came under the coaching guidance of none other than Nyandika Maiyoro. By 1959 his best mile was 4:15.6, and the following year he was accepted by Cornell University to study in their agricultural programme. During his first year he dominated the cross-country division that Cornell competed in, and (in appalling conditions) broke the Cornell mile record that had stood since 1914. Unlike most that would follow, Machooka had to work to help pay for his education, and this, coupled with the need to spend more time at his studies, led to less and less training. He gave up training completely before his final year, and managed to successfully graduate in 1964.

On his return to Kenya he had a successful academic and public service career, before succumbing to a heart attack at his farm in 2002. While his service to Kenya was in the field of agriculture, one of his main achievements was to show the US college system that Kenyans could run, could handle the academic requirements, and may well be worth some consideration when recruiting.

During his time in Montreal, Rono shared a room with Kip Ngeno, a hurdler who was on a scholarship at Washington State University. Back at WSU, Ngeno let the coach know of Rono's interest in joining him at the university. Samson Kimobwa (another fellow Kenyan) also told how there was a runner (Rono) better than him at home. No mean feat considering that Kimobwa himself would later break the world 10,000 metre record. As a result, by October 1976, Henry Rono was in Pullman as a student at Washington State. At the time, he would probably have been considered the second pick distance runner, as Australian Bill Scott was also recruited. Compared to Henry's best of 8:29 for the steeplechase, Scott's bests of 3:42.7 for 1500m, 13:28.6 for 5,000m, and 28:00.9 for 10,000m were probably superior. As it turned out, Scott never got to run for WSU as he was deemed ineligible, having previously attended a teacher training college in Australia.

To say there was a culture shock would be something of an understatement. Here was Henry, a black man from a rural background, with only a basic education and a similar grasp of English, thrust into a predominantly white, urban, college environment. As if that were not enough, his new coach would be John Chaplin – a fast talking extrovert, whose often over bearing nature made it easy for him to make enemies. However, he was one of the first college coaches to see what a valuable addition Kenyan runners could be to any athletic programme.

To a fair extent, the distance runners were left to their own devices. Chaplin himself had been a sprinter while a student at WSU. Certainly the training that the distance group undertook must have seemed easy compared to Henry's preparation for Montreal. Certainly there were no thrice daily sessions, with most days involving a morning run of 8-10 miles, followed by a session of long intervals in the afternoon. Usually twice weekly the group would drive out to Snake River Canyon and run some five miles to the bottom before making the return run to the top.

The weekly distance covered in training was in the order of 120 kilometres, the emphasis being more on quality than quantity.

To the wider world, the canyon was probably best known as the venue chosen by the dare devil motor-cyclist Evil Knievel for his attempt to jump across via motor bike. For the runners training with Henry, probably anything might have seemed preferable to trying to keep up with him on those return journies to the top of the canyon. He was running with world-class runners and making them look second rate. It was some weeks before Chaplin actually got to see Rono training in the canyon. One look convinced him that here was indeed a rare talent.

As a warm up for the biggest college harrier race of the year, Rono won the Northern Division Pac 8 meet on October 30. The Washington State Kenyans filled the first three places, but it was Oregon who would take the team title. A young Alberto Salazar- running for Oregon - would finish a minute behind Rono.

The NCAA cross-country was held on the golf course of North Texas State on November 22. Held over 10,000 metres, the Washington State trio of Rono, Kimobwa and Kimeto set off at a furious pace. The first mile was covered in 4:17, two miles in 8:40, and three in 13:27. The defending champion, Craig Virgin, ran well, but he was no match for the best Kenyans. Rono won the title convincingly in 28:07, ten seconds ahead of his team-mate Kimobwa, with Virgin a further ten seconds back. Kimeto would drift back from the leaders after four miles to finish twelfth in 28:56. After just seven weeks in America, Rono had gone from a virtual unknown to one that would no longer go unnoticed in any college meeting.

While his running was progressing rapidly, the same could not be said for other aspects of his life. Finding it difficult to adapt to such a different culture, Rono quickly adapted to finding solace in alcohol. Before too long, it was more a case not of drinking interfering with his running, but rather running interfering with his drinking. It was not unusual to finish a hard afternoon workout, and then head to the nearest bar and not leave until the early hours of the following morning. The constant physical abuse he was subjecting himself to, coupled with the stress and anxiety he felt (exacerbated at one stage by a death threat), resulted in treatment for stomach ulcers.

Despite his obvious illness and constant drinking, Rono put in a year of almost nonstop competition. Besides his college obligations, he also ran extensively in Europe, and to a lesser extent Africa. The year began with a series of indoor meets, probably the highlights of which were three miles in 12:56.1, and winning the NCAA indoor two miles in 8:24.8.

As the outdoor season got underway, it was increasingly obvious that Henry was in trouble. At the NCAA championships he failed to win the steeplechase, while in the 10,000 metres he could only manage tenth place, over seventy seconds behind the winner. It was shortly after this that he took time off to try and rectify his stomach problems.

In his absence, his Washington State team-mate Kimobwa helped fill the void. On June 30 in Helsinki he broke the world 10,000 metre mark. His time of 27:30.47 might have only been 0.3 under the old mark, but after only one day of rest he raced five times in five days in three different countries. Those races included a 5,000 metre PB of 13:21.9 and the third fastest 10,000 ever of 27:37.28.

Seeing these results was motivation for Henry to get back into action as soon as possible. After a couple of races in Africa (where he failed to qualify for the African world cup team), he headed to Europe. There he would finish his outdoor season with bests of 13:22.1 (winning in Rieti), and 27:37.08 (for the narrowest of seconds to Brendan Foster in London).

On his return to the US, his last race of the year was a successful defense of his NCAA cross-country title over ten kilometres. Second place was John Treacy who would later go on to medal in the 1984 Olympic marathon.

Considering his illness, let alone his problems with alcohol, 1977 had not been too bad a year. He had run some good times, and by the end of the year had shown that the worst was probably behind him. If he could run the times he had with his limited preparation, what might he do with no illness and a full training regime? While that question might have been asked by some, few would have been prepared for what happened the following year.

Rono's 1978 season would probably go down as one of the greatest ever compiled by a distance runner. Competing on the track (both indoors and out), on the road, and cross-country, he ran a total of fifty-two races in fourteen different countries, over distances between a mile and half marathon. Of those, he won forty. He won two Commonwealth Games titles and an African title. Against usually strong competition, that would itself be enough to be considered a standout season, but there were also four world records to be included.

Of Henry's twelve losses for the year, half occurred during the US indoor season. Of the other six, two were at distances really too short for him, while a third was when he took a wrong turn in the NCAA cross-country championships. Of the three remaining losses, one was in world record time, while another was at the hands of a future Olympic medalist. He ran against almost anyone, at any distance, in just about any country. When in reasonable form he was almost unbeatable.

His season began with a losing indoor two-mile competition on January 21. However, it was hardly a disgrace. In Los Angeles, on a 160 yard track, he finished a scant 0.3 seconds behind the future Olympic 5,000 metre silver medalist Nyambui in a fast 8:18.3. The next day, a different town and a different (larger) track saw him win the mile in 4:00.9.

In what became typical of his competitive schedule, six days later he was competing over 10,000 metres in Auckland, New Zealand. Winning in a fast 27:48.6, he won easily by over a minute – one of his victims being Lasse Viren, who was forced to retire. Another week, another country. Just seven days later, his next race was on the other side of the world, winning the San Blas half marathon in 64:46 against a strong field.

After that international interlude, it was perhaps not surprising that most of Henry's losses for the year came in the period immediately

June 24, 1978. Rono wins the British AAA championship over 5000m at Crystal Palace.

following those races. The half marathon was run on February 5, and five days later he was back running indoors in North America. In the next fifteen days he would compete six times – and lose all of them. His final indoor competition was a last place in the NCAA mile, after earlier finishing second over two miles. His indoor season may not have been great, but it did lay the basis for the great outdoor season that followed.

The early part of the outdoor season was dominated by collegiate competition. Henry demonstrated early in the season his ability to quickly transform from a good to a great runner in only a few competitions.

His first three races of the US outdoor season were over 5,000 metres. The first was in 13:31.8, the second in 13:22.7 (albeit in poor conditions). While both were excellent times and easy victories, they did not really prepare people for what was to follow in his third. Certainly Henry himself had not talked up his chances, although he was confident that he was capable of considerably faster than his recent personal best.

Unlike most modern day records that are invariably carefully orchestrated affairs with paid pacemakers, the race on April 8 was part of a triangular college meet held at Berkely. It was a pleasant spring after-noon, with perhaps 2,000 in attendance.

An opening lap of 67 seconds saw Rono, Kimobwa, and Kimeto - the three WSU Kenyans – together at the front. Slow running for the time he wanted, but laps in 63, 64 and 61 saw Rono pass four laps in 4:15, and with it, the chance of a record. Eight laps came by in 8:28, and Henry continued to push the pace. His last lap of 59.4 was the fastest of the race as he won by just on a minute. The time was a new world record, his 13:08.4 taking 4.5 seconds from Dick Quax's time set some nine months earlier.

In less than fifteen minutes he went from being only the third best on the Washington State all time list to being number one in the world. He also became the second Kenyan (after Kip Keino) to hold a world record at the distance. Running the fourth and fifth kilometres in 2:37 and 2:33.9 indicated that there was probably still something in reserve when he finished.

His record run would prove to be the third race in an unbroken string of twenty seven victories over distances between one mile and 10,000 metres (barring one where he retired with an injury) that would include a further three world records.

A week after his great five kilometre run, he showed that he had lost none of his steeple chasing ability. Running at the University of Oregon track in Eugene, Henry ran a fine 8:14.75, despite being ordered to slow his world record pace by coach John Chaplin – ostensibly because he did not believe that the Oregon fans "deserved" to see a world mark set on their track.

Henry had shown that he was capable of a new mark, and it would only be three more races before it happened. Running in Seattle on May 13, in far from ideal conditions, he easily accounted for Garderud's world mark with a time of 8:05.4. As with all his records, it was virtually a solo run – in this case winning by over thirty seconds. He had run kilometres of 2:42.0, 2:42.8 and 2:40.6, with halves of 4:03.2 and 4:02.2. Sadly, only some two hundred were on hand to witness this piece of athletic history being made.

As if his two world records were not enough to indicate what sort of form he was in, the NCAA championships would convince even perhaps the greatest of sceptics. Running in Eugene on June 1, Henry was initially entered in the 5,000, 10,000, and steeple. First up were heats of the steeplechase. Running a ridiculous pace for a heat, he finished over twenty three seconds clear of second place in a new championship record of 8:18.63.

As if that were not enough for one day, four hours later he was lining up for his 5,000 metre heat. Laps of 65, 61, 59 and 63 saw him pass the first mile in 4:08. He would finish in 13:21.79, over thirty seconds ahead of his nearest rival. After a day of rest he ran the steeple-chase final, his time of 8:12.39 being another meet record, sufficient to finish over eleven seconds ahead of second place. He did not contest the 5,000 metre final (run on the same day), but it is of interest that the event was won in a time just over thirteen seconds slower than his heat time. Since WSU had no chance in the all important team competition, he also did not start in the 10,000 metres. His college requirements completed, Henry headed for Europe. As the form distance runner in the world, meet promoters were clamoring for his services.

Eight days after his exploits in Eugene, he was in Vienna, making up for the 10,000m he did not run at the NCAA championships. There were only some five hundred in attendance for the late afternoon race, mainly made up of those who stayed after an earlier soccer match. The conditions were warm and still. For just over three thousand metres, the pace was set by the Dutch runner Jos Hermens (later to become Haile Gebrselassie's manager). After that it was a purely solo effort by the Kenyan. The first half took 13:49.0, but, aided in large part by a last kilometre in 2:36.9, he took just 13:33.4 for the second. His time of 27:22.47 took exactly eight seconds from the mark held by his WSU teammate, fellow Kenyan Samson Kimobwa. As was the custom for all his world record performances, second place was not even close. For the record, it was Domingo Tibaduiza of Columbia just over thirty seconds behind.

After this exploit there followed a quick trip to his homeland to qualify for the African and Commonwealth Games in both the 5,000 metres and steeplechase. Then it was back to Europe. Two more races – including the British AAA championship over 5,000 metres in 13:20.78 – and he was ready for his next record, this time over 3,000 metres.

The venue was the famed Bislett track in Oslo, and on June 27 Henry took aim at Brendan Foster's time of 7:35.2. After a first half in 3:49.5, he went to the front and ran the next three laps in an even three minutes. The seventh lap took only 59 seconds; the last two hundred metres 28.6. The longer the race went, the faster he ran, with kilometres of 2:34.0, 2:30.5, and 2:27.6. Second and third (Suleiman Nyambui and Nick Rose) became the fifth and sixth fastest ever – but they were over eight seconds behind! Whereas only meagre crowds had seen his first three records, there were at least some 13,000 on hand to witness his latest (and perhaps greatest) record. Considering the time (7:32.1), the ease of his victory over a top international field, and his strong finish, a more even pace may well have resulted in history's first sub 7:30 time. Even the normally reserved runner himself was of the opinion that with more pressure he could run 7:29.

The next day he was in neighboring Finland, winning the steeplechase at the World Games in Helsinki in 8:16.8. Two days later he was in Milan, Italy, winning the 5,000 metres against another strong field in

13:18.2. He was churning out excellent times, winning against strong opposition, with almost monotonous regularity.

After a break from competition of nearly three weeks he won the steeplechase / 10,000 metres double at the African Games. Taking another long break (eleven days on this occasion), he took another double, this time at the Commonwealth Games in Canada – over 5,000 metres and the steeplechase.

While Henry was running himself ragged in a wide variety of countries, his opposition was generally being far more conservative, and consequently better prepared for any confrontation. With this in mind, it was not surprising that toward the end of his European season his hectic schedule, coupled with his on-going drinking problem, would eventually catch up with him.

Returning to Europe after the Commonwealth Games, his first race was over 5,000 metres at the famed Weltklasse meet in Zurich. Winning in a good 13:16.12, it seemed that the natural order had been restored. However, he then had seven races in twelve days - and lost four. However, the four included defeats by the Pole Malinowski (the future Olympic silver medalist) in the steeplechase, a two mile loss to Steve Ovett (in world record time), and a loss over one mile to an up and coming runner by the name of Sebastian Coe. His final race of the outdoor season was a mile in Tokyo where he failed to finish.

Returning to the US, his one remaining college commitment of the year was the NCAA cross-country championship. What should have been a formality after his great year turned into a disaster, when after taking a wrong turn, he finished second last in a field of two hundred and thirty eight, the race being won by Alberto Salazar.

After his superhuman 1978 season, any year that followed would have to be something of an anti-climax. Rono returned to Kenya over the Christmas period, but after his return it was obvious that he was not in the form he showed the previous year. Although only racing about half as much, he lost more than he won. There were a number of contributing factors. Probably at the top of the list would be his ongoing drinking problem. This, coupled with an unhealthy liking for "junk food" that usually accompanied his drinking, did nothing positive for either his waistline or his fitness.

There were also increasing disputes with the governing body for Kenyan athletics, and his relationship with John Chaplin was an almost constant cause of tension. There was also the fact that he was spending more time on his studies, often to the detriment of his running.

Over the course of the year his results were very irregular. Whereas in 1978 he was in superlative form for just on the full twelve months, this year he showed only occasional glimpses of his past form. His best efforts for the year were a 5,000 in Rieti, Italy in 13:19.65, and a defense of his NCAA steeplechase title in 8:17.92. He finished the year with a trio of cross-country wins, including the NCAA title.

With 1980 being an Olympic year, Henry began with a trip to New Zealand and Australia in early January to mid February. By the end of his tour, it was obvious that he could be a real threat come Games time. His last two races were over 10,000 metres in Melbourne (in 27:31.68) and 3,000 metres in Brisbane (in 7:43.0).

However, there would be no Olympics for Henry – again! Before he began the Australian leg of his tour, the Kenyan government announced that it would be bowing to the wishes of the Americans and boycotting the Moscow Olympic Games. In a contentious move that divided both sporting bodies and governments, President Carter used all the diplomatic power he could muster to try and orchestrate the Olympic boycott. The motivation for the boycott was to put pressure on the Soviet government to withdraw their troops from Afgahnistan. The boycott had only limited success, and would have repercussions for the US four years later when the Games were held in Los Angeles. In light of subsequent events, it would not prove to be one of America's greatest foreign policy triumphs.

After the promising runs on his Australian trip, Henry continued his fine form with some good indoor results after returning to the US, the best of which was two miles in San Diego in 8:15.9. However, after that, it was mostly downhill. As the year progressed, some of his times came to resemble more that of a club runner than a multiple world record holder. Finishing tenth over a mile in 4:18.9 was hardly what might be expected from someone who had run 2:52 for 1200 metres in training. The same might be said of finishing fifteenth over 5,000 metres in a time over two and a half minutes outside his world mark.

However, even when only a shadow of his former self, he was still able to show glimpses of the runner he used to be. Within a week in mid July (in Sweden), he ran two 5,000 metre races. Although finishing only fifth and sixth, the times were good (one in 13:24.4, the other in 13:19.8).

By early 1981, Henry was back running for Washington State. Although winning more than he lost, it was hard to believe that he was the same athlete of three years earlier. His weight had gone up, his fitness had gone down, and the once clamorous European meet promoters saw him more as a liability than an asset.

One thing that Henry had shown throughout his career was the ability to train and race himself into shape quickly. If ever that was evident, it was during the 1981 season. His major sponsor – Nike – had sent him to Boulder, Colorado to try and have him sober up, and try to get in some sort of form for the upcoming European summer. It seemed a hopeless task. He was greatly overweight, and resembled more an out of condition office worker than an athlete hoping to take on the worlds best in a few months.

In April, while training in Boulder, he met up with Steve Cram, the world mile record holder. He told a somewhat bemused Cram that he intended to break a world record during the European summer. One did not need to be a world-class runner to see how unbelievable such a proposition was. Even more unbelievable was the fact that just over four months later, Cram himself would be pacing Rono in a race to do just that.

Before leaving for Europe, his last US race was a steeplechase. Finishing fifth, over twenty seconds behind the winner, in a time more than a minute outside his best was a fair indication of his fitness level.

The one positive thing he did achieve before leaving was to complete his college course.

Once in Europe, being accepted into races proved almost impossible. Meet directors took one look, and what they saw was not a pretty sight. Rather than the lean world-beater of 1978, they saw someone several kilograms overweight with a pronounced beer gut.

Talking his way into a couple of meets in Finland did not really help his cause. Of the two races (both over 5,000 metres), one was a third place finish, while in the other he was lapped twice, finishing fourteenth in 15:40.85. In a later race in July, in Oslo, he was reduced to acting as a pace maker in a 10,000 metre race, dropping out at the half way mark. Still, running 13:40 while so unfit was yet another indication of what might be possible in the future.

Later that month he decided that some consistent hard training might be the answer to his problems. He relocated to Germany and put in some solid sessions. The average day was made up of a morning run in the forest, followed by interval sessions each afternoon. No easy days, just constant hard sessions. Such sessions included standard repetitions of 400 metres. On July 19, the second day of his training in Germany, the best he could manage were twelve in 65-68 seconds. Four days later he could do the same session, with times between 61.5 – 63.2 seconds, with the last one in 58.5. Three days later, he could complete seventeen in 63 – 65 seconds, while the very next day he managed twenty-four, with the last one in 57.7 seconds. Between these days were sessions of 5 x 1,000 m, 24 x 200m or similar. Things were looking up.

After two low-key meets, he managed to get an entry into the British AAA championships. Although finishing fifth, some six seconds behind the winner (Eamon Coghlan), his time of 13:26.45 was a vast improvement on his recent previous efforts. Four days later he was in the central Finnish city of Tampere running 3,000 metres in 7:50.88, and a week later in Zurich for the Weltklasse meet. Originally only given permission to run in the "B" competition over 5,000 metres, he bluffed his way into the main event – and ran well enough for fourth in 13:27.71.

Promoters could see what was happening, and it suddenly became a lot easier to gain entry into the big meets. His next 5,000 metres race was in Koln four days later. The result showed further improvement – second place in 13:23.97. Although obviously improving, few would have predicted his next result. Three days later in Koblenz he improved dramatically to 13:12.15. As was common in most of his fast races, it was a comfortable victory – this time by over fourteen seconds.

A one day break was followed by a 10,000 metre race in Brussels as part of the Van Damme memorial meeting. After lagging well behind the leader, Julian Goater, he gradually reeled him in, and won going away in 27:40.78. A six day break, and then another 5,000 metre competition – this time in Rieti, Italy, the site of so many fast races over the years. The time was another 13:12 (13:12.47 to be precise). Although fast, two others finished ahead of him – the East German, Kunze (in a European record 13:10.40), and the Russian Abramov. Two days later and he was in England for the London Coca Cola meeting. Another 5,000 and another 13:12 – this time a winning 13:12.34.

His last three outings over five kilometres had all been within four and a half seconds of his world record, a feat that must have been a record in itself. Two days later (September 13) in Knarvik, Norway, Henry was ready to make good on his promise to Steve Cram, made earlier in the year in Colorado. Helped over the first four laps by British runners Cram, Ian Stewart, and James Espir, Rono then pulled steadily away. Until the final stages he set a remarkably even pace, with each of the first four kilometres taking between 2:38 and 2:38.5. However, he clearly had something in reserve, running the final kilometre in 2:33.2, his last lap taking just 56 seconds, finishing in 13:06.20. As was the case with all his world records, the win was convincing – this time just on thirty seconds. It would surely have been one of the great sporting comebacks of all time. The race was an example of Henry saving his best for last, as it would be his final race for the European season. Sadly, it would also be the high water mark of his career.

There would be a few more races that year, but clearly Henry was slipping back into his bad old ways with a vengeance. After his final world record, his weight started rising again, and his behavior became increasingly unpredictable and erratic. He was a hard man to rely on. However, as the holder of four world records, the last one still fresh in people's memory, he was still a drawcard.

With this largely in mind, Alberto Salazar, now the premier US distance runner, decided to invite Rono to Eugene to race over 10,000 metres, the idea being to enable him (Salazar) to break the US record. The race was scheduled for April 10. What seemed like a good idea at the time probably seemed like an increasingly bad one as race day approached. Henry, despite being guaranteed good appearance money, decided shortly before the meet that he would not run. Salazar, using a mix of bluff and bribery, finally got him to change his mind.

Race day was cold, wet, and windy. An obviously overweight Henry Rono would face up to one of the in form runners in the world. Rono's only real form guide was over 5,000 metres the week before in Stanford. Second place, over thirty seconds slower than his world record was not exactly encouraging.

A field of fourteen started the race, but it was obvious early on who the race was really between. Rono led at the first mile in 4:27.1, and by just over half way it was a race in two. Salazar was in front pushing the pace, but Rono just would not go away. With just over a lap to go, he went to the lead, but this time it was Salazar's turn to hang on. In the final straight, he narrowly took the lead, but Rono would not be denied. Beer belly or not, he held on for the narrowest of victories – 27:29.9 to 27:30.0. He would later say that it was the hardest race he ever ran. The simple fact is, that in adverse conditions; overweight, and only a shadow of his former self, he had come within eight seconds of his world record.

The rest of 1982 saw more losses than wins, but there were still the odd outstanding performances. At the Bislett Games he ran 27:28.67 for 10,000 metres, finishing fourth, and ten days later won over 5,000 metres in Stockholm in a fast 13:08.97. However, that would really be his last hurrah, as the next night in Oslo he would be in the very race that dethroned him as the five kilometre record holder. The Englishman, Dave Moorcroft took an early lead and went on to produce one of the most unexpected of all athletic records. His time of 13:00.41 took a huge chunk off the old mark, with Rono himself finishing in fourth place almost 25 seconds behind.

His last good run for the year was in the Weltklasse meet, but even there, his 13:16.14 was only good enough for seventh. After that, most aspects of his life went steadily downhill – except his weight. Whereas his best racing weight was about 63 kilograms (139 pounds), he was now an almost unrecognizable 100 kilograms (220 pounds). After a couple of early season runs in 1983 he essentially disappeared from the athletic landscape. For three years he did little – except continue to drink and indulge his liking for American junk food.

In 1986 he decided to make another effort. He lost some 21 kilograms (45 pounds), and despite still being well above his ideal weight, showed how quickly he could improve. His first competitive outing was a road ten kilometres. He finished thirty-eighth in 31:08. Within three weeks he was running the same distance (even if slightly downhill) in 28:10 for a win. On the strength of that run he gained an entry to the Van Damme meeting in Brussels, the traditional site of the years top 10,000 metre race. This time, unlike 1981, there would be no fairy tale ending. He was lapped twice by the leading runners, barely breaking thirty minutes for the distance, as Mark Nenow ran 27:20 for a new American record.

But wait. There was more! The following month the still obviously portly Henry lined up for the Chicago marathon. Despite it being his first venture over the distance, he still managed to drag his body, along with its several extra kilogrammes, over the distance in a very creditable 2:19:12 for twenty-sixth place.

Apart from one or two low-key efforts, that was pretty well the end of his career. It was then that the demons that had bedeviled his running career really took over. While training had served to modify the extremes of his drinking somewhat, not training had the effect of allowing more time for drinking. He had tried returning to his native Kenya, but disputes with the Kenyan athletic authorities, coupled with unease at the political situation, led him to return to the US.

His life continued to spiral downward. He had been drinking heavily while back in Kenya, and it continued after his return to the US. While a top athlete, he had been well paid both in appearance money and endorsements, notably from the sports-good giant Nike. In the early eighties, when it looked like he was a chance for the Los Angeles Olympics, Nike signed him to a multi year contract worth in excess of fifty thousand dollars annually. It was not long before the money was all gone.

For a number of years after his last race, Henry became – not to put too fine a point on it – an alcoholic vagrant. He had become his own worst enemy. The athlete who had been one of the most notable figures on the European circuit, earning in the region of $250,000 a year, had become both penniless and homeless. He would take any job, including a car park attendant, washing cars, even a brief stint as a used car salesman. He even approached his former sponsor Nike for a job as a cleaner, only to be turned away. His accommodation was in the form of homeless shelters. At one stage he was arrested and jailed while awaiting trial. It was in part due to his celebrity (long forgotten by most) that saved him from being the victim of mistaken identity.

After numerous failed attempts at overcoming his alcoholism, Henry finally succeeded, though the word "finally" is one fraught with danger when used in conjunction with such a problem.

Deciding that teaching was the area he was most interested in, he finally landed a high school teaching position. The early days proved as much an education for Henry as it was for his students. It was not easy. As he explained in his autobiography, his English left a lot to be desired, but he was not going to give up. Sticking with it, coaching a school team, and deciding to make yet another comeback (as a masters runner), seemed to be the elixir he needed.

He was training again regularly, he had explained with brutal honesty his trials and tribulations, and, most importantly he had regained his self esteem. Not to be under estimated in his recovery was his recognition that, whatever the speed, he just loved going for a run. Although still carrying considerably more weight than in his record-breaking years, he still has ambitions (at time of writing) to etch his name one last time into the record books. In light of his past history, it may not be wise to bet against him.

The story of Henry Rono is one of lost opportunity, of sadness, of human frailty. However, it is also a story of one of the greatest talents ever to set foot on a track. What he did in those eighty-one days in 1978 – not to mention the rest of that year – will likely never be repeated.

Had he not been denied his Olympic opportunities, and had he not succumbed to his alcohol addiction, he may well be remembered in a completely different light. It would probably not be over exaggerating to suggest that a fully fit Henry Rono may have been the first to run under 7:30 for 3,000 metres, 8 minutes for the steeple chase, and 13 minutes for the 5,000 metres.

Instead, we are left with the memory of someone who, for an all too short time, was perhaps the greatest talent seen in his pet events. And an example of human frailty.

HAILE GEBRSELASSIE

The little emperor

Haile Gerbrselassie- 2011
Vienna City Half Marathon.
1:00.18

WERE A PHYSIOLOGIST TO be asked to design the ideal distance runner, the result would probably not be a whole lot different from the real life Haile Gebrselassie. Short, slightly built, with relatively long legs would be the obvious external features, while internally, an inordinately powerful cardio-vascular system would be a given. Environmentally, living at high altitude and running long distances on a daily basis from an early age would serve to promote the development of any genetically based natural advantages. As the twig is bent, so it shall grow.

Standing a mere 1.65m (5 feet, 5 inches) and weighing just 56 kilograms (8 stone, 11 pounds), a figure of Haile's stature would not be out of place in many an upper primary school class. When watching many championship races, the small stature of many competitors is not readily evident, as most in the race are of a similar build. The advantage of being small and thin is that it aids in heat dissipation as well as having less weight to carry during the race – both key ingredients for success.

In many ways, the early life of Haile Gebrselassie was typical of so many in Ethiopia. Born to a poor rural family (on April 18, 1973), he was one of ten children, growing up in Asella, in the rural province of Arsi, some two hundred and fifty kilometres south of the capital Addis Ababa. Home was a mud-floored hut with no running water. The advantage – and that only from a running point of view – was that school was some ten kilometres away. The only mode of transport was of the two legged variety, and so from an early age Haile was running some twenty kilometres daily, barefoot, and split into a morning and afternoon session each of ten kilometres. Carrying his schoolbooks while running was just part of the routine. All this was at an altitude of some 2,400 metres (about 8,000 feet). For the young Haile, this was not training – this was life.

With this background, it is hardly surprising that the young Haile was attracted to running as a sport. Not just because it was part of his daily life, but also because of the influence of those who preceded him in the field of Ethiopian distance running. By far the most notable of these for Haile were Abebe Bikila and Miruts Yifter.

Bikila was a true national hero. Born in 1932, he later died in the same year that Haile was born. At the Rome Olympics in 1960, virtually overnight he went from unknown to national icon and worldwide phenomenon. That a barefoot runner from such a little known country could beat the best in the world – in the marathon no less – seemed more the fare of a 1950's comic strip hero than real life. That he could repeat the result four years later (this time in shoes), in a time that obliterated the world record seemed, if anything, even less believable. The only thing that prevented a third victory in 1968 at Mexico City was his enforced withdrawal during the race caused by a stress fracture. Despite his withdrawal, his understudy, Mamo Wolde, would take his place for the gold medal.

Tragically, later that year, Bikila was involved in a car accident that left him a paraplegic. Confined to a wheelchair, he took part in a variety of sporting activities, before sadly passing away only five years after his last attempt at Olympic glory. His funeral was attended by a vast crowd that included the then emperor, Haile Selassie.

Miruts Yifter was not unlike Gebrselassie - tiny. Born in 1938, he achieved considerable success from the late sixties, but it was not until the 1972 Olympic Games in Munich that he really made an impact on the world scene. In the 10,000 metre final he remained in contention until very late after the Finn Lasse Viren made his long drive for home. It was really only in the home straight that he finally had to settle for third place. In a time that was only just outside the existing world record, he had truly arrived as a force to be reckoned with.

Sadly, he did not get the chance for a second medal in Munich. Apparently misreading the start time for the 5,000 metre heats, he was a non-starter. In light of his great closing speed, he may well have performed better in that race than in the longer event. Little did he realize at the time that it would be another eight years - due to a boycott by many of the African countries in 1976 in protest at the New Zealand rugby team visiting the then racially segregated South Africa - before he got his second chance at Olympic glory.

There would be no timetable mishaps second time around. With a partial boycott of the Moscow games due to the Russian incursion into Afgahnistan (led ironically by the US in view of later historical events), the two longest track events became largely a tussle between Ethiopia and Finland. Ethiopia clearly came out on top, as Yifter used his blazing finishing speed in both the five and ten thousand metres to come home a clear winner. Of the boycotting nations, Kenya was the most notable absentee in the distance events. Gebrselassie would retain fond memories of listening to both victories on the family radio.

As was the norm for most boys his age, walking or running were usually the only means of transport. He won his first race when only eight, and completed his first (and only marathon for many years) when aged fifteen. This latter event proved harder than he might have imagined before starting. Despite his years of "unofficial training", and being able to complete the journey in two hours and forty two minutes, it would be a number of days before he could walk properly, rather than hobble.

As a fourteen year old in 1987, he won his first "proper" race – a school competition over 1500 metres. However, by the following year he was good enough to win his age group over 3000 metres at the national level. While his father had been a subsistence farmer, it was never Haile's ambition to follow in his footsteps. Never greatly enamoured with schoolwork, following Yifter's success he decided that a career as a runner would be his real aim.

There followed a number of local and national competitions, which resulted in first regional, and then national selection. By 1991 Haile was ready for bigger things. He qualified for the world junior cross-country with a fifth place finish in the national cross country over twelve kilometres. In the subsequent world junior event in Antwerp over 8.4 kilometres, he finished some twenty four seconds behind the winner (Sambu of Tanzania) in eighth place. Later in the year he showed more of his obvious ability by running his five kilometre leg of the Chiba International Eikiden relay in 13:35.

If 1991 was his "coming of age", the following year was when he really announced his presence on the world stage. After considerable pestering by a young Haile, the Dutch agent Jos Hermens agreed to be his manager (undoubtedly one of his more astute decisions). Hermens had been one of the top European (and world) distance runners during his competitive career, and Gebrselassie would much later break a world record that had been held by his manager.

While the more astute observers may have noticed Haile's ability in 1991, it did not require a lot in the way of predictive abilities the following year to see that a new and rare talent was about to make its presence felt on the world distance-running scene.

His first major international race for 1992 was the world junior cross-country, held in Boston on March 21 over 7.8 kilometres. In a race largely dominated by the East Africans, he finished second – some eight seconds behind the Kenyan, Ismael Kirui. A prodigious talent, Kirui would later go on to be a dual world champion on the track. Also of note in the same race was a young athlete named Hicham El Guerrouj in fourteenth place.

The following month Haile would finish fifth in an international field over 5000 metres in South Africa, some 9.7 seconds behind the winner in 13:58. While these results were promising, they were only a portent for the rest of his year. In mid May, at the altitude of the capital Addis Ababa, he won the national junior title over 10,000 metres in 28:45.0. Some four months later he was in Seoul for the World Junior Championships. Over three days (17-19 September) he qualified for the 5,000 in 14:00.1; won the 10,000m in 28:03.99, and returned the next day to narrowly win the 5,000m final in 13:36.6. In the latter race, Kirui was second, and El Guerrouj third. His last important race for the year was an Ekiden international relay in Berlin. Ethiopia was a clear winner, with Haile contributing the fastest time for his five kilometre leg – 13:24.

The year 1993 was Haile's first full year against senior competition. The first three months were dominated by cross-country events, the latter part of the year by track, with some road races included for good measure.

His first race of the year was a Dutch half marathon (no doubt reflecting the wishes of his agent). A fourth place finish in 64:29 served as a warm-up for a series of four cross-country events, each over ten kilometres. In each, the winner would be his countryman Fita Bayissa. In the first three of them, Haile would finish a close second, while in the fourth he would be one position further back. A road race over 20 kilometres (third in 59:36) was followed by two more cross-country events. The last of these was the World Championship in Spain. The event, over 11.75 kilometres, was won by the future world record holder over 10,000 metres, William Sigei of Kenya. Haile would finish 32 seconds behind the winner in seventh place.

With the cross-country season over, it was time for the track. In late March Haile won his first senior championship (over 5000 metres) in Addis Ababa in 14:03.6. A month later he was in Durban for the African championships. On June 25 he finished third over 10,000m in a personal best of 27:30.17 behind Sigei and Bayissa, and two days later, second in the 5000 metres. His time of 13:10.41 was another personal best – less than a second behind Chemoiywo of Kenya.

Some four weeks later he was in London for the TSB International Games (part of the Grand Prix circuit). Over 5000 metres he was a narrow third (in 13:15.10) behind Sigei and Bayissa, as per the African Championship 10,000m. Some twelve days later he was in Zurich for the famed Weltklasse GP meeting. As was typical, the field for the 5000 metres included just about all the top names – certainly all those with aspirations for the World Championships to be held ten days later. Less than a second separated the first four, with noted big finisher Khalid Skah of Morocco winning in 13:04.67. Gebrselassie was fourth, but significantly his time of 13:05.39 was his first national record. Just over a second behind him in fifth place was Ismael Kirui.

The 1993 World Championships were held in the German city of Stuttgart, and the two longest track events would be among the most dramatic ever witnessed. First up was the 5000 metres. Haile qualified in a fast 13:25.27, and the final was two days later. And what a race it was. The question that most people were asking was whether the field could withstand the withering finish of Khalid Skah. From very early on, Kirui, the youngest in the field decided that he would not die wondering. With some early help from his Kenyan team-mates he went to the front and proceeded to run away from the opposition. The rest of the field had to decide whether to go with him or hold back, assuming that he would pay for his seemingly suicidal pace later in the race. That they chose the latter was probably as much to do with just not being able to cope with the pace he was setting, rather than making any sort of reasoned decision. With his lead reaching sixty metres or so, the closest of those following included Skah and Gebrselassie, along with his Ethiopian team mates.

To most observers, it probably seemed only a matter of time before the pursuing pack would reel in the audacious front-runner. However, as the laps went by, it just was not happening. At times over the last two laps it seemed that Haile lacked more the confidence than the ability to strike out for the lead on his own. Finally, on the last lap he decided it was no good waiting for others to help – he would have to do it on his own. He rapidly detached himself from the chasing group and proceeded to gain ground on Kirui. In the final straight it looked like he might just do it. However, the race was over 5000 metres, not 5020, and he fell an agonizing 0.42 seconds short. In what was probably no consolation whatever, his time of 13:03.17 broke his own recent national record for the distance.

Aged eighteen years and one hundred seventy seven days, Kirui was the youngest champion ever. As a reward for courageous front running his race would have to have been one of the best ever. To prove it was no fluke, he came back two years later and defended his title in a manner completely different to his Stuttgart effort, running the field off their legs over the closing stages, rather than at the beginning.

Four days later Gebrselassie qualified for the 10,000 metre final in 28:17.95. The final two days later would be one of the most unusual and controversial ever run in such a major championship event. As if determined not to make the same mistake twice (i.e. let the runner in front build up too big a lead), Haile was within a stride or two of the leader for almost the whole race. The leader for much of the time, and especially the last half of the race was the Kenyan defending champion Moses Tanui. No matter what the situation, it was obvious that Haile had no intention of leading until the last possible moment. Tanui was clearly not impressed and made a number of gestures to have his Ethiopian shadow share pace making duties at the front. And then it happened. With a lap to go Tanui threw his arms in the air, partly in annoyance, but mainly because Gebrselassie had stepped on one of his feet, partly dislodging his shoe. After a few strides Tanui managed to kick off the offending shoe and sprinted for home. He immediately opened a sizeable gap, and for much of the last lap looked like a winner. But in the final straight, Haile managed to draw even and eventually pull away for a narrow victory. His time of 27:46.02 was just over half a second ahead of a justifiably annoyed Tanui. There were definitely no handshakes at the end of that race.

Tanui would go on to have an illustrious career. In addition to his first and second place finishes in successive World Championships, he would win the famed Boston marathon twice and become the first runner to break the one hour mark for the half marathon.

After the World Championships, Haile would finish the year with a series of relatively low key events, most notably a ten mile road race in Holland (finishing third in 47:07) and a track 5000m in Japan (first in 13:30.1).

As had become customary, the 1994 season began with a series of international cross-country events, culminating with the World Championship in Budapest. Often referred to as the most difficult race in the world to win, Haile finished a close third behind the Kenyan duo of Sigei and Chemoiywo, and just ahead of another Kenyan in Paul Tergat. He would be seeing a lot more of Tergat in the years that followed.

Following the cross-country there was a ten kilometre road race in Switzerland. In the closest of finishes, Sigei edged out Haile in 27:34. Then followed the world road relay championships. Morocco scored a significant victory over Ethiopia, despite Haile having the fastest time for his 7,195 km leg (19:27). Eleven days later he was a close second to his fellow Ethiopian Bayissa over 1500 metres in 3:41.74. He was obviously in good form. Six days later the world would see just how good.

The meet was the Adriaan Paulen Memorial, the event was the 5000 metres. In what was obviously an orchestrated attempt on the world record, a pace maker led at the first kilometre (2:36.6), and the second at 5:13.8. Just after the two kilometre mark Gebrselassie went to the front, but after that the pace was shared for the next four laps between Haile and his fellow Ethiopian Bikila, until he went to the lead for good with three laps to go. In Aouita's world record of 12:58.9, he had gone through 3000 metres in 7:46. The two Ethiopians passed the same mark in 7:50.86; but Haile had a lot more in reserve. Accelerating steadily over the last three laps he finished full of running. His last kilometre was under 2:29 as he finished well clear of Bikila in 12:56.96 – a new world record, the first ever by an Ethiopian.

Now definitely the man to beat, his very next race showed clearly that being the world record holder, and obviously in good form was no guarantee of victory. Less than a week after his record performance he was facing a top field in the GP meeting at Saint Denis in France, again over 5000 metres. It was obvious early in the race that the one man he had to beat was Khalid Skah. Skah's sole objective was to stick as close as possible to the new record holder, confident that if he was with Haile in the final straight he would be able to out sprint him. It was as if each man knew exactly what the other was trying to do.

For the whole race there was never much more than a stride separating the two. Finally, with about two laps remaining, Haile took off, with Skah going with him as the two cleared out from the rest of the field. It stayed that way until the final straight when the Moroccan went past. Even then, the race was in doubt until the last few metres, with Skah winning in 13:10.51 by a scant .28 of a second.

Early the following month Haile was in Lausanne, Switzerland for another GP meeting, this time over 10,000 metres. The result was a convincing win in 27:15. Then followed another GP 5000m in London (fourth in 13:11.87) and a 1500 in Belgium where his second place in 3:37.04 was a new national record. Three days later he was in Monaco for another GP event, this time over 3000 metres. The world 1500 record holder Morceli was in rare form and was determined to add the 3000 metre record to his collection. Gebrselassie, along with the rest of the field was outclassed. Despite his second place finish in 7:37.49, he was over twelve seconds behind Morceli's new world mark.

Haile's final track race for the season was at the Van Damme Memorial meeting in Brussels. The feature event as usual for this meet was the 10,000 metres, and once again a top field was on hand for the event. It contained no fewer than three future world record holders for the distance, with Haile winning in 27:20.39 from Salah Hissou. Rounding out the year was a 15 km road race (winning in 43:00) and two cross-country events (for a first and third place).

While 1994 had been a good year for Gebrselassie, it was little more than an appetiser for what was to come the following year. The early year cross-country season began with two victories as a lead up to the world title race in Durham on March 25. As usual, a top class field was on hand. Paul Tergat was simply too good for them all, and won from Ismael Kirui and Salah Hissou, with Haile in fourth position, twenty-one seconds behind the winner. By the end of the year, that defeat would be the only blemish in an otherwise perfect year.

After a three week break there would be a ten kilometre road race in Switzerland (winning comfortably in 28:02), before he really got to work. His first track race for the year was over two miles in the Dutch town of Kerkrade. Well ahead of the field, he passed the 3000 metre mark in 7:36.7, before finishing in the world record time of 8:07.46. As had become his usual modus operandi, he spent most of the time between his European races in Holland with his brother (also a runner). He did not have to wait long, or travel far for his next competition. As for last year it was in Hengelo for the Adriaan Paulen Memorial. As per last year for the 5000, this year it was an organized attempt on the 10,000 metre world record (held by the Kenyan Sigei).

Paced until the six kilometre mark (most notably by Bikila), he reached the half way point in 13:21.7. Bikila held on at the front for another kilo, and then Haile was on his own. Maintaining a near metronomic tempo, he lapped the entire field to finish in a time of 26:43.53. Two track races – two world records. 1995 was obviously going to be a good year.

After his great 10,000 metre run there were two more races before the World Championships. Both were over 5000 metres and against top competition. Haile won both in convincing fashion in fast times. Clearly he was in the best form of his life heading into the Goteborg World Championships.

Entering only the longest of his two pet events, to most observers it seemed a question of whether Haile would be up to the task of running a fast enough pace to negate the finish of Skah (again). However, the Gebrselassie of 1995 was a different runner to previous years. After relatively slow going early, the pace gradually picked up. Haile never led, and Skah was never more than a metre or so behind him. By the last lap there was a group of four – Hissou, Tergat, Gebrselassie and Skah. The pace was still steady, and at two hundred and twenty metres, any of the four could have won. Just twenty metres later, the answer was obvious. Haile went to the front and the race was over. His winning margin of 1.58 seconds over Skah flattered the Moroccan. Haile had run the last 200 in 25.1, finishing in 27:12.95. Tergat finished a close third. After this race and his earlier world records, there was no doubt who the best distance runner in the world was – and by quite a wide margin. Just how big a margin would soon become apparent.

On occasions there are records set (in just about all fields of human endeavor), that are so far beyond the expected norm that they invite a degree of incredulity. In distance running, two examples from Australia spring to mind. The 10,000 metre race where Ron Clarke took over thirty five seconds off the existing (already his own) world record. The other would be Derek Clayton in the marathon where (in 1969) he reduced the record from 2:12.00 to 2:09:36.4. In both cases, readers of the results could be forgiven for believing that there had been a misprint.

Eight days after his world championship win Gebrselassie would produce an example of such a performance. The meeting would be the Zurich Weltklasse, and the race was over 5000 metres. The record was no longer his, as it had been reduced from 12:56.96 to 12:55.30 by the Kenyan Moses Kiptanui. As it transpired, Kiptanui was running at the same meet, and in fact became the first to run under eight minutes for the steeplechase later in the meet. Thus he was the record holder for both the steeplechase and the 5000. Not for long.

As is typical for most of the big European races, pace makers set the tempo until – in this case – four laps remaining. Haile's last two kilometres took a fraction over 5:01, his last lap 56.69, as he finished in a hard to believe 12:44.39. He was clearly the best in the world over both classic distances. As if to emphasize the fact, in his very next race he outclassed the previous record holder, winning by almost eight seconds in a fast 12:53.19. He would finish the year with two further track races (over 3 and 5000 metres), and a 10k road race in Italy. In the latter race, Paul Tergat was second, as Haile won all three.

1996 was an Olympic year, and probably with a view to improving his already daunting speed endurance, Haile embarked on some indoor races, along with some – shorter than usual for him – 1500 metre competitions, in addition to the usual cross country races.

The year began with one of the World XC Challenge races. Second behind Haile was the Kenyan Daniel Komen – a name that would feature prominently for the rest of the year. Then followed two indoor events, both victories and both new world indoor records (5000 in 13:10.98 and 3000 in 7:30.72). Then followed the world cross-country championship. Paul Tergat would again prove to be the best as he disposed of another high-class field. Haile would finish fifth, but a measure of the quality of the field was that all those ahead of him were either future or present world record holders, world champions, or both.

His next important races were almost two months later. There were two over 1500 metres – victories both, including a new national record (3:34.64). His final race before the Atlanta Olympics was the 1996 edition of the Adriaan Paulen Memorial meet. Over 3000 he was a comfortable winner in 7:34.66.

Another two months later the weather would be warm and the track hard for the start of the Olympic track and field programme. Entered only in the 10,000 metres, Gebrselassie was the overwhelming favourite. As the world record holder, the reigning world champion, and with an almost unbeatable finish, the only debate seemed to be what the winning time might be, and who would take the minor placings. If only it were that easy. The early pace varied greatly, with some laps as fast as 62 and some 69. The warm conditions (80F and 75% humidity) and gradual quickening of the pace saw most of the field slowly drop off. At the business end of the race, the only one capable or willing to try and blunt the finish of the little Ethiopian was Paul Tergat.

With five laps to go, Tergat went to lead and put in a sixty second lap. Gebrselassie was the only one able to stay close enough to be a realistic threat, but Hissou was still some sort of a chance if both were to falter badly. Tergat gave it all he had, but with a lap to go Haile went by and the race was over. Not that it was easy. Both runners were suffering, but the early gap was enough to decide the winner. Hissou battled gamely for third place. The hard track (ideal for sprinters, not so much for distance runners) and weather conditions obviously exhausted not just those at the front, but the whole field. Finishing in 27:07.34, the effort required was deserving of a considerably faster time.

A little over a fortnight later was the Zurich Weltklasse meet. For many events it was like a re-run of the Olympics. The 5000 metres was somewhat unusual in that the main protagonists were runners who did not run that distance in Atlanta. As the world record holder (set at this very meeting the previous year) Haile probably deserved to start favourite but there were many who thought, with some justification, that the Kenyan Daniel Komen was really the one to beat.

Komen was a rare talent. One of fourteen children, he showed that talent at an early age and saw running as a means of breaking free from the grinding poverty of his home life. At his best, both in training and racing, he was virtually unstoppable. By the end of his all too brief career he could claim to be a dual junior world champion, a senior world champion, and a Commonwealth champion. But really, the titles he won, and the way he won them, were probably not as notable as the world records he set. At the time of writing (2019), he still holds world records for 3000 metres (indoors and out), and remains the only man to have run two miles in under eight minutes – and he did it twice. His outdoor 3000 metre record (7:20.67) is regarded by many as the best of all distance running records. Certainly no one has come close to it in the years since it was set.

Despite his talent, a fourth place finish in the Kenyan Olympic trials saw him miss the Atlanta games. Rather than despair at his misfortune, Komen used his Olympic disappointment as a spur to run fast times and make lots of money. He quickly learnt that the faster he ran, and the more often he ran, the bigger would be his take home pay. Almost every race he ran – and there were a lot – was fast. It seemed that just about every race he ran was a record attempt.

The Weltklasse race had all the hallmarks of a heavyweight title fight. The pack was in single file at the half-way point, and then, with five laps to go, everything changed. Komen ran that lap in 58 seconds and it quickly became a two man race. Komen's pace barely slackened, and it looked like the world record would go. Then with two laps to go the pace dropped slightly and two questions became one. Who would win, rather than would there be a new record. In the last lap, Komen lifted his pace yet again and with about 120 metres left, Gebrselassie was forced to concede. He jogged home over seven seconds behind, while Komen just missed the world record, finishing in 12:45.09. While Haile may have still been feeling the effects of his Olympic effort (especially the hard track), there was no denying the greatness of Daniel Komen.

While Gebrselassie was finished for the year (apart from a ten kilometre road race in Italy, winning in 28:42 from Tergat)), Komen continued to race. Two days after his Weltklasse effort he ran a personal best over 1500m (3:34.17) in Cologne, and then a few days later just missed the 3000m record in Brussels, running 7:25.87. By the end of August, it seemed that his relentless racing was finally catching up with him. A slow (for him) 5000 in Berlin would surely be the end. Rather than rest, Komen took a flight to the Italian town of Rieti. Seemingly saving his best for last, he followed pace makers for the first two kilometres before striking for home over the last kilometre. His amazing 7:20.67 took almost five seconds off Morceli's record. But even that was not the end. A few days later in Milan he won over 5000m in 12:52.38.

While Haile would be finished for the year in early October, he would be back again in the first week of February the following year. It would be hard to pick the best year of his long and illustrious career, but 1997 would be close. His first two races would actually be losses, but they were hardly upsets. Indoors against Hicham El Guerrouj over 1500 metres would be one of the toughest assignments in athletics. While Haile would run a new indoor national record of 3:32.39, Guerrouj would finish 1.21 seconds ahead in a new world mark. This was followed a week later with a fifth place 800m in 1:49.35, again indoors. Losses they may have been, but they showed that he was in great form nevertheless.

To round out his indoor season there would be a fast 3000 (7:31.27), a new world indoor record for 5000m in Stockholm (12:59.04), and victory over 3000m in the Paris world indoor championships (7:34.71). A fortnight later, and it was onto the outdoor track competitions.

First up was a comfortable 1500m win in Chemnitz (Germany) in 3:35.92. Then followed his traditional outing at the Adriaan Paulen Memorial meeting. The result was a new world mark over two miles, with his time of 8:01.08 showing that the chance of running two consecutive miles under four minutes was very real. This was followed by two

5000m events – comfortable victories both in 12:54.60 and 13:01.51. The winning margins of over eight and eleven seconds respectively might lead one to question the quality of the opposition, but that would be unfair. About the only notable absentees were Paul Tergat and Daniel Komen.

Despite his great races and fast times, they were only a prelude to the next phase of his season. The first event of this phase was at the famed Bislett Games in Oslo. Haile's 10,000 metre world mark from 1995 had been broken by Salah Hissou, and Bislett would give him the chance to reclaim it. As had become the norm in many such races, it was more a time trial than a race. In this instance the last of the pace makers were gone by the halfway mark, and it was a race against the clock from that point. Running almost even pace for both halves of the race, most of the field would be lapped as he finished in 26:31.32, some seven seconds under the old mark. With the World Championships a month away, it was obvious who the favorite would be for the 10,000. The question was: how to beat the fastest runner who also had the fastest finish?

The race itself was largely predictable, except for a twist at the end. For the entire race, Haile was never more than a metre or two from the lead, with Tergat and Hissou never more than a few strides from him. The expectation was that someone – probably Tergat - would make a long run for home. Lap after lap the steady pace continued, but no move from Tergat, or anyone else. Then, with 500 metres remaining someone went, and the surprise was that it was Gebrselassie. Most were expecting him to wait until the very end, but he caught them napping. Quickly the race was over. Tergat was the next to respond, but the gap was too great. The winning time was 27:24.58, with Tergat second and Hissou third.

Disappointingly for many, Haile only ran the longer race in Athens (as he had at nearly all major championships except as a junior). This left Komen as the favorite for the 5,000 and he did not disappoint. Running in the pack until about five laps to go, he rapidly put the result beyond doubt. Running 1:57 for 800 metres at almost any stage of a 5000 metre race will generally do that. He made the world's best look ordinary.

A week later the world's two best distance runners would meet again at the Weltklasse meet, again over 5000 metres. After what had happened in the last two versions of this event it was probably the most eagerly awaited race of the year. Despite virtually all the top performers over both five and ten kilometres at the recent World Championships being present, there was little doubt that it was really a two man race. And that is exactly how it transpired. Pace makers kept up a fast even tempo until 3000m (7:38.07), and then it was left to Komen to try and get rid of Haile as per last year. Paul Tergat was hanging on in third – but only just. With a lap to go, Tergat could not win, but either of the other two could. With just over two hundred metres remaining the difference between last year and this could not have been more different. Running the last 200 in 26.6, Haile finished full of running in a new record – 12:41.86. Komen finished in 12:44.90, the third fastest ever, while Tergat also finished under 12:50.

Despite such great running, there was still more to come for the 1997 season. Nine days after Zurich was the Brussels meet. While Haile had given the intervening meet in Monaco a miss, Komen had no such qualms. Against a strong field over 1500m he won in 3:29.46 – a new Kenyan record. As is often the case, the top athletes often avoid each other – sometimes to preserve their win/loss record, sometimes at the behest of their manager or meet promoter. Brussels was one such meet.

For the endurance enthusiasts, Brussels was about as good as it gets. All three of the longest track events were on the programme, with the 3000m first. Haile ran well, very well in fact, but despite his time of 7:26.02 being the fifth fastest ever, he was still some six seconds outside Komen's scarcely credible world record time.

Later in the meet was the 5000 featuring yet another record attempt by Daniel Komen. It seems somewhat redundant to say that with Komen, as almost every time he ran a record of one sort or another was under threat. And so it proved. With Haile watching, the pace maker reached 3000m in 7:37 before retiring and leaving Komen to press on alone.

With little apparent stress he finished with a lap of 59.44 to complete the journey in 12:39.74. The previous record had lasted all of nine days.

The final event for the evening was the 10,000m. The Brussels meeting had long had the reputation for having a high-class field for the longest of the track races and this year was no exception. The expectation was that Paul Tergat might finally get his name in the record books, but with former record holder Hissou and a number of very capable Kenyans in the field it would not be easy. A variety of different Kenyans brought the lead group to the halfway mark in 13:17. Shortly after six kilometres Paul Koech took the lead, followed closely by Tergat and Hissou. Realising that the chances of a record were slipping, Koech tried to increase the pace. Almost immediately Hissou lost contact. It stayed that way until Tergat took the lead with just over four laps remaining. His next two laps were just over 61 and 63 seconds. Following those laps he held on desperately to finish in 26:27.85. Koech finished less than nine seconds behind in the third fastest time ever (26:36.62). In one evening, Gebrselassie watched as both his world records were consigned to history.

Four days after Brussels was the ISTAF meet in Berlin. Haile won the 5000 from the Keyan pair of Koech and Nyariki in 12:55.14. However, the highlight of the evening was the attempt by El Guerrouj on the mile record. Of interest was the fact that one Daniel Komen was running. After the pace makers had done their job, Komen went to the lead with 500 metres left to run. The only ones who could stay close were El Guerrouj and the Burundian Niyongabo (later to be an Olympic gold medalist). It was as if there was another pacemaker in the field. With some 300m left, first El Guerrouj and then Niyongabo went past Komen. However, in the home straight Komen was moving faster than either, catching Niyongabo but just falling short of El Guerrouj. Just missing the world record, times for the first three were 3:45.64, 3:46.38 and 3:46.70. Haile finished his year with a ten kilometre road race in Italy, winning in 28:22.

1997 would have to go down as one of – if not the - greatest years in the annals of distance running. The careers of four of the all time great runners were at, or nearing, their peaks. The four were Gebrselassie and Komen, and at the shorter distances El Guerrouj over 1500m and Wilson Kipketer over 800m. Of the latter two, while El Guerrouj would have to wait another year to begin his record-breaking spree (outdoors at least), he was clearly the dominant runner over his favourite distance.

Over 800m the Kenyan born Danish citizen, Wilson Kipketer was the equivalent of Daniel Komen over that distance – always fast and rarely beaten. In his classic year of 1997 he first equaled the world 800m mark, and then broke it on two further occasions. Going into the world championships he had won all twenty-six previous races he had run. It was almost a formality that the world title was number twenty-seven.

Despite finishing with "only" silver and bronze medals from his Olympic appearances, he did win three world titles. Taking his career as a whole, a good case could be made for considering him one of the very best, perhaps even the best, 800m runners ever.

Like Komen, missing the 1996 Olympics – in Kipketer's case due to citizenship issues – gives some credence to the belief held by many that the importance of Olympic results is somewhat over-rated in the consideration of an athlete's career. Certainly in both their pet events the results in Athens could well have been much different had Komen and Kipketer been present.

Despite the great year that Haile had in 1997, a hard to believe fact is that he finished the year having lost all his outdoor world records – to Daniel Komen (twice) and Paul Tergat. It was obvious from his form early in the new-year that this was a situation he was determined to remedy.

He began the year by running six races indoors. First up was a new world mark over 3000m (7:26.15) in Karlsruhe, followed by what would be his only loss for the year – a sixth place finish over 800m in 1:50.39. Then followed two fast 1500m races. The first narrowly missed the world mark as he beat his own national record, running 3:31.76. He followed this a week later with 3:33.27. Another week, another world record. This time in Birmingham over 2000m in 4:52.86. The finale of his indoor season was an overwhelming victory over 3000m in Stockholm in

7:31.70. Haile had never been this fast so early in the year. He was in the form of his life.

A few weeks after the indoor season and a cross country in Paris (beating Khalid Skah among others), he returned to Addis for training. There was also time for two further good 1500m outings, including the national title win in 3:37.90 – good running indeed considering the altitude factor. Haile knew he was in record-breaking form, and the return home for training at altitude was the icing on the cake. However, over the last year standards had been pushed ever higher making the chances of regaining his records that much harder.

First up – as had become something of a staple in his outdoor seasons was the Adriaan Paulen meet in Hengelo, this year on June 1. In a specially arranged 10,000m it was obvious that there was only one aim –for Haile to reclaim the record. Following a variety of fellow Ethiopian pace-makers, the halfway mark was reached in 13:11.53, some six seconds ahead of Tergat's record pace. The last of the pacemakers – Assefa Mezgebu – held on for another kilometre before leaving Haile to complete the task he had set himself. Despite actually losing time to Tergat in the last half, his final lap of 58.1 was enough to do the trick, finishing in 26:22.75, some five seconds under the old time.

Twelve days later and he was ready for the second of his record attempts – this time at the Helsinki stadium – site of the 1952 Olympics and Zatopek's great distance running treble. Had he needed any further reminding of the history of the event, he may have seen the statue of Paavo Nurmi at the stadium entrance.

As per usual a quartet of pacers took Haile to a little over six laps. With the quantum leap in standards over the last two years, getting anyone able to hold the required record-breaking speed for anything beyond halfway was becoming very difficult. With six laps remaining, the last of the quartet was gone and it was Haile by himself against the clock. With 3000m coming in 7:38.93, a new record looked very hard; with four laps remaining and the clock showing 8:40 it looked almost impossible. It certainly seemed that way to the commentators on the European TV network covering the race. It wasn't until the last two laps that he made up the required time. Covering the last 800m in 1:56.93, and the final lap in 56.77 he finished in 12:39.36, taking 0.37 seconds off Komen's time. With a finish like that, perhaps it could be argued that the pace makers had actually hindered rather than helped. Second place, over twenty seven seconds behind, was the Kenyan Luke Kipkosgei.

With his rightful place at the top of world distance running resumed, the rest of the season was something of a coronation. No more records, but plenty of fast times and no losses. Three times under 7:28 for 3000 (two of those under 7:26), three more fast 5000m races, and a tactical win over 3000m in the Grand Prix final. Again he finished the season with a ten kilometre road race in Italy, winning in 28:59.1.

The 1999 season for Haile began indoors on January 24 at Karlsruhe, Germany. Over 3000m he showed that he was again in excellent form, running one of the fastest times ever (7:26.80). Then followed a fast 1500m in Stuttgart (3:34.28). A week later in Birmingham he gave another exhibition of just how great his form was with a new indoor record over 5000m (12:50.38). Following this there was another fast 3000m, this time in France (7:31.25).

Two more weeks and it was off to Maebashi, Japan, for the world indoor titles. Winning both the 3000m (in a tactical 7:53.57) and the 1500m (in a fast 3:33.77) added two more trophies to his burgeoning collection. With this conclusion to his indoor campaign, it was again off to the Adriaan Paulen meet in Hengelo to begin the outdoor season with a specially arranged two mile event. While in 1997 Haile had set a new world mark of 8:01.08, his time did not see the year out as Daniel Komen became the first (and twenty years later the only) to run the distance in less than eight minutes. No doubt hoping to regain his record, Haile fell just short in a time of 8:01.86.

This prefaced a series of fast winning times in the lead up to the World Championships in Seville. It included another attempt at the two mile record (just missing again in 8:01.72), and bests of 12:49.64 for the

5000m, 7:26.03 for the 3000m, along with new national records for both the 1500m (3:33.73) and mile (3:52.39).

The only questions regarding the 10,000m in Seville were what effect the hot conditions might have, and would anyone challenge Paul Tergat for the silver medal. The overwhelming consensus was that first place for Gebrselassie was pretty much a foregone conclusion. And so it turned out. Apart from a couple of minor attempts to speed up the pace, one at about the seven kilo mark, the other with a kilometre left to run, it was left to Haile to run the final lap in 54.4 seconds to finish in 27:57.27, some eight metres ahead of Tergat.

With 2000 being an Olympic year, Haile's racing schedule was only a fraction of what it normally was. With the Games being in the southern hemisphere – something of a rarity – all the major European competitions took place before the Games, none after. His preparation for Sydney involved four 5000m races, the last of which was the Weltklasse event in Zurich. Winning all four as expected, only in the Zurich event did he dip below thirteen minutes, and that was a very narrow win over Tergat. Despite winning, the close margins of all his victories could perhaps give an inkling that there was some vulnerability compared to previous years. The reality was that for some time Haile had been having treatment for achilles problems.

The informed thinking was that the 10,000m would end up a two man race between Gebrselassie and Tergat, with Tergat trying to run hard from a long way out to negate his opponent's closing speed. Those who thought this were only half right. The race unfolded the way many championship races tend to, with no single runner prepared to be the sacrificial lamb and set a pace that just might get rid of some of the main contenders. The pace varied, with the lead group dominated by the Ethiopians and Kenyans. The one constant was Haile's position just behind whoever was leading. The large crowd, along with those left in the leading group, seemed to be waiting for the inevitable to happen. With some 250 metres remaining, it did. The big surprise however, was that it was not Gebrselassie bolting into the lead, but rather Paul Tergat. Around the final bend Tergat held his narrow lead. In the finishing straight, Haile started to gain – but only just. With thirty metres remaining he was still marginally behind. In a finish that would do justice to a 100m sprint the final margin was .09 second. Once again the little man had found a way to win. The winning time of 27:18.20 was largely inconsequential, it was the final 200m – 26.0 for Tergat, 25.4 for Gebrselassie that was the real story.

The athletic world did not realise it at the time, but Sydney would be the last of Haile's World and Olympic victories. However, his career was far from over. Post Sydney the decision was made to operate on his troublesome achilles. In the short term that meant no running at all for two months, and then a gradual easing back into something like full training. The result was that by the time of the 2001 Edmonton World Championships he was still regaining full fitness and had not raced since the Olympics. As if that were not enough, he contracted a virus shortly before the championships. Suffice to say, if ever he was vulnerable this was it.

The race for the most part was uneventful. By the standard of most taking part it was slow with frequent changes of pace and frequent lead changes. As per so many of his big races, Haile was a constant presence near, but not in the lead. Once again it seemed that most were just waiting for the usual story to play out. The first half went by in 14:15.11, and although the pace picked up in the second half there was still a group of six making up the lead group with a lap to run. With a little over 200m remaining, as usual and as expected, Haile dashed into the lead. What was unusual and unexpected was that he was not running away from his pursuers. The Kenyan Charles Kamathi was third with 150m to go but finished full of running to win going away, while one of the other Ethiopians – Mezgebu – also passed the defending champion. The winning time was 27:53.25 with Haile just over a second back in 27:54.41.

By his own standards the rest of his season was decidedly low key, however the few races he did enter showed that his old form was returning, most notably winning the world half marathon title in Bristol in October (60:03), and a month later running a fine 15km road event in Holland, winning in an excellent 41:37.8.

2002 was, again by Haile's standards, a season of few competitions, but it did show something of what the future might hold. His only track event was an attempt on the rarely run one hour record in Hengelo. In a disappointing day he retired just short of fourteen kilometres, but there were highlights to his year. He won the Lisbon half marathon against top opposition in a fast 59:40, and ran a world best for ten kilometres on the road in Doha (27:02). Perhaps the offer on hand for breaking the record ($1,000,000) was sufficient inducement to make the trip to the capital of Qatar. However, the real interest in distance running circles in 2002 was the London marathon.

Priding itself on attracting the best runners available, this year was perhaps the greatest coup of all. Not only did they have Khalid Khannouchi, the world record holder, but thanks to a very large budget also enticed both Gebrselassie and Tergat. It was perhaps the most eagerly anticipated marathon ever run. The general feeling was that with arguably the two best distance men moving to the marathon a new record was just not possible, but probable. There was also a strong supporting cast.

In many such races, the pre race hype does not carry over to the race proper. This was not one of those instances. A series of pacers set a fast, steady tempo reaching the halfway point in 1:02.46. Shortly after, the pace makers picked up the pace before leaving the race at 25 kilometres. They had done their job well. With their departure, the lead group was down to eight, with Khannouchi, Tergat and Haile all present. A few kilometres later and the defending champion – the Moroccan El Mouaziz – began a long run for home. His bold attempt lasted until thirty-two kilometres, when Haile assumed the lead. Now there were just three remaining, all seemingly with a chance to win and break the world record in the process. The pace remained fast as Khannouchi and Gebrselassie dueled at the front with Tergat in close attendance. With a little over 3km to the finish the world record holder made his move. Haile responded, but not before Tergat had moved into second a stride behind the leader. It stayed that way for about a kilometre, and then Haile broke. When he broke it was sudden, when Tergat broke a little later it was a more gradual process. Khannouchi's winning time was indeed a new record – 2:05.38, finishing just ten seconds ahead of Tergat, while Haile finished third in 2:06.35. There were really no losers – certainly not the sport, certainly not Khannouchi, and for Tergat and Gebrselassie the race was a stepping-stone to greater things.

It may have seemed to many after his 2002 season that Haile's track days were behind him. What the 2003 season showed was that while he was not finished on the track, his days of almost absolute dominance were behind him – thanks initially to someone very close to home. The start of the year gave no such indication. His first race was a new indoor record over two miles (8:04.69), then followed a fast 3000m (7:28.29) and the world indoor title in 7:40.97. After a relative hiatus over the last 2-3 years, it looked like normal transmission was resuming. His very first outdoor race would tell a somewhat different story.

As was commonly the case his first outdoor race was in Hengelo, this year over 10,000m. Among his fellow countrymen in the field was a young Kenenisa Bekele. Bekele was hardly an unknown – anyone who has won the World cross country title four times (two short and two long course) is hardly a novice, but his credentials on the track did not really equate to his cross country ability. In the race, by halfway it was a race in three – Sihine, Bekele and Gebrselassie. The three had trained together so knew each other's strengths and possible weaknesses. Intent on a fast pace Haile went to the lead, probably assuming that the other two would gradually lose contact. It did not happen. With five laps remaining a frustrated Gebrselassie motioned for those behind to take a turn at the front. Sihine couldn't and Bekele wouldn't. With four laps remaining he surged, but Bekele covered the move easily. At the bell all three were still together. With 300 metres left Haile sprinted. Sihine lost contact, but Bekele did not. Gradually catching and then passing the little champion in the home straight, Bekele won in 26:53.70 to Haile's 26:54.58. Sihine finished just over four seconds further back. Haile was fit, he was in form, he ran well – but he still got beaten. This was not meant to happen.

Following the Hengelo race he had three 5000m races as lead ups to the World Championships in Paris. Despite running good times (a best of 12:54.3) he was beaten in two of them. His problem, one that had plagued him for some time, was his inability to sprint at the end of races as had long been his trademark. Heading into the championships he was fit, but lacked his usual explosiveness at the end of races. He was also up against Bekele again. It would not be easy.

As usual in major competitions his sole event was the 10,000m. The early part of the race gave no indication of what was to come. The first 3km passed in a slow 8:24.72, and then Bekele went to the front without changing the pace. The fourth kilometre took 2:46.05, and then Haile took over and the real race began. The next kilometre took 2:41.56 with the halfway mark coming up in 13:52.33. Although a lot faster than each of the preceding kilometres, the last five individual kilometre times would all be faster, in some cases a lot faster. Kilometres 6-9 each took between 2:34 and 2:38. The rest of the field dropped away and the race became an all Ethiopian affair. Sihine slowly began to lose contact as Haile did all in his power to lose his younger pursuer. He ran the penultimate lap in 61.75, but Bekele would not budge. With 200m to go he went past. Haile was still running fast, but Bekele just ran faster, covering the last 800m in 1:56.6. For both Bekele and Gebrselassie the last 5000m took under 13 minutes – 12:57.24 for the winner, 12:58.8 for second, as the winning time was 26:49.57. It would have to rate as one of the great races of all time.

Despite losing, Haile knew he was in great shape, possibly record breaking shape. He would find out in his next race, the Van Damme Memorial meet in Brussels over 10,000m. Set up as a record attempt and paced accordingly all was going well until the 3000m mark, then the pace began to slow somewhat, with 5000m being reached in 13:15.58. The drop in pace caused Haile to assume the lead and try to make up for lost time. The problem was that he had two Kenyans (one a "re-badged" Qatari) close behind. In effect he was now the de facto pacemaker for the pair. Any attempt to have them share pace making duties led to the pace dropping – not exactly what he wanted. With five laps remaining he decided that the record was beyond reach and concentration should be on winning. With 600 metres left to run Haile jumped into the lead, the Qatari / Kenyan Abdullah (aka Chepkurui) faded quickly, but the other Kenyan (Nicholas Kemboi) was a different matter. He slowly reeled Haile in, forcing him to sprint yet again. The result was a narrow victory in a fast time, 26:29.22 to 26:30.03 for Kemboi. It was Haile's fastest time since his world record run for the distance, and a huge personal best for Kemboi. Neither would run as fast again.

2004 being an Olympic year, Haile's aim was to make history by winning the 10,000m for the third time. The pre Olympic portents were not good. While he was far from his best, the rest of the world (mainly Ethiopia) had moved on. Bekele was fulfilling his obvious potential by claiming both the 5 and 10,000 records from Haile, while the man himself had trouble beating some of his lesser-known countrymen. Before the Athens Olympics, he was beaten indoors over two miles by Geneti, while outdoors he could only finish second to Sihine – and that over 10,000m.

The simple fact was that he was injured. He should not have run in Athens, but if you are the defending champion, a national icon, and as proud as he was – you run. After what had happened at the last World Championships, it was almost a foregone conclusion that an Ethiopian would win – the only questions were which one, and would it be a clean sweep for the medals. The early pace was slow, until just short of 3000m Haile went into the lead. Within a lap both Sihine and Bekele had joined him at the front and it was beginning to look like a repeat of last years World Championship race. With Sihine leading they passed 5000 in 13:50.87. Alternating the lead, it soon became apparent that Haile was not up to it. As the pace got faster he dropped off. Playing the ultimate team game Sihine and Bekele deliberately slowed the pace to allow their team mate to re join the lead group. By 8000m he had managed to regain contact with the lead group, but it was obvious that slowing for him would put an Ethiopian victory in jeopardy.

Once the decision was made Sihine and Bekele quickly built up a substantial lead, and in the last lap Bekele showed he was a class above the rest. Running the last lap in 53.02 he came home a comfortable winner in 27:05.10, over four seconds ahead of Sihine. Haile came home in fifth (27:27.70), not a bad result for someone who should not have even been running. He then had his second operation on both achilles tendons.

After that, the decision was made. While he would run the occasional track race, Haile would now turn his attention almost exclusively to road events. His training also changed significantly. Intense speed sessions on the track were a thing of the past, replaced by a greater emphasis on more mileage with a view to realizing his marathon ambitions. Such changes would prolong his career, partly by relieving the stress on his legs caused by both speed training and track racing.

2005 was the first year to put this new approach into practice. The results were encouraging – no injuries, seven races for seven wins, a world best over ten miles (44:23.0), and his first marathon victory (Amsterdam in 2:06:20). He was hoping that Amsterdam might be a world record, but the windy conditions largely put paid to that.

It was not as if training was any easier, just different. Whereas during his track career he completed sessions such as 18 x 400m, with the first 15 in 56 seconds and the last 3 in 53, and repeat kilometres at well under 2:30, now there were more long steady fast paced runs. For example, a fortnight before his ten mile record he had run 42:24 for 15km with the last 5km in 13:39 in a solo training effort on the road (at 8,500 feet). He was also completing forest runs of up to three hours and frequent road runs of 20 – 30 kilometres. In the month leading up to his Amsterdam win, in addition to his regular two hour runs, he completed a 20km run in 59:40 and 30km run (in tough conditions) at about 3:06 per kilometre. Ten days before the race he ran a "comfortable" 15km in

45:27 only running hard for the final 2km. Bear in mind, all this at over 8000 feet. While 2005 had been a good year it would be the next three years when Haile would establish himself as one of the really top marathon men.

2006 began well with a half marathon world record of 58:55 in Tempe, Arizona on January 15. This was followed by another half marathon, this time in Spain three weeks later, winning again in 60:07.6. His next "race" was over 25km in Holland. The race was actually over 20km, but Haile and six others ran an extra loop of the 5km circuit before the race proper began. Because of this unusual situation his world record time 1:11:37 for the rarely run distance was not accepted.

While obviously running well, this year was really all about the marathon, or more specifically, the world record for the marathon. In all he ran three marathons in 2006 – London, Berlin and Fukuoka. London was first (April 23) and it was disappointing, finishing ninth in 2:09:05 almost two and a half minutes behind the winner (Limo of Kenya). Some five months later and it was the Berlin marathon. Designed to give Haile a real chance at the record, it was more a high level time trial than a genuine race as he won by nearly five minutes in a much improved (but still no record) 2:05:56. The record was really lost over the last seven kilometres where he faded badly. His final race for the year was the Fukuoka marathon in Japan, held in early December each year. Before the relatively recent advent of the big city marathons, Fukuoka had been considered the unofficial world championship for the event, and while it no longer attracted quite the fields that it once did, was still considered one of the most prestigious to win – especially in marathon mad Japan. Winning in 2:06:52 showed that he was certainly coming to terms with the distance, and with perfect preparation and conditions he just might break the record.

2007 began with a cross-country win in Spain, then the London marathon. Again a disappointment for him as he was forced to withdraw at 30km. Next up was a rare track race – over 10,000m at his old haunt of Hengelo. Despite running a good 26:52.81, it was only good enough for fifth place in a race won by Sihine. Second in the race was a young Eliud Kipchoge who would much later go on to create his own history in the marathon.

No doubt buoyed by his showing at the Hengelo race, his next event would be another track outing – this time at Ostrava, Czechoslovakia – the scene of some of Emil Zatopek's more memorable records. The event would be an attempt on the world one hour record. Although run infrequently, the record had been held by some of the greats of distance running over the years – names such as Nurmi, Clarke and of course Zatopek among them. One such athlete that had in fact broken the record twice, was none other than Haile's agent and friend, Jos Hermens, whose best effort resulted in 20,944 metres being covered within the hour. The record now stood at 21,101 metres held by Arturo Barrios. Despite it not being attempted often, it was not an easy or "soft" record. Passing 15km in 42:18.70, 10 miles in 45:23.80 and 20,000m in 56:25.98 (a new world record), Haile managed a new best distance of 21,285m.

He was obviously running well, and some six weeks later a convincing win in the New York half marathon against some top opponents in 59:24 suggested that perhaps his time had finally come. In Berlin in eight weeks he would find out.

The record he was chasing in Berlin now belonged to his old friend and rival Paul Tergat and stood at 2:04.55, run in the 2003 version of this very race. To match Tergat's time would require each of the 42 kilometres to pass in an average of 2:57.6. He knew that after chasing the record for so long this was his big chance. With the help from pacemakers he was ahead of the pace required from early in the race (10km in 29:27) and after that it was a matter of running as evenly as possible. He never really faltered, passing 20km in 59:10, 30 in 1:28.56 and 40 in 1:58.08 for a final time of 2:04.26. The first half had gone by in 62:29, the second in 61:57, giving an indication that there was some chance he could perhaps better his time. He had now broken all the classic distance records, some on multiple occasions. His year finished with a win over 15km in Holland in 42:36.

The year 2008 began with a marathon in Dubai. Offering huge prize money and an almost dead flat course it was made for fast times. The main problem was that the early pace was a bit too fast. With a first 10km in 28:39, the first half went by in a fast 61:27 - there would be a price to pay later. At 30km Haile was still ahead of his Berlin schedule but then began slipping behind. With the second half taking 63:26, he would finish in 2:04.53, the second fastest ever.

Two months later he was in Lisbon for the half marathon, winning again in 59:15. Another two months and he was in Hengelo for one of his rare track appearances, as per last year over 10,000m. He improved three places and just over a second to finish in 26:51.20 to Sihine's 26:50.53. This would be his last race before the Beijing Olympics.

Prior to the Beijing games there was considerable concern about the degree of air pollution in the Chinese city. The rest of the world was realizing what the residents had known for years. It was a particular issue for athletes involved in endurance events. Haile, having had some asthmatic problems, was concerned that running a marathon under such conditions could be a real problem, and decided that it was not worth the risk. As it eventuated, Beijing got lucky. By a combination of strict government intervention and favorable weather conditions the air quality for most of the endurance events (not just athletics) was not too bad.

Deciding to forego the marathon, Haile joined Bekele and Sihine in the 10,000m. The race began slowly and with no one really happy to be in the lead, the first kilometre took over 2:50. The pace then sped up dramatically, with the second kilometre taking just 2:37. The third kilometre remained fast, but the next two dropped to 2:49 and 2:48. Because of the pace changes, the 5,000m time of 13:48.00 was probably more tiring than the time might indicate.

A kilometre later and Gebrselassie went to the front and immediately the pace quickened. It looked like the Ethiopian trio might do what they had done before – simply run away from the rest of the field.

Modern marathon running. Haile with pacers and Kamathi en route to new world record at 2008 Berlin marathon.

The race became a battle between the Ethiopians and Kenyans, with the Eritrean Tadesse also in attendance. Besides the Ethiopians, it was mainly Tadesse and the young Kenyan Micah Kogo pushing the pace as the rest of the field dropped off. The final kilometre just got faster and faster. The penultimate lap was 61.22 before Bekele really put the issue beyond doubt. The last kilometre took 2:27.10, the last 800m 1:54.66, and the final lap just 53.42 seconds as he finished in 27:01.17. Sihine was second in 27:02.77 with Kogo third in 27:04.11. Haile did not really falter, he just did not have the change of gear that Sihine and especially Bekele had at the end, finishing sixth in 27:06.68. Considering that his preparation had been for the marathon rather than the track, he could not have been too disappointed.

The Berlin marathon was some six weeks after the Beijing Olympics, and as the world record holder and defending champion, Haile was the favorite. The main interest was in what time he might run. The conditions were good (48F at the start 55F at the finish), the four pacers did their job well, and by half way (reached in 62:04) the chance for a new record was very real. One of the criticisms made of Haile's marathon career was that most of his races were largely orchestrated time trials rather than races against top competition. In this case it was something of a surprise that he had company after the pace makers dropped out. Two Kenyans in the form of James Kwambai and Charles Kamathi were still in contention. Kwambai was the last to lose contact, but not until the last 5km. He would take a huge chunk from his previous best in running 2:05.36, while Haile finished full of running to become the first under 2:04. The new record was 2:03.59. Haile now had the three fastest marathon times ever run. Another record of sorts was that it was now over fourteen years and three months since he set his first and last world records – longer than any other athlete.

Haile Gerbrselassie 2009 Fanny Blankers-Koen Games at Hengelo (in a group).

Haile Gerbrselassie 2009 Fanny Blankers-Koen Games at Hengelo (on his own).

Haile would finish the year with a trip to Australia for the so-called Great Australian Run over 15km. As a promotion, and a bit of fun, organizers set up a treadmill with the speed set at marathon world record pace. Members of the public, along with some top local sportsmen and women were invited to see how long they could maintain the required pace. Most were amazed at just how fast the required pace was. As in most sports the very best, such as Haile, make it look easy.

After 2008, his career was in gradual decline. Having set such a high standard for so long it would be unrealistic to expect anything else. Even so, he had wins and times that a lot of world class runners would consider career defining. In 2009 he won both Dubai (2:05.29) and Berlin (2:06.08) again, had a half marathon best of 59:50 but failed at the attempt on his one hour record (reaching 20,822m).

In 2010 he won at Dubai again (in 2:06.09) and convincingly won the British Great North Run (a half marathon) in 59:33. However, in two New York appearances, firstly the half, and then the full marathon he had to withdraw. Following the latter disappointment he announced his retirement, only to rescind his decision shortly afterwards.

The following year he had two victories each over both 10km and half marathons with bests of 28:10 and 60:18 respectively. He also had a 15km win in 42:44. However in the Berlin marathon he was forced to withdraw after the half way mark while the Kenyan Patrick Makau won in 2:03.38 to better Haile's world record.

He began 2012 with fourth place in the Tokyo marathon in 2:08.17, but ended the year by failing to finish the Fukuoka marathon. In between however, he was still good enough to run 27:20.39 for 10,000m on the Hengelo track. As if to emphasize the passing of time the winner was Bekele – but it was not Kenenisa, it was his younger brother.

Without doubt, the highlight of 2013 was that year's version of the Great North Run. It brought together three all time greats, and in running terms, it was almost like three generations – Haile, Bekele, and Mo Farah. Well and truly the veteran of the trio, Haile showed that he could still mix it with the best. While Bekele held on for the narrowest of wins in 60:41, Haile was only 32 seconds behind. He was also good enough to win in Bern over 10 miles in 46:59 and run 28:00 for 10km on the road.

Despite his best days behind him, he still ran, he probably always will, mainly because he enjoys it so much. With his seemingly boundless energy and enthusiasm, for the latter part of his career he was able to combine the multiple lives of a world class athlete, managing a growing business empire and family man – not to mention the time demands made on a national icon. He has frequently been mentioned as a future political leader if the mood so took him.

Of the characters that are the topic of this book, probably the closest in nature to Haile would be Zatopek. Both dominated their events and re-wrote the record book, both were national icons – adored at home and revered abroad. Both were affable and outgoing. Both had humble beginnings but rose in stature to almost transcend the sport they loved.

Looking back at Haile's career it is hard to believe that he ran so well, for so long, at such a variety of distances. He won world titles and / or set world records at just about every distance from 1500m to the marathon. But for some quite severe injuries (which were never publicized and never used as an excuse) his record may have been even more glorious. He was the precocious junior who just seemed to get better with age. As a role model for the sport he was it par excellence. At his best – fully fit and injury free – it was virtually an assumption that he would win. Eventually time, injuries, and other physical conditions would serve to slow him, but even then only by his standards.

In any consideration of the best of all time, Haile must surely be one of the first considered. But even that probably sells him short – not as an athlete, but as a person.

KENENISA BEKELE

"The secret to success is investing the time in trying to make it right."

Beijing 10,000 metre final.
Bekele winning the first
leg of his great double.

By a twist of fate, just as one candidate for the greatest of all distance runners was passing his peak, so another candidate for the same title was emerging. Making the coincidence striking was the fact that the newcomer was not just from the same country, but also from the same regional area. The country was of course Ethiopia, the area was the province of Arsi, and the newcomer was Kenenisa Bekele, who would go on to be a legitimate challenger to Haile Gebrselassie as the greatest of all time.

Bekele was born on June 13, 1982 in the town of Bekoji. Perhaps not a complete surprise in a country such as Ethiopia, he was not the only notable distance runner to be born in the same town. The Dibaba sisters notably Tirunesh and Genzebe would both be among the very best ever to compete. For a town with a population of some 17,000 to produce the winners of ten Olympic gold medals, along with almost as many minor medals, gives rise to the suggestion that there is some degree of genetic advantage bestowed on those living in the area. The dominance of Kenyan and Ethiopian runners on the world scene is such that it would be no surprise to find that there in fact is some inherent genetic advantage they have over their non East African counterparts. Whether it is this, the lifestyle, the diet or the altitude, or more probably a combination all these factors and more, is a topic of ongoing speculation and scientific research. Bekele himself believes that the East African success in distance running is a combination of genetics, living and training at altitude, and lifestyle.

Certainly one common thread is the stature of nearly all the top runners. Mention has already been made of Haile Gebrselassie. Bekele at 1.65m (5 feet 5 inches) is just one centimeter (about half an inch) taller. Eliud Kipchoge is 1.67m and Daniel Komen, who always looked quite tall running against Gebrselassie was only 1.70 (5 feet 7 inches). By comparison Mo Farah is something of a giant at 1.75m or 5 feet nine!

Bekele's claim to be the best ever is probably best summed up by his three Olympic gold medals (and one silver), five World championships, four World indoor titles, and eleven world cross-country titles. There were also the world records. But more than this was the way he won his races and the dominance he had over fellow competitors when at his best. Quite simply, if at his best he was, like his predecessor, virtually unbeatable.

To say that Bekele had a talent for running is a bit like saying Mozart was a good composer or that Michael Jordan had an aptitude for basketball. Typical of most boys his age he was keen on any type of ball game, especially soccer. It was only when one of his high school teachers suggested that he might have some ability as a runner that he decided to give it a try and began some training. From the very beginning a young Kenenisa showed what talent he had and what the future might hold. Records show that while a schoolboy in 1997 he won his school cross country championship, ran the mile in 4:25, and the 800m in 2:10 all without training, just natural ability. The following year with some training he ran two miles in 8:47. However the sporting world is littered with examples of talented juniors who fail to make the transition to senior ranks successfully.

In 1999, while still a sixteen year old, he won the junior provincial cross country for the Arsi region, and finished sixth against older boys in the national cross country title held in the capital Addis Ababa. As a result of that run he was included in the national team for the world junior cross county championships held in Belfast, finishing ninth over the 8km course. The senior long course race was won for the fifth time by Paul Tergat. It would take a while, but eventually Bekele would overtake both Tergat and fellow Kenyan John Ngugi to win the title six times.

Because of his age Bekele was still eligible for the world youth championships, to be held in the Polish city of Bydgosecz in July. Running 3000m he was good enough to finish second in 8:09.89. Few of those running would later make a name for themselves in senior ranks, but in fifth place there was an M. Farah from Great Britain.

The end of 1999 and the start of 2000 would be dominated by cross-country events for Bekele. While still a junior he was often competing in senior events and hence some of his placings were much lower than had he been competing solely against runners of the same age as himself. In December there would be two races (in Belgium and Holland) for sixteenth and third place finishes, and in January two further races in Spain (thirteenth) and in Holland (seventh). In May he had his first track race for the year. In the Dutch town of Nijmegen he finished just behind fellow Ethiopian Deberework over 5000m in 13:37.16. His next two races, also over 5000m were both victories. The first was again in Holland in a time of 13:24.36, the second in Estonia in 13:27.45. These times were all achieved while still just eighteen years of age.

His first race after turning nineteen was over 3000m in the German town of Ingolstadt. While his other races had been close affairs this one was not. Against none other than Daniel Komen he would finish over twelve seconds behind the Kenyan great in 7:50.45. His next race would be another over 5000m in which he failed to finish, the race being won by Gebrselassie in 13:01.07. His remaining track races for the year would include a fourth place in the African Championships (in 13:32.37), a victory over 3000m in 7:46.95, and second place over 5000m at the World Junior Championships in Chile (13:45.43). However, his fastest time for 5000m (13:20.57) would be his third place finish in Rieti — again well behind (over sixteen seconds this time) Daniel Komen.

The year ended for Kenenisa with two cross-country races and a ten kilometre road race, winning one of the two cross country events, and also the road race. First up in the new year were selection trials for the forthcoming World Cross Country championships. As an official IAAF championship the title began as a single 12km event held annually. In 1998 a 4km race was added to the programme with the aim of encouraging more shorter distance athletes to become involved. As we shall see, it did not quite work out that way. Qualifying by winning the selection trial at the shorter distance, the decision was made for Kenenisa to run both the senior event (over 4.1km) and the junior event (over 7.7km). The championships were held at Oostende, Belgium on March 24-25. First up for Bekele was the senior short course event. With the decision in doubt until the very end, he finished just two seconds behind the Kenyan Koech. The junior title the next day was about as convincing as it gets, with a thirty three second gap to the second place getter. He would be the third Ethiopian to win the junior title, and significantly all would go on to have successful senior careers, especially Million Wolde who would be a later Olympic gold medalist over 5000m. Of interest for the future was M. Farah of Great Britain in position 59.

The week after the cross-country championships there was a 10km road race in France (seventh in 28:54), and then it was home for preparation for the European track season, beginning for him in Hengelo on June 4 over 3000m. Despite actually losing this and every subsequent track race for the season, time wise there was a definite improvement. His slowest 5000m time was 13:25.86 at the Oslo Bislett Games — good enough only for nineteenth place. However in his four other attempts at the distance he ran 13:13 twice and 13:15 twice. That one of those times (actually 13:15.39 in Rome) was only good enough for sixteenth place says something about the standard of competition at the highest level. His 3000m best of 7:30.67 (finishing second) at the Van Damme meet in Brussels was a new World Junior record. Probably his best competitive performance on the track was in Melbourne, Australia for the Grand Prix final. He was a close second, just 0.24 seconds behind Paul Bitok of Kenya, despite his slowest time for the year at the distance (7:54.09).

Despite his steady improvement on the track, his competitive record at cross-country events was far superior to his achievements on the track. After his 2001 track season, leading up to the 2002 World Cross Country championships he would race five times over cross country and his only loss would be to Haile Gebrselassie - and that by one second. In between his cross-country outings he also had time to win on the road in Holland over 15km. His time of 42:42 was a new World Junior best. The last two of his races before the world titles would be the national trials (over 4km) and one of the more famous cross country events, the Cinque Mulini (five mills) over 12km in Italy.

The world championships were held in Dublin on 23-24 March and the nineteen year old Kenenisa was entered in both the senior short and long course events. First was the short race of just over 4km. Winning by seven seconds, unsurprisingly the first six place-getters included three Kenyans and two Ethiopians. What did surprise many was the tall figure of Craig Mottram from Australia in fifth place. The next day was the long course event. Dominated again by the African nations, Bekele won by six seconds, always looking in control, from the Tanzanian John Yuda. The next four after Yuda were all Kenyans.

It would be almost two months before resuming competition. Injuring his achilles tendon after the World Cross country he missed virtually the whole of the European track season. It would not be the last time that injury would make serious inroads into his career. His first race post injury would be the national championships over 5000m in Addis, finishing second to Birhanu in 14:02.0. Four days later over the same distance in Italy he was third in 13:26.58, but nearly twenty seconds behind the winner. Six days later he was back in Addis for the Great Ethiopian Run, a ten kilometre road event, finishing third behind Gebremariam and Sihine.

At the end of 2002 and in the lead up to the 2003 World Cross Country titles Bekele would race over cross-country five times at distances between nine and twelve kilometres, winning all convincingly. He would also run an Ekiden event in Japan, and as part of the winning national team had the fastest 5km leg of 13:07. He was clearly in the form to be able to defend one or both of his titles.

The championships this year were in the Swiss city of Lausanne on March 29-30. As expected both races were dominated by the large African contingent. In the short race, while he won by three seconds, the next four place getters were all Kenyan. In the longer race his winning margin was thirteen seconds with the first seven places being shared between the Kenyans and Ethiopians. The Kenyan Ivuti was second with fellow Ethiopian Gebremariam in third. A week later there followed another cross-country and another win, this time in Italy.

At this stage of his athletic career it looked like Bekele might be one of those athletes whose performances on the track would never quite measure up to their achievements at cross country - perhaps a little like Paul Tergat who had won Five World Cross country titles, but away from the country did not have quite the same impact. Of course, the fact that his career largely coincided with that of Gebrselassie did not help. In Bekele's case all that was about change - and a lot quicker than most would have thought.

After the conclusion of the cross-country season it was back to Addis Ababa and some serious training. Being in the national team meant that the top runners frequently trained together. Thus the likes of Bekele, Sihine, Gebremariam - and not forgetting one Haile Gebrselassie - were frequently on the same track training together (at about 2400m or 8000 feet). This made for the chances of rapid improvement along with being able to keep an eye on just how potential rivals were moving. Of the two nations that have dominated distance running over the last twenty years or so, it would probably be true to say that Ethiopia has made more of the talent it has than Kenya. While Kenya has a greater number at the top level, the Ethiopian system - such that it is - seems to be more centralised and is able to bring the best together for training more easily.

After five weeks of solid training leading up to the national titles, Kenenisa was second in the 5000m, but his time of 13:47.25 was almost twelve seconds behind the winner Sihine. It gave little indication of what was to follow. As with Gebrselassie, Bekele's manager / agent was Jos Hermens, thus it was no surprise that his first race for the European season would be in Hengelo. Named after the Dutch heroine of the 1948 Olympic Games (winning four gold medals) it would be at the Fanny Blankers-Koen Games on June 1. Despite having run numerous races beyond ten kilometres, it would be his first attempt at that distance on the track.

Except for his loss at the 2001 World Championships when injured, Gebrselassie had not lost a race at 10,000 metres for ten years. Few present thought the situation would change on this day. After achilles problems in 2001 and a calf injury last year Haile was back to something like his best. Indoors he had broken the world two mile record and won a World Championship. In fact, he was hoping that he might even better his own world record for the 10,000m set five years ago. On that occasion he had to run almost the entire last half by himself. This time he was hoping that his young teammate might be able to share some of the pace making duties later in the race. Not that he was taking his twenty year old rival lightly. Frequently training together, Haile saw Bekele as his heir apparent, just not yet. Like their shared manager Jos Hermens, he was of the opinion that Kenny - as he preferred to be called - had yet to really establish his credentials as a track runner.

When the topic of comparing himself to Gebrselassie was raised with Kenenisa, either out of deference or modesty he would downplay his part in any such comparison. Prior to his 10,000m debut he was quoted in an interview: "I am not as good as him on the track. I do not have the speed to finish like he can. I can only train like hell and pray to heaven that I will ever reach the level of Haile." His prayers were to be answered a lot sooner than he might have ever imagined.

With the somewhat warm conditions, a world record was out of the question from quite early in the race. After the fast early pace (3000m in 7:58.40 and 5000m in 13:22.72) there were just three Ethiopians left at the front — Haile, Kenny, and Sileshi Sihine. In almost any other country, or any other era, Sihine would have been an absolute star. Being in Ethiopia when he was, he spent most of his career playing second fiddle to arguably the two best distance runners ever to set foot on a track. While Haile was intent on pushing the pace, Bekele was intent on staying in contention for as long as possible and seeing what might happen at the end. Still leading at the bell, Haile began his final sprint with about three hundred metres remaining. Sihine lost contact immediately, but Kenny gradually closed the gap until slowly but surely moving ahead in the final straight. Bekele would finish less than a second ahead of Gebrselassie (26:53.70 to 26:54.58) with Sihine third in 26:58.76. On the track Ethiopia was definitely no longer - if indeed it ever had been - a one-man band.

While his victory was a shock, his very next race would prove that it was no fluke. Three weeks later he was in Oslo for the Bislett Games - always a highlight on the European athletic calendar. Running against a small army of high class Kenyans it all came down to a frantic half lap sprint. With a closing 200m of 25.3 seconds and a personal best by 21 seconds Bekele just held off Sammy Kipketer by 0.07 seconds in 12:52.26. Of special significance that would become more apparent a few weeks later was Eliud Kipchoge finishing a close third in 12:52.61— a new World Junior record.

After his Bislett breakthrough at 5000m he would have two more races over the distance before the World Championships, winning in Lausanne in 13:06.05, and finishing a close second to Chebii of Kenya in Rome in 12:57.14 to 12:57.34, with Gebrselassie third.

The World Championships for 2003 were held in Saint-Denis, France, beginning on August 23. The 10,000m was on August 25. As described in detail in the previous chapter, the race was not greatly exciting until just before the halfway point. It was then that the Ethiopian "team" - because that is effectively how they ran - took turns in the lead and simply ran away from the opposition. Both Bekele and Haile would run the last 5000m in under thirteen minutes as the now twenty one year old Bekele won 26:49.57 to 26:50.77. His final half in 12:57.24 was faster than the time Gebrselassie needed to run to break his first world record over 5000m in 1994. That 10,000m would be remembered as one of the truly great races, but for Bekele it was just the first of what he hoped would be the distance double.

The 5000m final was held three days later and brought with it the tantalising prospect of seeing the world's best over 10,000m up against the world's best over 1500m. The latter was of course the Moroccan, Hicham El Guerrouj. For a number of years El Guerrouj had been dominant in the 1500m. As the world record holder in both that distance and the mile, along with the times he had run and honours won he was really in a class of his own. The question was whether Bekele could put the race beyond doubt before the last lap, or whether El Guerrouj could hang on long enough to use his superior speed at the end. From the very start it seemed that conventional wisdom was being put into practice. At the gun Bekele immediately went to the lead, and unlike many such big races he pushed the pace. The first lap was just over 60 seconds and the first kilometre took 2:31.94. Still ahead but slowing slightly, 2000m came up in 5:07.27. The only problem was that his bold front running had not dislodged any of the main contenders - notably El Guerrouj and the Kenyans - Kibowen, Kipchoge, Limo and Chebii. After six laps he was left with two options - press on even faster, or slow somewhat to save something for the inevitable sprint finish. He chose the latter, but unfortunately for him whenever he slowed no one else showed any inclination to keep up a reasonable tempo. As a result, with a kilometre left there were still eight in contention for the win. With just over two laps remaining the newly minted junior world record holder Kipchoge moved into the lead. Not for long. With 800m left to run El Guerrouj went to the front and began his long drive for home. It looked like the inevitable story was playing out as he took 59.7 seconds for the second last lap. On the back straight El Guerrouj was in full flight while the young Kipchoge had moved into second. The final straight was like a 100m race with any of Bekele, El Guerrouj or Kipchoge a possible winner. In the end it was the youngest in the field that would triumph as Kipchoge won in 12:52.79 from El Guerrouj in 12:52.83 with Bekele a close third in 12:53.12. Given the fast early pace, a last 800m in 1:53.4 and a last lap in 53.52 were amazing. For Kipchoge it was an unexpected victory that would be just one episode in what would be a long and illustrious career. He finished the year as the World Junior cross-country champion, the World Junior 5000m record holder, and the senior World Champion for the distance, all achieved as an eighteen year old.

Kenenisa would have four more races for the year. In Monaco a fortnight after the World Championships he won over 3000m in the finale of the Grand Prix series against a mainly Kenyan field - the time: 7:36.98. Then followed a ten kilometre road race in Italy, the 5000m at the All Africa Games and a cross country in Spain, winning all three. At the start of the year Bekele was the undisputed king of cross-country, but the jury was still out on his track ability. In 2003 all that changed. He finished the year clearly the world's best over 10,000m. While his Hengelo performance may have been considered an aberration by some, his truly great run over the distance at the World Championships would have dispelled any doubters. Over 5000m he won four races from seven, but two of his three losses were by the slimmest of margins against top opposition. His only substantial loss for the year at any distance was his second place finish at the national championships over 5000m.

Bekele would start the new year as he had finished the old – with a cross country win over 12km in Milan, followed by another in Seville. Then it was on to the indoor circuit. His first race was over 3000m in Stuttgart, winning in a fast 7:30.77. The second was in Birmingham three weeks later. As a final race before the forthcoming World Cross-Country titles he showed that he was in great form to defend his titles, winning over 5000m in a new world record time of 12:49.60. Then it was home for more training before the world titles a month later.

The World Cross Country for 2004 was run on March 20-21 in Brussels. As the defending champion over both distances, having not lost a cross-country race for over three years, and obviously in great form, Kenenisa was the overwhelming favorite.

The first event was the short course race over 4km which he won comfortably from his Ethiopian team mate Gebremariam. The long course race the next day was over six 2km laps. Showing no ill effects of his race the previous day Bekele was content to stay in the main group for the first three laps, before applying the pressure in the fourth and fifth laps. Breaking clear he was able to slow somewhat over the final lap while still maintaining his comfortable lead. He would finish eighteen seconds ahead of Gebremariam (again), while Sihine finished a close third in a sprint finish. For the first time Ethiopia claimed the first three places, but probably even more important was the fact that they had broken the Kenyan stranglehold on the team trophy. Kenya had won the teams event for the previous eighteen years, and it was not as if it was a substandard Kenyan group, comprising as it did the reigning World 5000m champion, the 2001 World 10,000 champion, and the 2002 Commonwealth Games 10,000m champion.

Following his Brussels victories and some solid training at home Bekele was ready to start the track season proper as a lead up to the forthcoming Athens Olympic Games. And what a lead up it was. It began with a big win in the national championships over 5000m in Addis Ababa in 13:34.03 – excellent running at that altitude. Thirteen days later was the 2004 edition of the Fanny Blankers-Koen Games, and with it an orchestrated attempt on the 5000m world record.

The record of course was held by Haile Gebrselassie and stood at 12:39.36, set over six years before in Helsinki. Only Komen and Gebrselassie had ever run the distance in under 12:40. The two pacemakers for this attempt were the Kenyans David Kiplak and Luke Kipkosgei. The first kilometre took 2:33.24 – good running – but already slower than required if the record was to fall. The second went by in 2:32.23 – an improvement, but still too slow for the record. By halfway the pace makers were gone and it was just Kenny against the clock. The 3000m time was 7:37.34, good enough to win most races at that distance alone, but still too slow for the record. For the record to be broken a final 2000m in close to five minutes flat would be required. Apart from perhaps Komen and Gebrselassie, such running would be unthinkable, but Bekele was now in the same league. Covering the final 2km in 5:00.01, and the last lap in just over 57 seconds he finished in 12:37.35, a new record. Wondimu, who he had beaten for the national title a few weeks earlier ran well to finish second in 13:01.28, a long way behind. Craig Mottram ran a new Australian record – and finished a half lap behind in 13:10.47 and seventh place. Distance running was in a new era.

His very next race, eight days later would be on the Ostrava track made famous all those years ago by Emil Zatopek. To call it a race is something of a misnomer, as it was really a time trial. The pace that records now require means that only a select few can hope to keep up for little more than a fraction of the full distance. In this case, over 10,000m it meant that the pace maker (Martin Keino) could not keep the pace required for less than half the distance, and Bekele was forced into the lead with fifteen laps remaining to try and regain the time lost vis a vis the record. Passing 5000m in 13:14.42 he was still outside the pace needed, and even with a kilometre left a new record looked anything but likely, but Bekele did what he had to – a final kilometre in 2:31.46 and a last lap in 57.1 resulted in a time of 26:20.31. Two races for two world records.

Kenny's final race before the Athens Olympics was at Gateshead over 3000m. A convincing winner, he came home over nine seconds ahead of the Kenyan Paul Bitok in 7:41.31. His preparation for Athens had been close to faultless. He had not lost a race since the epic World Championship 5000m last year, had won both World Cross country titles, and set three world records (two outdoors, one indoors). He was without doubt the best distance runner in the world, and ready for the distance double.

The first of the double was the 10,000m on August 20. Following their great race in last year's World Championship over the distance, the Ethiopians were hoping for another clean sweep of the medals. However, a year on and injured, Gebrselassie was not up to the task. At the business end of the race Bekele and Sihine realised that trying to shepherd Haile into a podium position may well cost them their own medals, and were forced to leave him while they made their own run for home. With a last lap of 53.02 seconds, Bekele was simply far too good for both Sihine in second place and the rest of the field, winning in 27:05.10.

Five days later were the 5000m heats, followed three days later by the final. After the great race last year at the World titles, expectations were high. The three medalists from last year were all there along with a strong supporting cast. The same questions from last year were asked again: would Bekele, and after last year's heroics Kipchoge, be able to run fast enough to negate the finishing sprint of El Guerrouj?

Until Athens, Hicham El Guerrouj's Olympic career had been, by his standards and expectations, disastrous. In Atlanta in 1996, expected by many to challenge for the 1500m gold medal, he fell with a lap to go and finished last. In Sydney four years later, despite being the overwhelming favorite, he was beaten into second place by Noah Ngeny. Trying for some degree of atonement, in Athens he was attempting the 1500m / 5000m double – something not done since the bygone era of Paavo Nurmi. He came into the 5000m final after having already won the 1500m four days earlier. Any doubt about the task that lay ahead of the other competitors was the fact that he had run the final 800m of his gold medal race in 1:46.7.

What probably needed to happen, and what most expected would, did not eventuate. After last year's World Championship race logic would seem to dictate that Bekele, and probably also Kipchoge would push the pace for all they were worth over the full 5000m. Anything less and they were playing onto the hands of a fit and determined El Guerrouj. It just did not happen. With Bekele either first or equal first the opening kilometre took just over 2:58. It was no longer a 5000m race, at best it was now a 4000m race. First to raise the tempo was Gebremariam, then the Kenyans (notably Kipchoge), and then Bekele, but laps of 61-63 seconds would never be enough to dislodge El Guerrouj. With a kilometre to go, it looked like Kipchoge might be able to repeat his win of the previous year, but really, it seemed more like each of the main contenders thought that they had the best kick. Only one would be right, and that one was El Guerrouj. Covering the last 200m in 24.9, the last lap in 52.6, and the final 800m in 1:54 said it all as he won in 13:14.39 to Bekele 13:14.59 and Kipchoge 13:15.10. The final straight was like last year's race, only the ending was different. Post Olympics the only race for the rest of the year for Bekele was a cross country in Spain, winning as usual.

2004 had been a great year for Bekele. Apart from his close loss in the Olympic 5000m final he had won every race he entered. He had won two more World Championship cross countries, set world records for both the indoor and outdoor 5000m and 10,000m, and won gold and silver Olympic medals. He could justifiably look to 2005 with confidence. But just when it looked like life could not get any better, his whole world came tumbling down.

While his athletic life was excellent, so too was his private life. He was engaged to be married on May 8, his fiancée being Alem Techale. Like Kenenisa, Alem was also a world-class athlete and was highly regarded by the athletic hierarchy in Ethiopia. In 2003 she had won the world youth championship over 1500m, making the now eighteen year old the first Ethiopian to win any sort of world title over that distance. On Tuesday, January 4 the two were training together in a hilly area outside the capital Addis when Alem suddenly collapsed, later dying on the way to hospital. After a brief examination, the hospital doctors put the cause of death as being an undiagnosed heart condition. Alem was buried the next day. Kenenisa was distraught, and seriously considered giving the sport away. Coupled with his personal grief was the outpouring of sorrow from so many others – friends and strangers alike. In the end he decided to go overseas, and keep running, mainly as a means of dealing with his grief but also to leave behind the large number of well meaning people keen to offer their condolences.

Thus it was that twenty-five days after Alem's death he was in Boston racing over 3000m. Confusing the finish, he was second to the Irishman Alistair Cragg in 7:41.42, a win that Cragg readily pronounced as no more than a pyrrhic victory on his part. Three weeks later he was in Birmingham and again second, this time over two miles to his countryman Geneti. With just a month before the World Cross-country championships, his participation was by no means assured. In keeping with Ethiopian tradition when mourning, Bekele shaved his head, grew a beard, and wore black.

The cross-country championships this year were in St Etienne, France. His training had not gone well, and for the first time in a long time he looked vulnerable. He certainly did not look like the favourite. In the short race, half way through the second of two laps he had slipped some thirty metres behind Saif Shaheen, the world steeplechase record holder, but then managed to catch him and win by five seconds. In the longer race the next day he dominated a strong field to storm to a fourteen second victory. It looked like the Bekele of old was back.

Following his cross-country wins he spent time training in the US at Flagstaff and then at home in Ethiopia. He knew he was running well, probably well enough to try and improve his world record times. His attempt on the 10,000m record was at Hengelo six weeks after his world title wins. In cold, windy conditions the designated pace makers dropped off early in the race, despite which he was still able to run the fourth fastest time ever (26:28.72). The big surprise however was in second place. Abebe Dinkessa, a twenty one year old fellow Ethiopian improved his best by 53 seconds, clinging to Bekele for the whole race to become the fifth fastest of all time in 26:30.74.

Realizing that but for the conditions he may well have broken the record, he was back to try again a month later – this time in Paris over 5000m. He thought that this was the harder of the two records, but nevertheless thought a time of 12:33 – 12:36 was possible. As for his last race he had Dinkessa for company. In front of some 70,000 spectators, the 5000m was the feature event. For much of the race it looked like a new record was possible. Behind pacemakers the first kilometre took just 2:30.11, while 2km came up in 5:03.92. Leading well before 3km. he reached that mark in 7:32.71. Dinkessa was still in contention, but would drop off and finish well behind, albeit in a fast time. The fourth kilometre was where the damage was done, almost certainly by running too fast during the third kilometre trying to dislodge Dinkessa. Averaging under 2:31 for each of the first three kilometres, the pace dropped to almost 2:36 for the fourth, and with it went any chance of a new record. Despite a 2:32 final kilo and a 57.8 last lap there was no new record, just the fourth fastest time ever as he crossed the line in 12:40.18. Dinkessa would finish second in 12:55.58 with Gebremariam third in 12:58.60.

Two more races would serve as the warm up for the forthcoming World Championships in Helsinki. During this period Bekele was not living in Ethiopia, preferring to avoid the sadness that it brought by training overseas – mainly in New Mexico. He could be a lot more inconspicuous there than he ever could in Addis. As a member of the national team he was expected to be in Addis training with the rest of the team, but at the start of training he was not there. Not that the capital was a good place to be at that particular time. A disputed election, an unpopular government, police shootings during protests and troops patrolling the streets meant that the often inclement weather was the least of the team's problems. Although late, Bekele did arrive. He said he had been training well and was in good shape. His mental state was still an issue however, but when you are as big a star as he was you get special consideration. Certainly the rest of the team was delighted he was there.

The Helsinki World Championships 10,000m was on August 8, and like so much of the championships the conditions were cool and wet. For much of the early going it was the two Ethiopians Sihine and Dinkessa at the front pushing the pace, but not fast enough to drop any of the main contenders, as half way passed in 13:51.10. Less than a kilometre later Bekele went decisively to the front, the pace rose quickly, and with the three Ethiopians first, second and third, it looked like they may run away with the race as per the 2003 World Championships. But when he looked for others to help with the pace they were either unable or unwilling. At all times, Kenny looked like the one in control even when not in the lead. He seemed as interested in the team result as in his own, continually looking around to check where others were. At the bell there were nine still in contention for the win – or so it seemed. When the real running started on the last lap Dinkessa dropped back quickly (he would eventually finish seventh), and in the final straight it was a battle between Bekele and Sihine. Sihine never really looked a winner, and Bekele never really looked a loser as he finished in 27:08.33, winning by 0.54 second, with the Kenyan Moses Mosop third.

Eleven days after his 10,000m victory he was at the always high class Weltklasse meet in Zurich, this time over 3000m. In weather conditions similar to Helsinki he crushed a top field that included the gold and bronze medallists from the 5000m in Helsinki, winning by almost five

seconds in 7:32.59. Those finishing behind him were probably thankful he had not attempted the distance double a couple of weeks before!

A week later and it was Brussels for the final big meet of the European season, the Van Damme Memorial, and with it the usual high class 10,000m. Realising that he was running as well as he ever had, the decision was made to attempt to better his existing world record for the distance. Once again, the event was more a time trial than a race, but it did give some others the chance to run personal best times. Early in the race it was obvious that the designated pace makers found the pace required too demanding – not all that surprising since in most cases it was so close to their personal bests for much shorter distances. There was one runner that could help out however - another Bekele in the form of his younger brother Tariku. Himself a world class athlete, earlier in the season he had run 12:59.03 for 5000m and so was willing and able to help out for at least some of the distance. He did his job well, reaching 5000m in 13:09.19, his second best time ever for that distance. Also hanging on were two Kenyans – Nicholas Kemboi and Sammy Wanjiru – as Kenenisa went to the front to try and run the second half as fast if not faster than the first. Kemboi almost immediately dropped out of contention, while Wanjiru held on for another kilometre before slowly losing contact. He would still finish third in an excellent 26:41.75, a new World Junior record, something of a precursor to becoming for a time the world's best marathon runner before his tragic death a few years later.

With ten laps remaining he was running well, but not really well enough for the record. As he slowed almost imperceptibly Wanjiru actually closed the gap somewhat, and with the ninth kilometre being the slowest of the race, it looked like the record bid was a lost cause. However, when it counted he managed to find that something extra, that something this time was a last lap in 56.9 seconds – the difference between disappointment and a new record. The record now stood at 26:17.53, second was the Ugandan Boniface Kiprop in 26:39.77, with Wanjiru third. A total of six would run under 27 minutes. Three weeks later he would finish his 2005 season with a 3000m race in Shanghai. The winner was K. Bekele in 7:36.36, second was T. Bekele in 7:36.53.

As was customary for the start of a new year it began with a cross-country event, this time in Edinburgh. Also customary was that Kenenisa won despite facing quite a strong field. Despite some setbacks, he had been undefeated in cross-country events for a long time. This was the only cross country he ran before this years edition of the World Cross country championships, his other races being on the indoor circuit. First up after Edinburgh was the Wanamaker mile in New York as part of the Millrose Games. On the tight track (over ten laps to the mile), he was convincingly beaten by Bernard Lagat, running 4:01.57. A fortnight later he was in Birmingham, and it was a one – two finish for the Bekeles over two miles as Kenny won in 8:05.12 from younger brother Tariku whose 8:13.32 was a World Junior indoor record. His final race before the World Cross country was the World Indoor championship in Moscow, winning over 3000m in 7:39.32.

The 2006 cross-country titles were held in the Japanese city of Fukuoka, famous for its annual marathon. After a close win on the first day over the 4km course, the next day for the 12km event he faced the usual strong field on a sodden course made worse by a howling gale. It was by no means easy, but despite not looking his usual dominant self did enough to win by three seconds from team mate Sihine. At the ripe old age of twenty-three he had now won a total of ten World Cross country titles, prompting him to suggest that he may not try for more.

With no major championships for the rest of the year, Bekele ran a total of nine 5000m races, two over 1500m and one over 3000m. At 5000m he won seven of nine, including three below 12:50, and a further two below 12:52. At 1500m his two attempts were 3:33.08 (winning in Stockholm), and 3:33.13 (second to Augustine Choge in Shanghai). Probably the biggest surprise was losing by more than four seconds to Craig Mottram in the World Cup 3000m.

2007 arrived, and with it came a change of heart on the part of Kenenisa not to try and add to his tally of cross-country championships – a change he would later regret. It would certainly not be due to any lack of form on his part. He would have four races leading up to the championships, and each would show that he was in as good form as ever. The first two were cross-country events, both against top fields. In Edinburgh on January 13 he won by ten seconds over Tadesse, with Kipchoge third, and eight days later in Seville it was another Bekele double as he beat his younger brother Tariku by just two seconds, with Chebii of Kenya third and Dinkessa fourth.

Then it was on to the indoor circuit, beginning with a 2000m event in Birmingham, winning comfortably in a new World Indoor Record time of 4:49.99. Three days later (February 20), he was winning again, this time in Stockholm over 3000m in a fast 7:30.51. The world titles were five weeks away.

Occasionally the athletic authorities, at least applied to the distance events, get it wrong. The marathon in the 1954 Empire Games in Vancouver would be one such example, the Mexico City Olympics would be another. Holding the World Cross-country titles in Mombassa, Kenya would be another. When most people think of Kenya and distance running, they think of the generally temperate climate and high altitude of the Rift Valley. Mombassa is neither of these. It is at sea level on the Indian Ocean coast – and it is often very hot and very humid – and it was both of these for the championships.

For the Ethiopians it was certainly a lot different from training in Addis Ababa. In Addis it never really gets very hot or very cold – certainly nothing like the conditions they would be competing in at Mombassa, where on race day it was 33C and 73% humidity. Earlier it had been both hotter and more humid. With the hope seeing a Kenyan victory an estimated crowd of 30,000 turned out. Opting only for the longer race, some indication of what was in store was provided in the women's race as a number were in a state of collapse at the end of the race. It was not as if the Ethiopian team had not prepared for the conditions – they had spent time training in a similar environment in the lead up to the race.

On the penultimate lap Bekele had built up what would normally be a winning lead, but due to confusion, exhaustion, or a combination of the two, failed to realize that there was still one lap remaining. He was caught by Tadesse and dropped out with 800m left as Tadesse went on to win from the two Kenyans – Mosop and Kipyego, with Kenyans filling six of the first eight positions. Tadesse credited his win in part to training under similar conditions in Spain, while Bekele said it was by far the worst he had ever felt in a race, and feared for his well being. He had won all of the previous twenty-seven cross country races he had entered. Of the 134 starters, 29 failed to finish, and remember this was not a local fun run, this was a World Championship.

As if to underscore what an aberration the race was, it would be his only loss for 2007 apart from his very last race for the year. Two months after his ill fated cross-country, he began his outdoor season, once again in Hengelo. Winning over two miles in 8:13.51, he followed up with a fast 3000m three weeks later in Sheffield, beating Craig Mottram convincingly in 7:26.69 with a last kilometre in under 2:24.

The World Championships this year were in Osaka, and in the month before, Kenny had three races, winning over 3000m in 7:29.32 and then over 5000m in 12:49.53, before another 3000m in a fast 7:25.79. In the last two in particular he simply thrashed the opposition. His build up to the championships had been well nigh perfect. The only potential problem was that the predicted weather for Osaka was not a whole lot different from what had been experienced in Mombassa, but at least it was not quite as severe – from a distance running point of view unpleasant, rather than almost unbearable and a danger to health.

Running just the 10,000m Bekele was the obvious favorite to defend his title, but in light of his Mombassa experience and the Osaka weather there were some questions to be answered. From the start Tadesse started looking for answers. His intention was obvious – try to make the race as hard as possible and hope that the pace and weather combined would have a similar effect as it had five months earlier. Considering the warm and humid conditions the pace was fast. The opening kilometre was 2:44.15, halfway was 13:49.90. There was still a large group following Tadesse's pace with the four Ethiopians always near the front. The problem for Tadesse was that steady laps of 64-66 seconds were not fast enough to cause his main opponents (i.e. the Ethiopians) to drop off. For the rest of the field it was a war of attrition as they gradually succumbed to his relentless front running, such that with four laps remaining there were just four in the lead group.

With three laps to go the Kenyan Mathati began what looked like a long run for home. Instantly Tadesse was gone, but Bekele did not respond as would normally be expected – he looked vulnerable. For much of the last lap Sihine looked a winner; he had gone past Mathati and his more fancied teammate had slipped some five metres behind. Gradually drawing on whatever resources he had left, Bekele made a supreme effort, gradually catching, and finally pulling away in the home straight. His margin of victory (3.13 seconds) belied how hard the race had been. The last kilometre had taken just 2:30.32 for a final time of 27:05.90 with Sihine and Mathati second and third.

The outdoor track season for Kenenisa finished with a 10,000m at the always high class Van Damme meet in Brusells (winning in 26:46.19) and then a close second over 1500m in Shanghai in a personal best 3:32.35. The winner in Shanghai was Daniel Komen – not that Daniel, but Daniel Kipchirchir Komen – another top 1500m runner from Kenya.

Off the track his private life took a big turn. On November 18, thoughtfully well after his last race for the year, and well before the start of the next athletic year, he was married. In what could best be described as perhaps the social event of the year in Addis Ababa, he wed actress Danawit Gebregziabher in a church ceremony followed by a glittering evening reception in the Sheraton hotel.

It would be hard to decide which year of Bekele's career would be the best, but 2008 would have to come close. An indoor world record, yet another cross country championship and two Olympic gold medals, and his only loss coming in his very last race of the year when injured. As much as his times and titles were noteworthy, it was probably more the way he won and those he beat, that made it such a memorable year. As had been evident for virtually his whole career, when at his best he made his opposition, with few exceptions, look second rate.

His year began with the Great Edinburgh cross-country, and with it the chance to gain some degree of redemption against Tadesse, the winner at Mombassa last year. It was their first meeting over the country since that race. In a closely fought encounter, Bekele finished just one second ahead, with Kipchoge in third place. He then moved on to two indoor races, firstly over 3000m in Valencia (winning in 7:36.08), and then in Birmingham. Over two miles he finished in a new World Record time of 8:04.35, winning from the Kenyan pair of Koech and Chebii. After last year's disappointment, he was back to try for another World Cross country title.

At the longer course he was tied on five titles with the Kenyan duo of Paul Tergat and John Ngugi, but of course he also had the additional five short course titles to go with his collection. In conditions much more to his liking than last year he was at or near the front from the very start, but after some two kilometres disaster struck, or at least it could have been for anyone other than Kenenisa. Someone had dislodged his shoe in the crowded conditions. Showing no signs of panic, he stopped, replaced the shoe, and re-joined the race, all the while losing valuable time to the lead group. Gradually threading his way through the field, he eventually caught the leaders, ran with the group for a while before surging away with some two kilometres remaining. Once he made the break, the result was never really in doubt and the three second margin to Leonard Komon in second place probably flattered the Kenyan, as Tadesse finished third. There was probably not much doubt now who was the greatest cross country runner of them all.

With the cross country and indoor seasons behind him Bekele would now have four track races as preparation for the forthcoming Beijing Olympics. Beginning with the African championships in Addis Ababa, anything but a win at home would have been almost unthinkable. Over 5000m he won in a fine 13:49.67 (at altitude) but his winning margin was a scant 0.24 seconds over the Kenyan Isaac Songok. His next race was in Hengelo, and over 5000m he crushed his opposition, winning by almost fifteen seconds in 12:58.94. A fortnight later and he was lining up for the 10,000m at the Prefontaine Classic in Eugene, Oregon. It was hoped that he might be able to set a new world time, but he was always just outside, and came home in 26:25.97, the fourth fastest ever. Only he and Gebrselassie had ever run quicker. His final race before Beijing was a 5000m event in Rabat, winning in 13:06.38. There would now be two months training before Beijing.

Realising how well he was running, the decision was made to enter both the 5 and 10,000m. First up was the longer race on August 17 with a big field of thirty-eight. At the start, both Bekele and Tadesse dashed to the front – and then almost stopped. It stayed that way for about 600 metres before the other Eritreans took over at the front, and despite a big pick up in pace, the first kilometre still took 2:50.15. The faster pace continued, the second kilometre taking just 2:37.17. Things then settled to a more even tempo with the Eritreans (but not Tadesse) at the front. All the Kenyans and Ethiopians were in the lead group. At six kilometres Gebrselassie went to the front and the pace quickened again (2:40.99 for the seventh kilo). Then it was Tadesse in front and the pace was faster again as most of the field dropped off. With three laps to go the lead group was down to seven – three Kenyans, three Ethiopians, and Tadesse. By the final lap it was a race in two as Sihine dashed into the lead, and then, as he had so many times before, Bekele closed the gap and won going away. You do not lose many 10,000m races with a final kilometre of 2:27.10 and a last lap of 53.42. He had successfully defended his title, winning in 27:01.17, finishing 1.60 seconds ahead of Sihine with Kogo of Kenya third.

Six days later it was the 5000m final, and with it came Kenenisa's hope of becoming the first runner to complete the distance double since his fellow countryman Miruts Yifter achieved the feat twenty-eight years previously. He would join a very select few if successful. At the gun, he went straight into the lead, and then proceeded at little more than a jog for the next lap. Nobody showed any inclination to do anything different - so he did. He increased the pace dramatically with brother Tariku and fellow team-mate Abreham Cherkos in tow. The pace then settled to a more even 63-64 second pace, at this level honest, but not ridiculous. Most in the field could hang on, but not easily. Despite the dawdling first lap, the first kilometre took 2:45.49, the second 2:36.80, both being led by the younger Bekele. Then it was time for Kenny to take over as the third kilo went by in 2:38.56, 3000m being reached in 8:00.85. The leading group was running at 13:20 pace, but the real racing was only just about to begin.

With five laps remaining Bekele ran that lap in 59.96. Instantly the lead group dropped to six, and it included just the one Ethiopian. The fourth kilometre was 2:31.67 but the main Kenyan threats were still there. At the start of the final lap both Kipchoge and Soi were within striking distance, at the end of the lap they were well beaten as Bekele simply exploded away from them. He finished the race with a 53.87 final lap, a last kilometre in 2:25.30 and the last 2km in 4:56.97 as he easily broke the Olympic record with his 12:57.82. Kipchoge, a great runner, lost five seconds on the last lap as he finished second in 13:02.80, with Soi third in 13:06.22. As a demonstration of his absolute brilliance it would be hard to beat.

At the Weltklasse meet six days later he repeated the dose, crushing a top field again over 5000m in 12:50.18 by almost ten seconds, running the last kilometre in 2:23.66. He truly was in a class of his own. He finished his track season with another big win – this time over 3000m in Gateshead in 7:31.94, winning by more than six seconds. It seemed that he could do no wrong, and then came his last race of the year.

The event was a fifteen kilometre road race in the small Dutch city of Njimegen. It was hoped that he might be able to break the existing world best for the distance, held by the Kenyan Felix Limo at 41:29. In training for the event he had sustained bruising to both his heels, the

2009 World Championships. Tadesse leading from Bekele in the 10,000m final.

Kenenisa Bekele 2009 World Championship 5,000m final.

problem being such that he was advised by doctors not to run. However, after warming up he felt better and decided to take part. It was definitely not one of his best decisions. After a first 5km split of 14:03, and a second in 13:45 he was well on track for the record. By the end of the race he could not stand and had to be carried from the finish after completing the distance in 43:41.9 for third place. On crutches, unable to climb stairs or drive, he was advised complete rest for at least two months. It would be more than six months before he was in condition to compete again. It would also be the first of a series of injuries that would have a profound effect on the rest of his running career.

His return to competition was not good. On June 1 at Hengelo he failed to finish over 1500m in a race won by the Kenyan Asbel Kiprop. There was good news however – he would win every other of his races for the year. Following a two week break after Hengelo, he ran three 5000m races in Berlin (13:00.76), Oslo (13:04.87), and Rome (12:56.23). His final race before the forthcoming World Championships in Berlin was over 3000m in Paris. Winning convincingly in a fast 7:28.64 would have been a good confidence boost especially as Bernard Lagat, expected to challenge Bekele if he tried the double, was over four seconds behind.

At the Berlin World Championships he decided to try for the 5 and 10,000m double. The first event was the 10,000. Tadesse did all he could to get rid of his Ethiopian nemesis before the last lap, but try as he might Bekele just absorbed the fast pace, confident that if it came to a final lap sprint he had all the answers, as he did. As a result of the pace set by Tadesse, the winning time was a fast 26:46.31 with Bekele finishing 3.81 seconds ahead of the game Eritrean, with the Kenyan Masai third. He showed that he could win off a fast pace, but could he win against a renowned sprinter in a slow race?

Coming into the championships Bernard Lagat was the defending champion in both the 1500m and 5000m - he was also the second fastest 1500m runner ever. Earlier in the meet he finished third in the 1500m and it was assumed that the faster the pace the more exposed he might be. The way the race was run it was almost as if Kenny was putting that theory to the test. He led for nearly the whole race, including a second lap of 75.62 seconds and an opening kilometre of 2:54.35. The second kilometre was reached in 5:34.17, the third in 8:14.63. At this pace the whole field was bunched with Lagat and Kipchoge in particular shadowing Bekele. The pace increased in the fourth kilometre, but a kilo in 2:37.69 did nothing to split the field. Kipchoge led briefly but with four laps to go Bekele was back in the lead.

At the bell just about anyone could have won – in theory. In fact, at this pace it would come down to a two man contest. When the real sprinting started with about 200m left Kipchoge dropped back; at the top of the final straight Lagat and Bekele were side by side before Lagat moved ahead. With forty metres remaining Bekele moved up, and then passed Lagat, edging ahead to win 13:17.09 to 13:17.33, with the Kenyan / Qatari James Kwalia Kurui third in 13:17.78. The last kilometre took just 2:24.87.

Victory in the 5000m made Bekele the first to ever achieve the distance double at the World Championships. The way the two races were run was vastly different, but he dominated both. Hard to believe at the time, his 5000m victory would be his last ever win in a major championship.

Five days after his Berlin heroics it was time for another 5000m at the Zurich Weltklasse meet, where he crushed an almost all Kenyan field in a fast 12:52.32. A week later, and at the Brussels Van Damme Memorial he won another, but much closer 5000m, finishing just 0.35 seconds ahead of fellow Ethiopian Merga in 12:55.31. His season finale would be the so-called World Athletic Final in Greece where he repeated his Berlin finish against Lagat. Over 3000m he won in a slow 8:03.79, his margin of victory actually decreasing compared to Berlin – from 0.24 down to 0.21.

Following his great year of 2009 it would have been reasonable to expect his dominance to continue, but as his predecessor Gebrselassie showed, even the greatest are brought back to the field by injury. In Kenny's case it was a combination calf, knee, and achilles problems. Just when all seemed healed, training or competition would cause the problems to recur. He just could not get an uninterrupted block of training. As a result, the Bekele of 2010 was but a shadow of the all conquering 2009 Bekele. He raced only once, and that for fourth place in an Edinburgh cross-country on January 9.

The following year (2011) was not a whole lot better. He did not race again until August 28, and that would be over 10,000m in the World Championships. Apart from his ill fated cross-country in early 2010, it would be his first race in almost two years! He stayed with the lead group until halfway, but then lost contact and dropped out at six kilometres. The race itself finished in dramatic fashion. Coming into the race, Mo Farah had broken the European record for the distance running 26:46.57 in Eugene earlier in the year. With Bekele dropping out and Farah seemingly in control in the last lap his victory seemed assured, You do not lose many 10,000m races with a last lap in 53.36, but he did. It was an Ethiopian storming through to take the lead with just metres remaining, but it was certainly not the one most would have expected. Ibrahim Jeilan had been the World Junior Champion in 2006, but after failing to make the team for the 2008 Olympics and the 2009 World Championships, decided to relocate to Japan – in retrospect a decision it would be hard to argue with. He won in 27:13.81 to Farah's 27:14.07.

Probably almost as big a shock occurred nineteen days later. At the Van Damme Memorial, none other than Kenenisa Bekele posted the fastest time for the year for 10,000m. A few more days training, a few more days to get over his injuries and he went from dropping out just over half way to running 26:43.16, supplanting Mo Farah as the years fastest. His third and last race for the year was a loss over four miles on the road, coming second to Yator of Kenya in 17:11.

2012 was a bit like 2011 for Bekele, only more races. There was the occasional glimpse of the old Kenenisa, but in the main his physical problems caused him to be more a shadow of his former self. His start to the year gave some indication to what lay ahead, as the most decorated cross country runner ever could only finish eleventh in the Great Edinburgh cross country. Some three months later he was in Dublin for the Great Ireland Run – a ten kilometre road race. In what must have been something of a first for him he was the only world class African in the field, perhaps explaining why it would be one of his only two wins for the year, as he came home first by almost a minute in 27:49.

Then followed a 3000m race in Doha, finishing seventh (!) in 7:40.00, over nine seconds behind the winner. Next were three 5000m races, the fastest of which was at the Bislett Games in 13:00.54, good enough only for fifth. The other two were fourth and fifth place finishes. That he was improving was shown by the fact that each of his races was a little faster than the one before, and in the 10,000m to select the Ethiopian team for the London Olympics he won narrowly from his brother in 27:02.59. The last race before the Olympics was the Diamond League event at Saint-Denis over 5000m. In one of the fastest and deepest fields over the distance for some time, Bekele ran his best time for almost three years (12:55.79). The problem was that it was only good enough for ninth place, and there were four other Ethiopians ahead of him.

With the Olympics a month away the big question for Bekele was whether he could improve enough to get back to his best – or close to it. In the end it was a case of almost, but not quite. In front of a huge home-town crowd Mo Farah made a long run for home and Kenny just could not keep up, finishing 2.02 seconds behind in fourth position in 27:32.44. Brother Tariku finished one place ahead, while the American Galen Rupp was second. Considering the injuries and the racing missed, it would have to be one of his best performances.

2013 was a continuation of the story that began almost four years ago – recurrent injury problems preventing the steady consistent training required to get back to his best. Times that would have been easy training runs when at his peak were now all out competitive efforts. His best times for the year were 13:07.88 and 27:12.08, almost 30 seconds and a minute respectively outside his world record times. Probably his best race for the year – certainly the most memorable – was The Great North Run, an annual half marathon run in Newcastle. Bringing together three of the all time greats, it pitted Bekele, Farah, and Gebrselassie against each other. Between them they had dominated distance running for the last twenty years. Gebrselassie's best years were well past, Farah was the reigning double Olympic champion, and Bekele was an unknown quantity due to the various physical issues he was dealing with. And the winner was – Bekele, by one second in 60:09. There might have been a winner, but really there were no losers. Haile showed that even though officially a veteran he could still mix it with the world's best, Farah showed that at almost any distance he was a threat, and Bekele showed that when healthy, or close to it, he was still as good – or better – than anyone.

The first Ethiopian athlete to become famous – really famous – was Abebe Bikila. Winning two Olympic marathons in succession, one in bare feet, the other easily beating the best time ever run for the distance really says it all. It is hardly surprising that so many top runners from the same country have similar aspirations, especially since the event is now so much more popular and there is so much money to be made. Victory in one of the big marathons can be life changing for a runner from Ethiopia (or Kenya), such is the prize money (and later appearance money) to be made relative to average incomes in either country. Almost inevitably Bekele would one day try the marathon. That day would come in 2014.

Like Haile before him, the lure of the marathon was twofold. Firstly the tradition of the event, especially in Ethiopia; and secondly the less intense training would hopefully lead to some improvement on the injury front. With the ongoing injuries he had, almost anything was worth a try. The year began with a return to Edinburgh for the Great Edinburgh Run, a four kilometre cross-country. In his first race since his half marathon win four months previously, he came home in fifth place. Another four months and it was a ten kilometre road race in Manchester, winning from future marathon rival Wilson Kipsang in 28:23. Three weeks later (June 4) he would be lining up with 42,000 others for the Paris marathon, chosen as a somewhat easier option than the more competitive London marathon the following week. Despite his long term injury concerns and his somewhat unpredictable results over the last four years it would be the most eagerly anticipated debut at the distance since Gebrselassie.

Despite putting on a brave face prior to the race, his preparation had not been ideal and he would later say that he was not at his best for the race. Bekele would be one of a small leading group until accelerating at the twenty-seven kilometre mark. The group quickly split up with only fellow Ethiopian Tamirat Tola able to follow the faster pace. Seven kilometres on there was a problem with cramping of his left hamstring, but he managed to run through it, winning in 2:05.04. Another Ethiopian, Getachew finished second 1.45 behind. It had not been easy, although he pronounced himself satisfied with the result. In reality he would almost certainly have expected something a little faster. Eight months later he would try again, this time against a stronger field in Chicago.

The course record for Chicago was 2:03.45, set the year before by the then current world record holder Dennis Kimetto. Being a big city marathon there were always going to be a number of high class Kenyans, and Chicago was no exception. Foremost among them in this race was Eliud Kipchoge. Bekele and Kipchoge knew each other well – over the years they had met on many occasions, with probably the best remembered meeting being the 2003 World Championships over 5000m when an eighteen year old Kipchoge (although later he did claim to be nineteen at the time) upstaged his older and more highly regarded rivals. Eleven years later and he was in the process of forging a marathon career that would have him regarded as probably the best ever over the distance.

The problem for Bekele was that he simply had not done the training needed to take on the very best over the marathon. According to Hermens, his preparation specifically for this race was seven weeks. On the track, his natural ability and dominance over his opponents was such that he could largely get away with it, not so in the marathon. Finishing fourth in 2:05.57 was hardly a disgrace, but the fact was that a trio of Kenyans each finished well over a minute ahead of him put it in perspective. Kipchoge won in 2:04.11 from Sammy Kitwara (2:04.28) and Dickson Chumba (2:04.32). After Chicago, with the prompting of Hermens, he began a coaching relationship with the Italian coach Renato Canova, hoping that it might result in the greater commitment required for success at the highest level.

For his third marathon it was decided to try Dubai. On an almost dead flat course with few turns, not to mention the huge prize money on offer, Dubai was tailor made for fast times. Almost since its inception as a big money event it had been like a magnet for Ethiopian marathon runners. For this years event there were no fewer than twenty from that country with times under 2:10, of which six had run below 2:06 and a further three below 2:05. No doubt first prize of $200,000 was a powerful incentive.

Hermens claimed that Kenny was in his best marathon form since taking up the event. All looked promising as he was with the lead group as they reached half way in 62:02, but before 30km he had lost contact with the leaders and subsequently dropped out, citing hamstring and achilles problems. Ethiopians filled the first fourteen, and seventeen of the first twenty places. And of their top twenty entrants, which one was the winner? None of them. First place went to little known Hayle Lemi Berhanu who had never before broken 2:10 – his time: 2:05.28.

It would be fifteen months before Bekele raced again. One certainly could not accuse him of avoiding tough competition, as his first race back after injury was the 2016 London marathon against, among others, Kipchoge. Kipchoge had only ever lost one marathon, and that was his first, and it took a world record to beat him on that occasion, as he came second to Kimetto when he set his record in Berlin. Bekele had never made any secret of the fact that he was after the world record – not necessarily in this race, but certainly at some stage in his career. After the ten mile mark passed in 46:32, and half way in 61:23 there was definitely a chance. Approaching twenty miles there was a leading trio of Kipchoge, fellow Kenyan Stanley Biwott, and Bekele. Slowly Kenny started dropping back. Kipchoge and Biwott kept at close to world record pace until Kipchoge made his winning move with over a mile to go. He would finish just eight seconds outside the world record in 2:03.05, with Biwott second in 2:03.51. Bekele was third in 2:06.36.

Considering it was his first race for so long, and the fact that he could run at record pace for twenty of the twenty-six mile distance could perhaps give him some cause for optimism. His next two races would possibly serve to temper that optimism. A month after London he won the Great Manchester Run over ten kilometres in 28:08. Of some future significance was Wilson Kipsang finishing seven seconds behind in second place. Five weeks later it was the Ethiopian championships (on the track) over 10,000m, but not in Ethiopia, but Hengelo. In keeping with his now somewhat unpredictable career, he dropped out. Although his next race was three months away, it did not look good.

Berlin has a deserved reputation for being a close to ideal course for setting fast marathon times, a bit like Dubai only with more enthusiastic spectators. Bekele's best marathon time of 2:05.04 dated back to Paris in 2014; it was also his only win over the distance. Since then his marathon results had been a fourth, a third, and a retirement. The favourite was probably Wilson Kipsang, the former world record holder who had announced his desire to reclaim the record. With the record standing at 2:02.57, intentions were made obvious by an opening 5km in 14:19 and 10km in 28:59. By the half way in 1:01.11 the attempt was definitely on, with a lead group of seven and another two only a few metres off the pace. By twenty-five kilometres the field was down to six and shortly after the last of the pacers was gone.

Nearing thirty kilometres Kipsang surged, and with that kilometre taking only 2:49 he was exactly on world record pace as Bekele dropped back some 4-5 seconds. Of those dropped he was the only one able to bridge the gap, only to have Kipsang surge again at 34km and again open a gap of 4-5 seconds. Yet again Bekele closed the gap and by 38km they were side by side, as the pace slowed in anticipation of a big finish. Just who the big finish would come from was answered emphatically just before the 41km mark – and it came from Bekele. Running the forty first kilometre in 2:49, and the forty second in 2:47 he cleared away from Kipsang who still ran his best ever time, his 2:03.13 being faster than his world record run. Kenny however was ten seconds ahead, his 2:03.03 being the second fastest ever. He was now faster than Kipchoge, and had it not been for the slow down before the 40km mark it may well have been a new record. He was also now the new national record holder for the event.

The Berlin marathon had been on September 25. Realising how close he had been, he was keen to try again for the record, and the next obvious choice was Dubai on January 20. There was the double incentive of the world record and the $200,000 prize money. Both Kenenisa and Jos Hermens had talked about a 2:02 being possible in the lead up to the race, but realistically that would have been somewhat optimistic given the warm and humid conditions. With a view to avoiding the worst of the conditions there is a 6.30 a.m. start for the race, the only problem with that being for the TV coverage. Watching the first hour of a marathon in the dark makes for less than compelling viewing.

Bekele was ready, willing, and judging by his last race probably able. Then the improbable happened. In a somewhat disorganized start, as the gun went he was knocked down. Having to catch the lead group while they are running 14:26 for the first 5km and 28:58 for 10km is not easy. By 10km he was five seconds off the pace, and by fifteen he was eighteen seconds adrift of the leaders. By the time the lead group reached half way in 61:36 he was 1:16 off the pace and dropped out shortly afterwards – his second failure to finish in Dubai in three years. Tamirat Tola, the

Olympic bronze medallist over 10,000m was the winner in 2:04.11 as Ethiopians filled eleven of the first twelve places. As a result of his fall the old injury curse returned – this time it was a combination of back, hip and calf problems.

The injuries sustained in Dubai persisted for two months, meaning that his next marathon – the always high-class London event – would be done on seven to eight weeks proper training. There might not be Kipchoge, but there were a number of others not that far behind him. Canova, who had been advising Bekele with his preparation, knew a bit about what was required to compete at the highest level. Knowing the training he had done, and more importantly the training he had not done, he could not think of anyone else who would be capable of running below 2:10 on such a preparation.

As the race unfolded, with some fifty minutes left to run and the pace makers gone, twenty four year old Kenyan Daniel Wanjiru found himself in the lead with Bekele only twenty metres behind. At 23 miles he still had an eight second lead, But Bekele was closing. Luckily for Wanjiru he still had something – in fact quite a bit – in reserve. He ran mile 25 of the 26 mile race in 4:27, but the gap really did not change as he won in 2:05.48 to Bekele's 2:05.57. Considering his limited preparation, it would be one of his best races at any distance and a testament, as much as anything, to his great natural talent.

Five months later he was back in Berlin, and after last year's epic battle with Wilson Kipsang and the presence of Kipchoge in this year's field, hopes were high for another classic race and possibly a new record time. Unfortunately the weather conditions conspired against a new record, with rain and high humidity anything but ideal for a record attempt. Perhaps Kipchoge did not realize that, as with the pacers he hit 10km in 29:04 and half way in 61:29 – almost spot on world record pace. Shortly after, Bekele dropped back and later retired, as did Kipsang. With his two main challengers gone it would be expected that Kipchoge would run on to an easy win, but it did not quite turn out that way. As the race progressed, unheralded Guye Adola from Ethiopia not only challenged

Kipchoge, but looked on more than one occasion that he might well go on to win. Slowly but surely, the Kenyan world number one reeled him in by forty kilometres and then pulled away for the win – 2:03.32 to 2:03.46. Adola's time was the fastest ever for a first time marathon, while Kipchoge would say that it was the hardest he had ever run.

After the race, long time agent and friend Jos Hermens had a frank discussion with Kenenisa. Essentially the problem was what he saw as his lack of application and professionalism. Comparing him to the now undisputed number one in the event he said that whereas Kipchoge prepared meticulously over a long period, Bekele would rely too much on natural ability and not enough on looking after himself and preparing in the best possible way. For so long on the track, Kipchoge had to work hard and consistently to get where he did, but Bekele was nearly always his superior. Marathon running was a different game altogether. Anything less than near total commitment would leave even a talent as great as Bekele exposed, hence the turn around in fortunes between the two.

Following his disappointment in Berlin and his conversation with Hermens, he had one final race for the year. Some eight weeks after Berlin he was lining up for a rarely run 25km race in Kolkata, India. In much more favourable conditions than Berlin, he ran what was more like a high class training run than a race, winning easily in 1:13.48.

The London marathon would again be on his agenda for 2018. Following his run in India the most positive sign was that he seemed to be fit and – probably more importantly – injury free. Joining the more than 41,000 starters on April 22 was the usual array of top marathon talent. Notable among those was the 2017 winner Daniel Wanjiru, former world champion Abel Kirui, Mo Farah, and of course Eliud Kipchoge. Probably the main opposition for most however, would be the weather. At more than 24C it was the hottest London marathon on record.

After the usual fast start (an almost ridiculous 13:48 first 5km) Kipchoge was on record pace for a good deal of the race. Even so, he still had six others (including Kenenisa) company at halfway, reached in 1:01.00. In a war of attrition the rest gradually dropped back as he too proved to be human and slowed somewhat in the later stages. Even so, his time of 2:04.17 was great under any conditions, let alone London on that day. The Ethiopian Kitata was a fine second in 2:04.49, while local hero Mo Farah was third in 2:06.21. Bekele finished in sixth position in 2:08.53, two positions and one minute forty two seconds ahead of last year's winner, Daniel Wanjiru. Only a month later he was in Bern racing over ten miles, winning in 46:47 – a good time, but still 44 seconds outside the course record set fourteen years previously by Tadesse.

His last race for the year was the Amsterdam marathon on October 23. Although not one of the really prestigious marathons such as London or Berlin, Amsterdam did have the reputation of being a potentially fast course attracting a high-class field. The course record stood at 2:05.09. What Bekele had not disclosed before the race was that while training had generally gone well (in his opinion), three weeks before the race he had sustained a hip injury.

The field was led by the usual pacers, most notably by the Kenyan Edwin Kiptoo, who kept a fast steady pace until the 30km mark. Bekele was with the leaders at half way (62:12) and was leading at 29.5km. When Kiptoo dropped out however, Lawrence Cherono, obviously intent on maintaining the pace went into the lead and began to draw away. Bekele dropped back as the only others who made some attempt to stay close to Cherono were two other Ethiopians – Mule Wasihun and Solomon Deksisa. Although slowing, Bekele was still on pace for a finishing time of just over 2:07 when he pulled out with only a kilometre to go. Cherono finished well to win in a new course record of 2:04.06, from Wasihun (2:04.37) and Deksisa (2:04.40).

One result of this disappointing run was another discussion with Hermens, very much the same as after the 2017 Berlin marathon. Bekele had made his intention clear that he still thought the world record was possible (although since Kipchoge had posted a new time of 2:01.39 in Berlin), few would probably agree, and that he intended to try for the Olympic title in 2020 in Tokyo. As Hermens made clear, while his intentions are good, putting it into practice is another issue altogether, claiming that he is just not organized or single minded enough. Again comparing him to Kipchoge, he made the point that while the latter would be resting or preparing, Bekele would be spending time on business interests and other pursuits, and would need to decide whether it was worth continuing if his outlook did not change markedly. The problems only continued into the new year. Entered for the Tokyo marathon on March 3 he withdrew with a stress fracture. One Ethiopian out, another one in, as twenty four year old Birhanu Legese won convincingly in 2:04.48 from a pair of Kenyans in Bedan Karoki (2:06.48) and Dickson Chumba (2:08.48)

When embarking on his marathon career, Bekele made no secret of the fact that he found the training required relative to his track training somewhat boring. Certainly running up to three hours in the forest is a bit different to repeat kilometres in 2:28 or 800m repeats in 1:57. Clearly the biggest obstacle to a successful marathon career has been Bekele's injury count, which was a problem well before he took up the event, and has only seemed to worsen over the years.

For almost any athlete other than Bekele his marathon career up until this time (April 2019), would probably be considered an unmitigated success. How many athletes could look back on a career that included a victory in Paris in their first race at the distance, a win in Berlin in the second fastest time ever, and a close second in the London event, and consider it disappointing? He has run ten marathons in total for two wins, a second, a third, a fourth and a sixth, but also four in which he failed to finish. Possibly the biggest threat to his ambition for an Olympic medal in 2020 will be actually making the Ethiopian team. With so many fast times and big wins to their names, any of perhaps twenty Ethiopians could legitimately stake their claim for team membership.

Whatever the future might hold, the possibility of an injury free Bekele becoming highly motivated to put in the long term consistent preparation that he has largely lacked in the past is an intriguing thought.

The 2017 London marathon. Despite again missing much training due to injury, Bekele finishes second.

If that were to happen, it would be a brave person to bet against him in almost any race against any opposition.

Looking back on his career, his record over all forms of distance running is largely unequalled. His record in cross country marks him as the best ever in that field, his record in major championships – indoors and out - puts him in a class with Gebrselassie, and his marathon record, while by his standards the weak link in his resume, is by almost any other comparison up there with a select few.

THE FUTURE

One of the major changes in distance running over the last twenty or so years has been the rise of the big city marathons. Almost in parallel has been the demise of the 10,000m as a track event. Apart from major championships, it is now rarely run, so the chances for new records over the distance have diminished accordingly.

As a consequence of the popularity (and money) now involved in marathons, many runners (most notably East Africans) who would have been potential five and ten thousand metre runners are almost exclusively marathon competitors. Many of the world's best rarely, or in some cases never, compete on the track, further lessening the chances of new records being set over the 5 and 10,000 metre distances.

In large part the recent explosion in marathon times has been because so many talented runners who in the past would have been track competitors, have chosen to bypass the track and gone straight to road events. Of course the fact that there is the potential to earn so much more, both in appearance and prize money, for the top runners plays no small part.

The only certainty is that the 5,000m and 10,000m records (as of August 2019) will be broken. Despite the longevity of the present records, sooner or later there will be others who come along with the necessary physical and mental requisites to run better times. It will not be easy. The last three record holders in both distances have been exceptional talents living in almost ideal environments from a distance running viewpoint, in addition to undertaking excellent (and hard) training. But broken they will be. Nothing is more certain.

PHOTOGRAPH ATTRIBUTIONS

#	SUBJECT/CAPTION	CREDIT
1	*Vladimir Kuts winning the 5000m at the 1956 Olympics in 13:39.6 – a new Olympic record*	CC
2	*Every picture tells a story. Nurmi in typical stance. Aloof, alone, unsmiling after victory in the 10,000m at the 1920 Antwerp Olympics.*	CC
3	*The 1924 Olympic 5000m final. Ritola leads from Nurmi and Wide.*	Popperfoto/ Getty Image
4	*Alone and in front. Nurmi leads the Finnish marathon trial for the 1932 Olympics.*	CC
5	*1939. Mäki finishing his record breaking 5000m in Helsinki in14:08.8.*	Acme Photo
6	*Mäki winning over three miles in New Orleans as part of the Finnish relief fund tour in 1940.*	Acme Photo
7	*Mäki in training for his American tour. New York, 1940*	Acme Photo
8	*Mäki & Nurmi during their U.S.A. Goodwill tour March 1940*	
9	*Zatopek training in Helsinki before his historic Olympic triple victory. The only runner to have won the 5000m, 10,000m and marathon at a single Olympics.*	c/-Trevor Vincent
10	*The 1948 Olympic 5,000m final. Zatopek leads from Ahlden (Sweden) and eventual winner Gaston Reiff.*	Hulton Archive/Getty Images
11	*The final bend of the 1952 Olympic 5,000m. Zatopek leads from Mimoun and Schade, Chataway having fallen.*	CC

CC=Creative Commons

#	SUBJECT/CAPTION	CREDIT
12	*Iharos and Wood after both breaking the two mile World Record, Iharos winning.*	CC
13	*Mihály Iglói in his competitive days.*	personal collection c/-T. Iglói
14	*The coach and his runners. 4x1500m world record, July 1955. L to R.Mikes, Iharos, Iglói, Rózsavölgyi, Tábori.*	Sports Museum Hungary
15	*Three of the greats. Iharos, Chataway and Tábori. White City, May 1955.*	PA Images / Alamy
16	*Athlete and coach. Iharos and Iglói after breaking the world 10,000m record, his last record. Budapest, July 15, 1956*	Sports Museum Hungary
17	*Kuts convincingly winning the 1956 Olympic 5,000m. But for a soft track his time would almost certainly have been a new world record.*	CC
18	*Kuts finishing the 10,000m in Melbourne after his epic battle with Pirie.*	CC
19	*One of Clarke's great breakthrough runs in 1965. The first man to run under thirteen minutes for three miles.*	Keystone Press / Alamy
20	*Finish of the 10,000m in Tokyo. Shock winner Billy Mills from Gammoudi, with Clarke third, passing lapped runners.*	CC
21	*Ron Clarke 5th July 1966 Stockholm – world 5,000m record:13:16.6 – the last of his 5000m records.*	©Svenska Dagbladet
22	*Ron Clarke-5th July 1966 Stockholm Alone at the front again, later in the race.*	©Svenska Dagbladet
23	*Photo to a friend. A lean, tanned Clarke training at Lake Tahoe before his ill-fated Mexico Olympic races.*	c/- Trevor Vincent
24	*Finish of the Munich 5,000m. Viren winning from Gammoudi and a fast finishing Ian Stewart.*	Getty Image/ Allsport Hulton/Archive
25	*The master and the apprentice – but not for long. Vaatainen leads from Viren in a domestic race prior to Viren taking over his mantle as the pre-eminent Finnish runner..*	

CC=Creative Commons

#	SUBJECT/CAPTION	CREDIT
26	*Munich 1972. Viren leads from Yifter, Haro and Puttemans in the closing stages of the Olympic 10,000m.*	Getty Image:/ Tony Duffy / Allsport
27	*1980 Viren leads from Martti Vainio in a domestic race. Vainio won the 1978 European championship over 10,000m and broke Viren's Finnish record for the distance.*	Reijo Pasanen// Helsingin kaupungin-museo -
28	*June 24, 1978. Rono wins the British AAA championship over 5000m at Crystal Palace.*	Keystone
29	*September 9, 1978. Henry Rono wins over 10,000m as a guest runner in GB v Finland meet at Crystal Palace.*	PA Images / Alamy
30	*Haile Gerbrselassie- 2011 Vienna City Half Marathon*	CC Alexxx86
31	*Modern marathon running. Haile with pacers and Kamathi en route to new world record at 2008 Berlin marathon*	CC Dirk Ingo Franke
32	*Haile Gerbrselassie 2009 Fanny Blankers-Koen Games at Hengelo (in a group)*	CC Erik Van Leeuwen
33	*Haile Gerbrselassie 2009 Fanny Blankers-Koen Games at Hengelo (on his own)*	CC Erik Van Leeuwen
34	*Beijing 10,000 metre final. Bekele winning the first leg of his great double.*	Stu Forster/ Getty Images
35	*Kenenisa Bekele at Golden League 2006, Gaz de France, Paris Saint-Denis 9th July*	CC Thomas Faivre-Duboz
36	*Kenenisa Bekele 2009 World Championship 5,000m final.*	CC Erik van Leeuwen
37	*2009 World Championships. Tadesse leading from Bekele in the 10,000m final.*	CC Andre Zehetbauer
38	*2012 Olympics. Bekele and Farah in the 10,000m. Bekele finishing fourth despite missing a lot of training due to injury.*	CC Robbie Dale
39	*The 2017 London marathon. Despite again missing much training due to injury, Bekele finishes second.*	CC Julian Mason

CC=Creative Commons

CPSIA information can be obtained
at www.ICGtesting.com
Printed in the USA
LVHW111224140520
654604LV00005B/100